It Gives Me Further Pleasure

by

Michael Kilgarriff

Further ruminations upon the art of the music hall chairman, plus over six hundred ready-made song introductions

Samuel French — London
New York - Toronto - Hollywood

Copyright © 1996 by Michael Kilgarriff
All Rights Reserved

IT GIVES ME FURTHER PLEASURE is fully protected under the copyright laws of the British Commonwealth, including Canada, the United States of America, and all other countries of the Copyright Union.

ISBN 978-0-573-19007-0

www.samuelfrench.co.uk
www.samuelfrench.com

The introductions and back announcements included in this book may be freely used in performance. However, permission to use any of the songs referred to in this work must be sought from the appropriate source, or, if this is not known, from The Performing Rights Society.

The right of Michael Kilgarriff to be identified as author of this work has been asserted in accordance with Section 77 of the Copyright, Designs and Patents Act 1988.

CONTENTS

Acknowledgements v

PREAMBLE vii

IT GIVES ME FURTHER PLEASURE
1. Your Genial Host 1
2. Decline of the Halls 2

BUILDING AN INTRODUCTION
1. Prime Considerations 4
2. Advance Warning 4
3. Keep It Simple 5
4. How Much Should The Chairman Give Away? 5
5. Song Narrative: Subjective or Objective? 6
6. Two Introductions Analysed: 7
7. Opera 8
8. Past or Present 8
9. Genesis of a Song 9
10. Scenery 9
11. Vocabulary 10
12. Lyricists and Composers 10
13. Song-sheets 10
14. Entrances 11
15. Exits 11
16. Back-Announcements 12
17. Developing Your Style 13

SONG INTRODUCTIONS 15

SONGS FOR TWO-HANDED OR CONCERTED PERFORMANCE 199
SONGS OF LONDON 201

INDEX
1. Artistes 203
2. Lyricists and Composers 209

ACKNOWLEDGEMENTS

Grateful thanks are offered to the following for their kind co-operation and assistance:

Katie Barnes, Boosey & Hawkes, Mick Booth (*Campbell Connelly*), Geoffrey Brawn (*Players' Theatre*), British Library Music Department, Robert J Bruce (*Bodleian Library*), Peter Charlton, Johnny Dennis, English Folk Dance & Song Society, John Foreman, John M Garrett, Terry Lomas, Public Record Office, Theatre Museum, Len Thorpe (*Warner Chappell Music Ltd*), Max Tyler, and John Whitehorn (*EMI Music Publishing*).

Lyrics for *Joshua* (words and music by George Arthurs and Bert Lee) © 1910, reproduced by kind permission of Redwood Music Ltd and Francis Day and Hunter Ltd, London, WC2H OEA.

Lyrics for *Molly O'Morgan* (words and music by Will Letters and Fred Godfrey) © 1909, reproduced by kind permission of B. Feldman and Co Ltd, London WC2H OEA

By the same author published by
Samuel French Ltd

It Gives Me Great Pleasure
Three Melodramas
Three More Melodramas
Three Comedy Sketches
Music Hall Miscellany
Make 'Em Roar (Vols I & II)

PREAMBLE

In 1956, the year I made my professional debut, men and women yet to draw their pensions had witnessed Music Hall's last grand flowering, for George Robey had been dead for only two years, Little Tich for twenty-eight, Marie Lloyd for thirty-four, and even the great Dan Leno for only just over half a century.

Personalities, songs and catch-phrases of the Victorian and Edwardian Halls were still vivid in the national consciousness. Bingo was yet to invade so many prime-site Empires and Grands and Opera Houses, vast gloomy buildings with vertiginous galleries, inadequate ventilation, bad sight-lines and uncomfortable seating. Performing in these doomed theatres was a dispiriting business, for many—notably the Howard & Wyndham chain—had long since ceased to pay their way, only justifying their existence as tax-loss assets before being sold to local authorities who in turn soon sold them off for re-development.

Then in December 1958, while rehearsing for a pantomime at the dingy Pavilion Liverpool, I caught a glimpse of the real thing: an "Old Time" tour starring GH Elliott, Albert Whelan, Marie Lloyd jnr and Randolph Sutton. The weather was vile, with flaring Tilley lamps doing little to alleviate the biting cold in the Lodge Lane shops, but that show gave me the chance to witness, through the fog which cast an icy haze between stage and auditorium, the authentic style of a dying tradition.

GH Elliott in his invariable white suit sang and yodelled *Lily of Laguna* with all the verve of a man half his age. He had his generation's penetrating high-pitched pre-microphone delivery with its over-enunciated consonants and nasal vowels, though the spontaneity of his reaction to the Shepherdess's Call and ecstatic soft-shoe dance showed that at sixty-eight he still knew his business; off he went in a welter of mutual affection.

The seventy-seven year old Albert Whelan walked slowly down centre supported by a stick— he had lost a leg the year before—whistling as always *The Jolly Brothers* and, punctuated by orchestral stings, treated us to his immaculately timed comic recitation *The Three Trees*. Marie Lloyd jnr was never in the first rank—her own mother once said "that one will never be an artiste as long as she's got a hole in her arse"—though it was quite something to see the original *Don't Dilly Dally* linnet cage.

Randolph Sutton's irresistibly charming *On Mother Kelly's Doorstep* made the strongest impression. After decades of performance every gesture, every move, every piece of business had been considered, polished, honed to perfection; we were offered not just another sentimental chorus song but a controlled and directed presentation. Not for him the routine cry of "All together now!" He gently gestured for us to join in the chorus, raising a hand to an ear to see whether we wished to accept the invitation. And so much did we crave the performer's goodwill that we responded full-throatedly, to be rewarded with a seraphic smile which remains a sharp-etched memory. To this day "All together now!" is banned from my own productions.

Five years later I was engaged for a play at the Glasgow Citizens' Theatre, my first visit to that vibrant city. During rehearsals I saw all the shows in town, including the Variety bill at the Empire—

Mike & Bernie Winters topping tumultuously and Hetty King in support. While I have to admit that male impersonation has never been my favourite style of act Miss King, the last of her kind, was an education.

The Glasgow Empire in 1963 could not have been the most sympathetic forum for an Englishwoman of eighty, especially when singing *Piccadilly*, but any initial reservations were soon dispelled by her extraordinary energy and attack. She also gave us *Ship Ahoy!*, the song she had introduced fifty-four years earlier and which she was still working with spectacular *élan*. As with Elliott nothing was left to chance. All the famous business with the quid of baccy, the pipe and the kitbag was executed with mesmerising finesse.

Only on grainy black and white film can we now observe the charm, the energy, the attention to detail and the high-definition precision with which performers of that generation invested their essentially trivial material.

I say "trivial" because, like melodrama, the Halls were intellectually undemanding. They cheered up the lower orders, wrote Max Beerbohm, "by showing them a life uglier and more sordid than their own", a comment reinforced by many observers. Ernest Foy, himself a Music Hall performer, said "in those days the working class wanted someone to look down on ... if they could see someone who was a little lower, or a bit dafter, it gave them a laugh". "The poorer the audience", declared JB Priestley, "the more desperate the laughter".

In contrast to French and German equivalents British popular culture rarely penetrated below the skin. Its exploration of the human condition was essentially superficial. Politically and sociologically the Halls were unengaged, and though there was burlesque there was little true satire. Working-class audiences wanted to be diverted on their precious nights out, not to watch earnest dissertations on their own drudgery and poverty. There was no statutory censorship in Music Hall, the only brake on song and patter content being the anxiety of managements not to offend the local licensing magistrates. This is not to say that political movements and social upheavals were ignored on the Halls, but their expression tended to be filtered through a thick veil of sentimentality and above all leavened with humour. The British Music Hall audience had no time for sociology lectures; it preferred its light entertainment to be kept light.

In 1964 I was invited to appear in Music Hall myself for the first time. This was in the first-floor saloon of the Green Man, Blackheath Hill, a pub in south-east London where Ewan Hooper was putting on shows to raise funds for the rebuilding of Crowder's Music Hall as the Greenwich Theatre.

The Green Man had been licensed as a Music Hall from 1850 to 1902, and in the six years before its demolition I appeared on and off in that handsome, high-ceilinged room as Chairman, soloist, and director. I wrote sketches and devised scenes; I played the piano and made my first attempts at instrumental arranging. I even did a saucy juggling act. Some things worked and some didn't, but that lively London audience, mostly young and sprinkled with fellow-pros, soon let you know what they thought. The majority of the performers were like myself from the legitimate theatre, and for many of us this stand-up experience was to lead to a parallel career.

* * *

It is significant that Music Hall, as it developed in Britain, never translated to any other country, not even to the major colonies. Individual performers such as Vesta Tilley, Marie Lloyd and Little Tich may have been hugely popular in the United States and Europe, but these were purely personal triumphs. The Halls as an institution remained firmly and uniquely British.

And perhaps this is the source of their undying appeal. Music Hall projects the Gaslight and Glory vision of a fair-minded, generous-spirited, humorously-inclined nation, policing the international community firmly but incorruptibly through *Pax Britannica* and supported by an Empire upon which the sun never set. The Halls perpetuate a powerful folk-memory of simpler times and sunnier days, of fortitude and certitude. So let us embrace this cosy if bogus nostalgia, just for a couple of hours. It does no harm, and it gives a lot of pleasure.

Michael Kilgarriff
Ealing, 1995

IT GIVES ME FURTHER PLEASURE

1. Your Genial Host

In his heyday Mr Chairman was celebrated for his gleaming macassared hair (or as was more often the case his wig), for his dazzling starched shirt-front, for the dubious quality of the studs therein, for the even more suspect gentility of his vowel sounds, and for the hyperbolic grandiloquence of his vocabulary. To sit at the Chairman's table and ply him with drinks was considered a signal honour—Harry Cavendish of the London Pavilion even used to charge half a crown for the privilege. Of Harry Fox, Chairman of the Middlesex Music Hall in Drury Lane it was said "he had a nose that might shame Cyrano, and a complexion of rich old mahogany", and at the sound of his deep voice "a gallery full of the scourgings of the Dials, thieves and their trulls, and similar gentry, would subside into awed silence".

Few chairmen were known to refuse the offer of a drink from a patron, and even fewer would refuse a tip from an artiste—indeed, not to tip one so close to the management's ear could materially affect your chances of a return booking. Most chairmen were ex-comics or singers who had settled for a regular wage and a non-touring existence. They could be surly, venal characters, not at all the jovial and educated figures of legend. There were no star chairmen; they were never more than local celebrities of little more eminence than a Hall's manager, musical director, or indeed its barmaids—in some establishments (notably the original 1861 Oxford) the latter were held in far greater esteem.

Nonetheless Mr Chairman has come down to us as a genial and good-natured fellow, the very pivot and focus of Victorian popular entertainment. So let us not try to dispel any illusions but present him as current perception would portray. Let him be imposing but now and then unexpectedly vulnerable: a touch déclassé perhaps, forever one of life's Remittance Men.

The first gavel-wielder of note was one John Rhodes. In the 1820s he was the proprietor of the notorious Coal Hole in Fountain Court just off the Strand, then as now London's principal artery between the City and the Court. Rhodes was "a facile mime, a ready wit, had an excellent memory, was past master in the art of the raconteur and possessor of a really admirable baritone voice".

It was he who extended and developed the role of the Chairman from that of the private Catch and Glee Clubs of the Georgian Era to the professional Song and Supper Rooms—the immediate forerunners of the Victorian Halls. With his brother William (Chairman at the equally insalubrious Cider Cellars in Maiden Lane) Rhodes offered entertainment for "the most depraved propensities" and in which their clientele "were content to dwell in indecencies for ever. When there was a burst of unwonted enthusiasm, you might be certain that some genius of the place had soared to a happy combination of indecency with blasphemy."

2. Decline of the Halls

Although the early Music Halls which proliferated with extraordinary rapidity in the 1850s after Charles Morton's pioneering experiments at the Canterbury in Lambeth had much in common with the male-orientated Song and Supper Rooms—a Chairman, community singing, food and drink—the new rooms and the entertainment they offered were designed to appeal to a broader-based and less raffish audience. It was the emergent lower middle-classes categorised by JE Ritchie in *The Night Side of London* as "respectable mechanics or small tradesmen with their wives and daughters" who flocked to the new Halls rather than the old Free-and-Easies "members of both Houses, the pick of the Universities, and the bucks of the Row".

Despite Morton's and his imitators' raised tone of programming the spectre of licentiousness was forever to haunt the halls and the carriage-trade firmly kept its distance. Later managers did their best to upgrade Music Hall's louche image by dispensing with the bibulous Chairman, by building ever-larger and ever-ornate "Theatres of Variety", and by exercising quality control over performers' material—as noted in the Preamble the Lord Chamberlain's writ never ran to the Halls.

This striving for respectability by the Mosses, the Butts, the de Freces and the Stolls finally bore fruit in the 1912 Royal Music Hall Performance and a rich harvest of entrepreneurial knighthoods. But it was too late. As early as 1890 Percy Fitzgerald was writing in his booklet *Music-hall Land* "There is little genius or originality of art exhibited... An assiduous course of attendance at a Music Hall is indeed likely to induce a state of hopeless dejection." And by 1910 Charles E Hands was stating in the Daily Mail on behalf of the working-man "We have not left the Halls, the Halls have left us". Managerial aspirations had killed the Golden Goose; the old Music Hall audience was dwindling with the younger generation increasingly seduced away by the more up-to-date attractions of revue and musical comedy, and above all by the intoxicating transatlantic rhythms of ragtime and the tango. Not until half a century later when the Beatles exploded on the world scene in the early 1960s was the impetus of popular song to return to Britain, by which time even Variety, the successor of the Halls, was on its last legs.

Yet folk-memory endures of the Halls offering a lively fun-packed night out, so who are we to dispel our audience's expectations? Let the songs be both jolly and mawkish, the jokes childish and saucy, the atmosphere knowing and ingenuous, the Chairman both pithy and loquacious.

BUILDING AN INTRODUCTION

1. Prime Considerations

"What would you like me to say?"
"Oh, anything you like."
"What have other chairmen said?"
"I don't know. I don't really listen."
"What do they say when you've finished?"
"Oh, I'm always rushing back to the dressing-room."

There you have the first rule for building an introduction: don't expect any help from the artistes. It's surprising also how often they forget to warn the Chairman of a patter interchange so that as you sit there wondering whether your planned back-announcement is entirely appropriate you are suddenly accosted; terrified of saying the wrong thing you waffle and flounder and the gag dies on its feet.

Another infallible way of upsetting your artistes is to pre-empt their jokes. Check your witticisms with the performer concerned; it may be the entire act is built around a jocularity you're intending to casually squander just to get him on.

Jokes, by the way, I firmly believe should be left to the comics. Nothing is more tedious than the stage-struck Chairman who insists upon telling reams of funny stories between each item. Such an approach slows the pace of the show to zero and quickly exhausts an audience's patience, besides incurring the enmity of comic acts about to follow. The Chairman should be amusing, certainly, but without trying to be funnier than the act he is introducing. Let his humorous remarks be confined to one-liners and his intros be designed more to set a mood, to whet the appetite and to heighten anticipation rather than to elicit peals of mirth. His function is to support the artistes, not to undermine them or consider himself as a star tiresomely interrupted by inadequate turns.

2. Advance warning

Music Hall songs are often amenable to a wide variety of interpretations, so be on your guard for the unexpected approach to a familiar title—in my time I've introduced *Has Anybody Seen My Tiddler?* sung by a children's nanny and *Seaweed* sung by a monk! Another trap is the misleading title; the lyrics of *The Postman's Holiday* never once mention postmen and *Paddle Your Own Canoe* has absolutely nothing to do with canoeing.

3. Keep It Simple

Many intros need comprise no more than the title of the song and the name of the performer. A simple number is best announced simply, e.g. *"Ain' It Nice?* declares Miss N, and I am sure you will agree with me when I say ain' *she* nice?, ladies and gentlemen, as we welcome that demure and dimpling damsel Miss N!" Similarly for, say, *If I Had a Girl as Nice as You* the title encapsulates the entire lyric; there are no surprises, nor need there be when introducing a song whose strength lies chiefly in its melodic interest. Straightforward numbers need not be fussed over.

4. How Much Should The Chairman Give Away?

As an artiste enters the audience has to absorb a great deal of information. If a woman is attractive and wears a pretty dress both must be admired and appreciated; if a man is wearing a fright wig and a grotesque costume both must be digested and laughed at; if there is a backcloth depicting Scarborough Sands or Piccadilly Circus the location must be identified; if the setting features furniture and properties these must also be registered. Nor is this all: is the artiste cooingly genteel or raucously comic? Do we like the voice, the personality, the general demeanour?

So many decisions to be made, so much to be sorted and filed, and all *during the first verse*. If essentials of plot or character are being established during those first few moments—and the average verse lasts only thirty seconds—they may well be missed, the audience never quite catches up and the whole turn goes off at half-cock. Sometimes this danger can be averted by the performer starting with a chorus, a self-defeating solution if (as in *Now I Have to Call Him Father* or *Come Down and Open the Door*) the last line prematurely discloses the comedic basis of the entire number.

Even when on the song-sheet some titles should not be announced if they are likely to give the game away too soon, other examples being *He's Going There Every Night, Father's Got the Sack from the Waterworks,* or *I Want to Play with Little Dick.*

An indication of the artiste's costume may be worth a mention therefore, especially for a comic item in which, for instance, a man dressed in ragged clothes might be described as the "scourge of Savile Row", or "dapper and debonair" or "attired in some of the less well-known items from our extensive wardrobe". A woman eccentrically dressed can be "gowned by Worth of the Leytonstone High Road (or local)" or "arrayed in the finest dress available at this price-range".

Previous appearances may be referred to, e.g. "Mr N whom you may recall appeared earlier as *The Galloping Major* now effects a complete change of character in order to regale us with etc., etc." Such a statement as "Miss N delighted us a short while ago as a little girl with *Daddy Wouldn't Buy Me a Bow Wow* and now demonstrates her versatility in a very different style of song with..." both help the audience to keep track of what might be an unfamiliar cast and also mightily please the artiste.

5. Song Narrative: Subjective or Objective?
When considering your introduction look first at the lyrics: is the singer describing his own experience? Or someone else's? An example of the subjective lyric is *Don't Dilly Dally*:
> "We had to move away,
> 'Cos the rent we couldn't pay..."

Here the moonlight flit, being the performer's own personal experience, is described in the first person, whereas in *Joshu-ah* the doleful events are suffered by a second party as the opening line makes clear:
> "Joshua courted Miss May
> To be correct I should say -
> She courted him, for he was so shy..."

Since the lyrical stance affects the nature of the performance so should it influence the intro. If Harry tells you he has broken a leg your sympathy is invoked directly, but if you are told Harry has broken a leg by someone else your sympathy is expressed at one remove. And even if at some point—often the chorus—the singer assumes the character of the protagonist we are still aware that we are watching a comment on the story-line rather than personal involvement.

So if a lyric features what the drama calls the Alienation Effect how should the Chairman handle it? Does it matter? Perhaps in

Building an Introduction   7

many songs not all that much, but if wielding the gavel is your chosen mode of self-expression why not aim for excellence rather than mere competence? Don't sell the office of Chairman short: subtlety and sensitivity need not be confined to the soloists.

6. Two Introductions Analysed:

(a) *The Ballad of Sam Hall*
In this famous song we follow a condemned murderer from his cell to the public scaffold, to the very instant of his death by hanging. Obviously a suitable mood needs to be established, especially if the preceding item has been broadly comic. I settle the house down by telling them that "We come now to a most interesting song, one which lays claim to be the very first popular Music Hall song of them all—from the 1840s: *The Ballad of Sam Hall*. We meet Sam in the condemned cell, the night before his execution. Perhaps he deserves his fate; nevertheless he remains defiant and unrepentant to the last, asking for no pity and no favours. A grim tale indeed, given a performance of power and intensity now by Mr N." The performer's name is uttered quietly (the lights having dimmed *during* the intro) and the gavel tapped very gently.

This takes only 30 seconds, the important background is related succinctly and an atmosphere established for what can be a quite harrowing few minutes. That the audience knows Sam is to die adds to the drama of his first appearance, the unequivocal nature of his guilt allied to a total lack of remorse making him a repellant yet fascinating figure, for even in the shadow of the gallows his uncompromising stance compels our admiration. The back-announcement should of course stay in keeping, e.g. "A remarkably powerful performance indeed by Mr N... Well, ladies and gentlemen, contrast is what we aim for in our productions, and there could scarcely be any greater contrast between that item and our next, as we continue now with etc., etc." Definitely no jokes about "Poor Mr N—always kept hanging about."

(b) *Molly O'Morgan*
Another number which needs careful setting-up is the more light-hearted *Molly O'Morgan*. Its sub-title is *The Irish-Italian Girl*, though the lyrics inform us that while Molly is certainly Irish her Italian-ness is assumed. Let's look at the first verse:

> *Patsy left Dublin, for London town bent,*
> *Weeks passed away, but no letter he sent,*
> *So Molly, his sweetheart, soon thought of a plan;*
> *She left for London to find her young man!*
> *And there hired an organ and costume so fine,*
> *Then in search of Patsy, each morning at nine:*
> *Chorus: Molly O'Morgan, with her little organ, etc.*

This is an bewilderingly complex plot-line, launched into within seconds of the appearance of a doubtless winsome ingenue wearing a *"costume so fine"* and in all probability carrying an organ prop. All these distractions will almost certainly combine with her ravishing form and face, raven tresses and seductive tones to obscure the story beyond recall—unless Mr Chairman has paraphrased those essential first four lines in his intro as follows: "and now a treat for all those admirers of Miss N—and who is not?—as she informs us in number X of one Patsy Burke who came from Dublin to London looking for work, and of Molly O'Morgan who came looking for *him*, the spalpeen! So let us now follow the fortunes of the gorgeous and guileless Miss N!"

No cracks, please, about Molly's organ ("showing it to all and sundry", "last night it started squeaking", "for a little girl her organ's quite big, isn't it?") either before or after the number.

7. Opera
If the Chairman's duty is to maximise audience receptiveness it's always helpful to outline the background of an operatic aria, no matter which language it is sung in. A sentence or two giving the context of, say, *I Dreamt that I Dwelt in Marble Halls* heightens appreciation very considerably, for although the melody may be familiar the plot-line may not be so well-known. And don't omit the name of the composer. It'll be on the music, and does so raise the tone.

8. Past or Present
Another dimension of the Chairman's art often overlooked is that of tense. Operatic arias usually either advance a continuing plot or treat of a character's current emotional state, whereas Music Hall lyrics as we have seen in *Joshu-ah* ("*Joshua courted Miss May*") and *Molly O'Morgan* ("*Patsy left Dublin*") often deal with past events.

Building an Introduction 9

On the other hand the storyline of *Sam Hall* is obviously occurring here and now (*"My name it is Sam Hall"*) and so should have a present tense intro ("We meet him in the condemned cell, etc").

9. Genesis of a Song

Historical events—wars, politics, royal marriages—were all grist to the song-writer's mill, as were novelties on the social scene. Johnny Danvers' *I've Got the Ooperzootic* referred to the first women doctors, Jack Norworth's *Kitty the Telephone Girl* to Alexander Graham Bell's invention and George Leybourne's *Up in a Balloon* to the first Aeronautical Exhibition held at the Crystal Palace in 1868 (and not, as is so often stated, to the 1870 Siege of Paris). Although not written as such *I'll Make a Man of You* became a notoriously effective First World War recruiting song while *All Round My Hat* laments a lover sent to Australia under the cruel transportation laws which were not repealed until the 1850s.

10. Scenery

Capital can be made out of stage settings—"For this item, ladies and gentlemen, we feature for the very first time tonight: a *prop!*" An intake of breath from the house will greet this astounding revelation, just as a good reaction can be elicited from mocking reference to the back-cloth—"The scenic marvels you are about to witness as the curtain rises ... very much against its better judgement ... are intended to represent the superb formal garden of a grand English country mansion at the height of its summer glory... I have to tell you that 'cos you'd never know just by looking..."

Even no setting at all can be a source of humour: "when the plush curtains part you will see before you a tastefully arranged empty space...!" If you have to set a chair or other prop you might observe "Now for a complete change of scene ... voila!... As must be apparent even to the meanest intelligence, the stage is now instantaneously transformed into a sumptuously appointed boudoir, fit for a queen. Or fit at least for that queen of all our hearts Miss N, who glides seductively into view with etc., etc."

For non-comic items "now we take you to..." or "we find Miss/ Mr N in..." will suffice. Alternatively, you may prefer not to mention the setting at all: it's all a matter of judgement, especially if your scenic-artist is of paranoid disposition.

11. Vocabulary

For your next birthday ask Aunt Augusta for a dictionary of quotations or a copy of Roget's Thesaurus. The first will give you access to the telling phrase and the second will help you to vary your synonyms: both will help you to avoid the crass "Put your hands together" and "So let's hear it for...", injunctions which belong to the club compére and never to the august figure of the Music Hall Chairman. Imaginative and elegant phraseology in your utterances compliment both artiste and audience.

Leonard Sachs in BBC TV's *The Good Old Days* popularised the string of alliteration which while perfectly acceptable can, I feel, be overdone. I usually include one or two introductions of this kind since I know audiences expect them, but I'm also aware that they can swiftly pall. Be sparing also with "Your own, your *very* own..."

12. Lyricists and Composers

As suggested in the paragraph on operatic arias the writer of a song may be given if the name is well known—that *Beautiful Dreamer* was written by Stephen Foster, for instance, is certainly worth mentioning. I always introduce *On the Road to Mandalay* by giving out the lyricist/poet (Rudyard Kipling) and the composer (Oley Speaks) before mentioning the title, and more than once I've been anticipated from out front. *The Lost Chord* was written by Sir Arthur Sullivan as a tribute to his dying brother; the lyrics of *The Holy City* were from the pen of Fred E Weatherly who was also responsible for *Danny Boy* and *Roses of Picardy*. Details of this kind all help to flesh out an intro and can be useful if you need to "pad" for a scene or costume change.

13. Song-sheets

Don't mention song-sheet numbers immediately prior to an artiste's name or every head will drop to scan the programme just as the performer makes that all-important entrance. Be prepared to pause to enable specs to be donned and lyrics to be chuckled over.

Even when you do not announce a song-sheet number many in the audience will still try and find the chorus, in which instance I generally say something on the lines of "This song is not on your song-sheets—your services are not required for this item ... we thought you'd like a rest..." And if a chorus has been missed off the

Building an Introduction

song-sheet you can say "This is not on your song-sheets but I'm sure you'll know it well..."

14. Entrances

It may be that on occasion you will wish to mention a soloist's name during the course of an intro as well as at the end, so if you are to avoid the embarrassment of stopping the band or even worse of the artiste coming on too soon you must make it clear to the entire company that the cue for an act to start is the bang of the gavel *and not before*.

Remain standing until the artiste has entered and graciously acknowledged your presence. Only then should you sit down, but do not imagine you can relax. For should you not continue to take an interest in the proceedings you have just announced with such enthusiasm? You must sing all the choruses, laugh at all the jokes, and be ready to respond to any asides thrown in your direction. In other words don't switch off, especially if the lighting does not stretch to a Chairman's "special" which can be dimmed out, putting you in welcome semi-darkness during the turns.

It is a well-remarked phenomenon that appreciation of comedy is enhanced by sharing. On a punch-line an audience will look at one another as they rock with laughter; not infrequently they will look to the Chairman for confirmation of a joke, so he should not have his nose buried in his notes or be gazing abstractedly at the floor wondering whether the pubs will be shut before the show comes down.

15. Exits

At the conclusion of an act rise and applaud, calling the artiste back as many times as you think appropriate, for you must be the arbiter of audience mood and stamina. The physical effort of clapping can be tiring for elderly audiences and as a rule I do not call an artiste back more than once unless the house has a broader demographic mix, though it is a great mistake to presume that a less than thunderous reception implies lack of enjoyment.

Performers must be asked to wait in the wings until it is clear they will not be summoned back further. When an audience is displaying frenzied enthusiasm nothing is more annoying than to be waving like a demented semaphorist, shouting out "And again!"

only to realise that the artiste has disappeared to the dressing-room. Audiences like to see their appreciation acknowledged. To snub a warm reception steers close to insolence.

16. Back-Announcements
As well as an irrelevant joke-festooned intro avoid topping an act in your back-announcement. When a performer has brought the house down it is very bad form to try and go one better—"Thank you, Mr N. That reminds me of a chap I met in the pub the other day. He said to the landlord etc., etc." Even worse are those chairmen so insensitive as to essay a sexual innuendo after the female balladeer has just delighted with an aria or gently sentimental number—"Thank you, Miss N, a lady celebrated in many fields, especially the one behind the Fire Station." (Nor would we ever *dream* of introducing her by asking for "a warm hand on her opening", would we? Give the girl a chance.)

Watch that your jokey back-announcements don't become too waspish and dismissive. I once saw a Chairman of considerable experience completely demolish the efforts of a couple who had just sung a ballad of blighted hope by saying "Well, that's cheered the party up..." Another time after an excellent performance of *A Fallen Star* this same Chairman said "Thank God I shan't have to sit through that for another week!"

Such reduction of artistes' efforts to gag-fodder may raise a snigger or two but the bulk of the audience may well be alienated. Genuine artistry and sincerity, whether dramatic or comedic, should be respected and a Chairman's constant dipping down to humour's lowest common denominator only demeans the performances he should be enhancing. If not entirely sure of the impact of a performance in advance I jot down two or three back-announcements on my notes, using the one that seems most appropriate when the time comes. And if none of them is right I just fall back on simplicity and straightforwardness—"Well done, Miss N, as splendid as ever".

If a comedy turn has reduced the house to hysteria it's not a bad idea to allow a breathing space before continuing. Just stand and smile as they tell each other how funny it was; when you feel they've calmed down give a little chuckle of appreciation and go gently into the next intro.

Building an Introduction   13

A comment such as "I'm sure we'd all agree you'd have to go a long way to hear that ballad better sung" or "How wonderful to hear that delightful old song so delightfully rendered" often elicits a murmur of agreement and sometimes even a further round of applause. And after a tricky accompaniment it is always a popular move to acknowledge the pianist: "Beautifully sung by N, and I am sure you'd all like to show your appreciation for a most sensitive accompaniment by Maestro N." All these little touches help to bind the house and the company together, the essential function of the Chairman.

17. Developing Your Style
The stature of the Chairman is perceived as one of relaxed authority so don't try to "act" the part by overplaying the heavy mock-pomposity. Be natural; imagine yourself as a host welcoming friends to a dinner-party and your style will emerge. Adjust my Introductions to suit the performances and practise till you feel comfortable with what you intend to say. Attend as many company rehearsals as you can to try out different ideas and test reactions.

There are of course many other aspects of the Chairman's role—opening and closing the show, introducing the orchestra, dealing with hecklers, announcing the interval, filling in for costume and/or scene changes, etc., etc—which need thought and attention; these are all discussed in *It Gives Me Great Pleasure* (Samuel French), the companion predecessor to this volume.

If your first few essays at raising a laugh fall flat don't panic—give them a chance to get to know you. Experience has taught me that if my witticisms don't set the house aflame with merriment thirty seconds after I've walked on they probably will by the time we finish, which is why I avoid upbraiding an audience for not responding boisterously right from the off. Go easy on the "that'll go better second house" and "please yourselves" type of put-downs—let them like you before you insult them. As I said earlier the Chairman should not consider himself a comic, so take things gently to start with and don't squander an audience's initial goodwill by demanding raucous participation almost before they've got their coats off.

Despite its responsibilities the Chairman's role offers very considerable rewards, for Music Hall is a form of entertainment which still attracts audiences uniquely ready and willing to enjoy themselves, to collaborate with each other and with the performers—who of course include the Chairman—in playing a game of make-believe. They want to have a good time and they want to like you. I'm sure they will.

SONG INTRODUCTIONS

As well as the scores of thousands of songs written specifically for the variety stage many operatic arias, musical comedy hits and parlour ballads found their way on to the Halls, those listed below being within my direct experience as Chairman. The Gilbert and Sullivan canon is excluded, as are folk songs which like most G&S tend to sit uneasily in a Music Hall programme.

Broadly speaking my cut-off date is 1920 though some later songs of appropriate style such as *Ain' It Nice, Don't Have Any More Missus Moore, Turned Up, On Mother Kelly's Doorstep, Nobody Loves a Fairy When She's Forty* and *The Marrow Song* virtually demand inclusion.

Many songs are amenable to a variety of interpretations, so if an entry does not suit your needs look up a number of similar type. Some cross-referencing—American, Army, Children, Country, Irish, Navy, Scots, Seaside, etc—is indicated. A list of songs which can be performed as two-handers and/or concerted items is given on page 199. Songs to do with London are listed on page 201.

As I said in *It Gives Me Great Pleasure* you should not regard my introductions as Holy Writ. They work for me but may not necessarily be suitable for you, so look on them as blueprints from which to devise remarks consonant with your own style, personality and delivery.

* * *

Underneath each song title lyricists and composers are given in brackets with lyricists to the left of the colon. Joint lyricists and/or composers are linked by an ampersand. The dates indicate either a song's first recorded appearance or first publication, whichever is the earlier. Original and/or significant performers where ascertainable are listed in alphabetical order.

All theatres mentioned are in London unless otherwise stated.

Remarks after the slash sign (/) are "back-announcements" to be made after the artistes have taken their calls. Whatever comment is made the performers' names should always be given.

ACROSS THE BRIDGE   1888
(Fred Bowyer: George Le Brunn)
Charles Godfrey

(*For concerted version*) The magic of dear old London Town lures countless visitors from every corner of the globe. They come to see the Tower of London, Westminster Abbey, the Changing of the Weather, and also to enjoy the historic appeal of London's bridges, whose cold stones bear mute witness to tragedy, comedy, drama—indeed, all aspects of the human condition. Let us imagine that we are those old stones as we observe the comings and goings: Across the Bridge!

(*See page 199 for other possible concerted items, also page 201 for further songs of London*)

AFTER THE BALL   1892
(Charles K. Harris)
Originally sung by Ann Whitney but popularised by J. Aldrich Libbey. In the UK sung by Charles Godfrey, George Lashwood *et al.*
Interpolated into "A Trip to Chinatown", Madison Square and Hoyt's, New York. London: Toole's, 1894.
Vesta Tilley sang a version by Fred Bowyer & Orlando Powell (1893) with the melody for the verses re-written and with fresh lyrics throughout. Fred Bowyer & Orlando Powell also published a parody in 1894 for Arthur Roberts. Only the original is sung today.

No X on your song-sheets is that haunting ballad After the Ball, and while the chorus is well known the verses are not perhaps so familiar. And a touching tale of misunderstanding and heartache they tell, rendered to the utmost advantage for us now by (*local's*) favourite vocalist: Mr N.

For girl in female dress: One of the first British artistes to sing No X, After the Ball, was Miss Vesta Tilley, but to put our next artiste, Miss N, a lady whose femininity is positively incandescent, into male attire would be a blunder of the first magnitude. So now becomingly befrocked with this touching tale of misunderstanding and heartache, is Miss N. / Thank you, N for letting us hear After the Ball- and well done yourselves, ladies and gentlemen, for singing up so well.

AIN' IT NICE?   1923
(R. P. Weston & Bert Lee: R. Harris Weston)
Daisy Dormer

Song Introductions   17

Now we present a young lady, eagerly yet tremulously contemplating courtship and marriage and all that is implied thereof. Ain' it Nice? declares Miss N, and I am sure you will agree with me when I say ain' *she* nice, ladies and gentlemen, as we welcome that demure and dimpling damsel Miss N! / Wasn't that enchanting?

ALABAMA JUBILEE   1915
(Jack Yellen: George L. Cobb)
Elizabeth Murray

We here in Britain export the best of our popular music so it is only right that from time to time we import the best. From the United States a celebratory song entitled Alabama Jubilee, a ragtime melody—I believe that is the correct technical term, maestro?—to be given in dashing and diverting style by Mr N. / Any Americans in…? How nice for you to come all the way to *(local)* to see an American song *done properly!*

(*See also* Alexander's Ragtime Band, Are You from Dixie?, Beautiful Dreamer, Bill Bailey Won't You Please Come Home?, Bowery, Dancing on the Streets, Everybody's Doin' It, Everything is Peaches Down in Georgia, Frankie and Johnny, Hitchy-koo, How Ya Gonna Keep 'Em Down on the Farm?, I Want to Be in Dixie, I Want to Go Back to Michigan, I Want to Go to Idaho, Swanee)

ALEXANDER'S RAGTIME BAND   1911
(Irving Berlin)
The Two Bobs, Emma Carus, Arthur Collins, Byron G. Harlan, Al Jolson, Ethel Levey, Billy Murray, Clarice Mayne, Ellaline Terriss, Maud Tiffany

That rising young American composer Mr Berlin has come up with a new song which has swept the world. It concerns a Mr Alexander who has his own band. But not just any old band—a ragtime band. No X on your song-sheets, to be given a rousing performance not just by any old artiste—oh, no!—but by Our Man in Dixie Mr N!

(*See also* Alabama Jubilee *etc.*)

ALGERNON, GO H'ON!   1914
(Worton David & Bert Lee)
Florrie Forde

A perky little song, sung by a perky little person: Miss N, who celebrates her return with No X, Algernon, Go h'On. Why the lyric should feature an intrusive "h" I couldn't say, nor does it much matter when into view comes tripping the suggestible and susceptible Miss N. / Miss N—wasn't that a pretty dress? Took me hours to get that hem straight.

18   It Gives Me Further Pleasure

ALGY, OR THE PICCADILLY JOHNNY WITH THE LITTLE GLASS EYE
(Harry B. Norris)   1895
Vesta Tilley

A celebrated Music Hall song follows, in which our Miss N gives us the latest intelligence of Algernon Brown, a young swell who surveys the social scene through a monocle. I refer to Algy, the Piccadilly Johnny with the little Glass Eye, a young blade with more money than sense. Details now from the faultlessly fashionable Miss N. / An immaculate performance there from the immaculately attired Miss N.

(See page 201 for further songs of London; for further "eye" songs see Could You Be True to Eyes of Blue?, Green Eye of the Little Yellow God, I Can't Take My Eyes Off You, I Just Can't Make My Eyes Behave, I've Got My Eyes on You, Two Lovely Black Eyes, When Irish Eyes Are Smiling*)*

ALGY'S ABSOLUTELY FULL OF TACT   1927
(Fred Chester)
Fred Chester

A fashionable man-about-town now demonstrates the exquisite sensitivity and tact that are the hall-marks of the well-bred English gentleman. He has asked me not to announce his name—he doesn't want his family to know he's been appearing in a common Music Hall, especially in front of you lot—so he prefers to remain synonymous. I shall simply introduce him therefore as the Roguish Rascal of Rotten Row (*or local*)! / Mr N. He takes a lot of beating ... enjoys it too, so I believe.

ALICE BLUE GOWN   1919
(Joseph McCarthy: Harry Tierney)
Edith Day, Anna Neagle
From "Irene", Empire

Most ladies, so I believe, have a favourite dress and our Miss N is no exception—hers being not a little black number but an Alice Blue Gown. So to tell us of *her* favourite dress is our favourite singer, the elegant and ever-beguiling Miss N. / "It wore and it wore and it wore"—I think Miss N is wearing pretty well, too, don't you?

ALL HANDS ON DECK   1909
(C. W. Murphy & Dan Lipton)
George Lashwood

Avast behind!... Nothing personal, madam, just getting into the mood, into the swing of things, because we now welcome a member

Song Introductions   19

of the Senior Service, the Royal Navy. With No X, All Hands On Deck, comes scudding the pride of the squadron, Seaman N!
(*See also* All the Nice Girls Love a Sailor, Down Went the Captain, Fishermen of England, Married to a Mermaid, My Boy's a Sailor Man, Oh Jack You are a Handy Man, On the Good Ship "Yacki Hicky Doo La", Sailor's Farewell, Ship I Love, Sons of the Sea)

ALL ROUND MY HAT   c1830
(I. Hansell: trad air arr. John Valentine)
W. H. Williams

It's not so long ago that our penal code permitted the cruel and inhumane punishment of transportation, sundering husbands from wives, parents from children, and sweetheart from sweetheart. That is the background to our next ballad: All Round My Hat, and few artistes can tug at the heartstrings more powerfully than Miss N. / You'd have to go a long way to hear a ballad better sung than that, I'm sure you'd agree.

ALL THAT I ASK OF YOU IS LOVE   1905
(Edgar Sellen: Herbert Ingraham)
Frank Morell, Violet Romaine, Bessie Wynn

All that I ask of you is Love ... yes, I'm talking to you, madam. It's not much to ask, is it? No, that's the title of our next song: All That I Ask Of You Is Love, No X. No doubts at all what the ladies'/our response should be, for the person hungry for affection is none other than the smouldering Mr/Miss N. / That scorched your song-sheets, didn't it? Mr/Miss N, asking for love, and not in vain, I'm sure.

ALL THE GIRLS ARE LOVELY BY THE SEASIDE   1913
(Worton David & Bert Lee: Harry Fragson)
Harry Carlton, Harry Fragson, Ella Retford

(*For concerted version performed in bathing costumes*) No fewer than three gentlemen now aver that All the Girls are Lovely by the Seaside—an observation I most heartily subscribe to, and which is also the title of our next song, to be placed at the talents and moustaches of that topping trio: The Margate Mashers! (*Or local variant such as Brighton Beaux, Dorset Debonnaires, Morecambe Madcaps, Scarborough Scallywags, etc.*)

(*See also* Bathing, Bobbing Up and Down Like This, Brighton (*Gilbert*), Brighton (*Rubens*), By the Beautiful Sea, By the Sea (By the Beautiful Silvery Sea), I Do Like to Be Beside the Seaside, I Love to Go Swimmin' With Women, On the

Prom Prom Promenade, She Sells Sea-shells (*chorus only*), Seaside Girls, Seaweed, Swim Sam Swim, Swimming Master, They All Walk the Wibbly Wobbly Walk, They're All Single by the Seaside, You Can Do a Lot of Things at the Seaside that You Can't Do in Town. *For other two-handers and/or possible concerted items see page 199*)

ALL THE NICE GIRLS LOVE A SAILOR (SHIP AHOY!)   1905
(A. J. Mills: Bennett Scott)
Hetty King, Ella Retford

(*For male impersonation*) A nautical number now from our Miss N, an artiste always very ship-shape and Bristol fashion, as I'm sure you've noticed. All the Nice Girls, she declares in No X, Love a Sailor. So let us sling our hammocks and splice the mainbrace as over the horizon steams the delightfully able-bodied Miss N. / There she goes, taking her little bell bottoms with her.

(*For male*) There follows a naval ballad—nothing to do with oranges—but one which extols the virile charms of Britain's seafarers because as we know All the Nice Girls Love a Sailor—No X. So let us pipe aboard our own jolly jack tar ... he comes from Epsom—he's one of the Epsom Salts ... here he is, bringing his very able body into view, Mr N. / Goodbye, sailor...

(*See also* All Hands on Deck *etc.*)

AMATEUR WHITEWASHER, THE   1896
(Fred Murray: Fred W. Leigh)
Frank Seeley

Mr N—for it is he—comes to us from a long engagement and a short marriage, and a further disaster in his private life, according to No X, was the occasion on which he attempted to whitewash the garden wall. I don't know why we have to be subjected to this sordid story of low-life ineptitude, but let us just sit back and think of England as we witness the dire domestic doings of Mr N! / Poor chap—he's been suffering from distemper ... perhaps we should have him put down—what do you think?

AMOROUS GOLDFISH, THE   1896
(Harry H. Greenbank: Sidney Jones)
Marie Tempest
From "The Geisha", Daly's

An aquatic aria now, an exquisite number from the popular musical comedy "The Geisha" by Mr Sidney Jones and entitled The Amorous

Song Introductions   21

Goldfish. And the singer? Well, I'm delighted to welcome back to the stage the intensely and ichthyologically interesting Miss N. / Miss N—wearer of the face serene, and bearer of the form divine.

AND HER GOLDEN HAIR WAS HANGING DOWN HER BACK
(Felix McGlennon: Monroe H. Rosenfeld)   1894
Yvette Guilbert, Seymour Hicks, Alice Leamar, Eunice Vance
Interpolated into "The Shop Girl", Gaiety

A cautionary tale of what happened on the first visit to London of an innocent young virgin... (*to woman in audience*) how's your memory, love?... and as you can see in No X it is entitled And her Golden Hair was Hanging Down—oh, you know her, do you? Yes, she gets about ... sung for us now by that essence of urbanity Mr N! / Well done, Mr N. That song reminds me of my wife. She's got golden hair hanging down her back. None on her head, just hanging down her...

AND THE BAND PLAYED ON *See* BAND PLAYED ON, THE

AND THE GREAT BIG SAW CAME NEARER AND NEARER   1936
(R. P. Weston & Bert Lee: R. Harris Weston)
Leslie Sarony

(*For two-handed version*) Sometimes in our programmes we offer comedy and sometimes we offer tragedy, and sometimes ... it's difficult to tell the difference. Be that as it may And the Great Big Saw came Nearer and Nearer is the highly significant title of the saga about to be given a finely-honed performance by those two ornaments of the legitimate theatre Sir Herbert and Lady Beerbohm Bush! / Our thanks to Miss N and Mr N for that item, known in theatrical circles not so much as a tour de force as a forced to tour.
   (*For other two-handers and/or possible concerted items see page 199*)

AND THE LEAVES BEGAN TO FALL   1904
(J. P. Harrington: George Le Brunn)
Marie Lloyd

Miss N now commands our attention with a song entitled And the Leaves Began to Fall. We all know what that did to Adam and Eve, so a few minutes of naked passion now from the properly delightful and delightfully proper Miss N. / One of the great advantages of sitting here is the propinquity of the female form, no more devastating than when displayed by Miss N.

AND THE PARROT SAID 1907
(Worton David & Orlando Powell)
Daisy Jerome, Marie Lloyd

Music Hall songs are sometimes written about the most unlikely subjects, and our next number deals with a domestic pet of the feathered variety, in this case a parrot. An avian aria therefore from a lady known to her friends as Psittacosis Sal, but known to her adoring public as Miss N. / My wife hates parrots ... she doesn't mind a cockatoo but she hates parrots.

ANNIE LAURIE c1700
(William Douglas. Revised 1835 by Lady John Douglas Scott)

In Maxwelton in Scotland in 1682 was born one Annie Laurie, a lassie greatly admired by a local laddie William Douglas. Though she married another, the bewitching Annie has achieved immortality through William's lovelorn verses no less than his lovely tune. So let us hear Annie Laurie once again, beautifully sung for us now by (our own Scottish songster) Mr N. / Bringing tears to the eyes, there, Mr N. (*If followed by comic*) And someone else to make you weep is our next artiste...

(*See also* I Belong to Glasgow, I Love a Lassie, I'm Ninety-Four This Mornin', Johnny Morgan's Sister, My Ain Folk, Roamin' in the Gloamin', Saftest O' The Family, Stop Yer Ticklin' Jock, Wee Deoch-an-Doris, We Parted on the Shore)

ANY OLD IRON? 1911
(Charles Collins & E. A. Sheppard: Fred Terry)
Harry Champion

This is where the show takes a dip ... and at this point I'd like to prevent—present a man who as we can see in No X has recently received a legacy from his old Uncle Bill, so stand well back for the man with the winning smile and the losing face: Mr N! / Thank you, Mr N, who likes to describe himself as a self-made man, thus relieving the Almighty of a grave responsibility.

(*See other "legacy" songs:* 'E Dunno Where 'E are, Where Did You Get that Hat?, Wot Cher!)

ARCHIBALD, CERTAINLY NOT! 1909
(John L. St John & George Robey: Alfred Glover)
George Robey

Our Mr N as you may know comes from a very large family. In fact

Song Introductions 23

he's the fourteenth of thirteen children, which makes it very difficult for him to afford original material. And that's why the next number which was once made famous by Mr George Robey will now be despatched into oblivion by Mr N! / Mr N, who did offer to sing an encore but I said "Mr N, certainly not!"

ARE WE TO PART LIKE THIS, BILL? 1903
(Harry Castling & Charles Collins)
Kate Carney

We continue with No X, Are We To Part Like This, Bill? a song which as the title implies tells of a ordinary enough event—a woman who loved not wisely but too well—and lifted out of the commonplace in a powerfully emotional performance by Miss N. / A tragedy in miniature from Miss N.

ARE YOU FROM DIXIE? 1913
(Jack Yellen: George L. Cobb)
The Two Rascals & Jacobson

Just to ring the changes we go across the old herring-pond for our next song—Are You From Dixie? To be delivered by an artiste brought over especially from the United States at—*enormous* expense... we've put him up at the Waldorf Hysteria. So here now complete with deep-south accent and matching trousers is Mr Mason Dixon! / That was your very own Mr N with his soft-shoe dance. Next week he's promised us his hard-sock routine.

(*See also* Alabama Jubilee *etc.*)

'ARF A PINT OF ALE 1905
(Charles Tempest)
Gus Elen

Mr N now claims our time and attention with a discussion of his favourite beverage. Why on earth he should think we'd be interested I really don't know. Be that as it may here now—if he can find his way to the stage—and performing under an assumed talent, is Mr N. / There he goes—as piss-istently plastered as ever.

(*See also* Champagne Charlie, Clicquot, Come Home Father, Don't Stop My 'Arf a Pint of Ale, Down at the Old Bull and Bush, Glorious Beer, Please Sell No More Drink to My Father, We Used to Gather at the Old Dun Cow, What I Want is a Proper Cup of Coffee)

24   It Gives Me Further Pleasure

ARMY OF TODAY'S ALL RIGHT, THE   1914
(Fred W. Leigh: Kenneth Lyle)
Vesta Tilley

A song with a military feel now—I love to feel the military, don't you? The Army of Today's All Right, stoutly insists Miss N in No X. So here she is in full patriotic flow, the pride of the regiment, Miss N. / Thank you very much, Miss N. That's made all our hearts beat faster, hasn't it? Off she marches, back to her Officer's Mess...

(*See also* Belgium Put the "Kibosh" on the Kaiser, Blue Bell, Captain Ginjah O.T.!, Galloping Major, Good-bye Dolly Gray, Good-bye-ee, Here We are! Here We are!! Here We are Again!!!, How Ya Gonna Keep 'Em Down on the Farm?, I'll Make a Man of You, It's a Long Long Way to Tipperary, Jolly Good Luck to the Girl Who Loves a Soldier, Keep the Homes Fires Burning, Macdermott's War Song, Major-General Worthington, Now You've Got Yer Khaki on, Old Brigade, Pack Up Your Troubles, Since I Walked Out with a Soldier, Sister Susie's Sewing Shirts for Soldiers, Soldiers of the Queen, Take Me Back to Dear Old Blighty, Where are the Lads of the Village Tonight?, Who'll Care for the Children?)

'ARRY 'ARRY 'ARRY   1902
(Fred W. Leigh & Fred Murray: George Le Brunn)
Fred T. Daniels, Alec Hurley

A Cockney ditty now as Mr N tries to bring his pal Harry—or 'Arry as they say in the vehicular—up to the starting-post in the old matrimonial stakes. See what you can do with the choruses—No X—while the verses will be sustained by the crafty and cunning Mr N. / That's one of my favourite songs, especially when sung by Mr N.

ART IS CALLING FOR ME   1911
(Harry B. Smith: Victor Herbert)
Louise Bliss
From "The Enchantress", New York, New York

Aka as I Want To Be A Prima Donna, *though this can cause confusion with a quite different American song of the same title (Malone: Sherman, 1909) sung by Maggie Cline*

And now we meet a princess with ideas below her station, because she longs to be a prima donna on the stage—like Tetrazzini or Melba. This is the celebrated aria from Mr Victor Herbert's "The Enchantress", so here is our very own enchantress, that sensationally spectacular soprano: Miss N. / A vivid performance indeed from Miss N. Art Is Calling For Me—what a lucky chap...

Song Introductions   25

ASK A P'LICEMAN   c1885
(E. W. Rogers: A. E. Durandeau)
James Fawn

Our next song has one of the most celebrated lines in the Music Hall canon: "If you want to know the time...?" (*Audience:* "... *Ask a p'liceman!*") It has been said that bobbies obtain their watches by half-inching them from drunks too sozzled to resist. I don't believe it, do you? An appalling slander on a fine body of men, and so here is a fine body of man if ever there was one: P.C. N. / Before joining the Force P.C. N was principal ballet master with the Brigade of Guards.
    (*See also* Gendarmes' Duet *and* P.C. 49)

AT THE VICAR'S FANCY BALL   1915
(Worton David & Bert Lee)
Ernest Shand

As I expect you know we are situated here in the parish of St Moribund's, and I've heard that the vicar's a bit of a card because he recently held a fancy dress ball. To report on the excitements and jollifications we are honoured to have with us the curate of St Moribund's, the moderately reverend Mr N. / I don't live in this parish myself. I live in St Michael's-Under-Ware.
    (*See also* Leave a Little Bit for Your Tutor, Vicar and I Will Be There)

AT TRINITY CHURCH I MET MY DOOM   1894
(Fred Gilbert)
Tom Costello

(*For gloomy, hangdog performance*) Twelve months ago, as you can see in No X our Mr N indulged himself in the old nuptials. Here then, brimming over with all the buoyant optimism that his youth and manly vigour can generate, is Mr N! / In our next programme Mr N will be singing an operatic aria, and I'm sure we all look forward to his execution.

AYESHA, MY SWEET EGYPTIAN   1908
(Joe Burley & Cecil Johnson: Maurice Scott)
Evelyn Taylor

Now we take you to the burning sands of Egypt, to the trackless wastes of the desert where we meet not the great Nefertiti nor the even greater Lotsatiti... but the legendary Queen Ayesha. Here she comes barging up the Nile as reincarnated in the person of Miss N! / That act has been purchased for the nation by the British Museum.

BACHELOR GAY, A 1916
(F. Clifford Harris & Valentine: James W. Tate)
Thorpe Bates

From The Maid of the Mountains, that most popular of Daly's Theatre shows, we have now one of its most popular numbers, showing that whatever a man's age—whether a callow seventeen or a mature thirty-five—he is ever vulnerable to feminine allure. May I ask you now to stamp, whistle and applaud for the ever-dashing and debonair Mr N.

BACK ANSWERS 1923
(Charlie Coverdale)
Robb Wilton

Some bizarre back-chat now—and they don't come more blatantly bizarre than our next artiste. He's new to me so just before the show I said to him "what's your name?", "he said "who?", I said "you", he said "me?", I said "yes," he said "it's Mr N! I / Mr N, with memories of the much-loved Robb Wilton.

BALLAD OF SAM HALL, THE c1840
(trad)
W. G. Ross
Based on an original of at least a century earlier

We come now to a most interesting song, one which lays claim to be the very first popular Music Hall song of them all—from the 1840s: the Ballad of Sam Hall. We meet Sam Hall in the condemned cell, the night before his execution. Perhaps he deserves his fate; nevertheless he remains defiant and unrepentant to the last, asking for no pity and no favours. A grim tale indeed, given a performance of power and intensity by Mr N. / A tremendous performance there of the Ballad of Sam Hall by Mr N.

BAND PLAYED ON, THE 1895
(J. F. Palmer. Often erroneously attr Charles B. Ward)
Lillian Russell

The Irish are celebrated amongst other things for their sociability, and so Miss N now tells us of a Mr Matt Casey, who as you can see in No X formed his own social club so that he could "waltz with a strawberry blonde". And which gentleman here would not wish to dance the night away in the arms of the bountifully beauteous Miss N! / Wasn't that a real treat?

(*See also* Bedelia (1), Cockles and Mussels, Danny Boy, Dear Little Shamrock,

Song Introductions   27

Has Anybody Here Seen Kelly?, Is Your Mother in Molly Malone?, Lark in the Clear Air, Little Annie Rooney, Macnamara's Band, Macushla, Molly O'Morgan, Mother Machree, Nora Malone (Call Me by Phone), Paddy McGinty's Goat, Phil the Fluter's Ball, Rose of Tralee, When Irish Eyes are Smiling)

BANG WENT THE CHANCE OF A LIFETIME   1908
(George Robey & Sax Rohmer)
George Robey

A few curious anecdotes and far-fetched reminiscences now from a gentleman who despite draining life's cup to the dregs remains unblooded and unbowed. Who else but that superannuated Piccadilly playboy (OR *epitome of eccentricity*) Mr N. / Mr N, a fine artiste and an awfully good chap to boot.

BATHING   1898
(J. P. Harrington: George Le Brunn)
Marie Lloyd

Now a reminder of summer holidays by the sea, as Miss N poses an interesting moral dilemma: should the sexes bathe together? A burning question of the day examined by a lady much sought after and indeed much yearned after for reasons which will become immediately apparent as we welcome the wickedly winsome and watery Miss N! / (*If in revealing costume*) There's a girl who likes to grin and bear it.

(*See also* All the Girls are Lovely by the Seaside *etc.*)

BEAUTIFUL DREAMER   1864
(Stephen Foster)
Christy Minstrels

To the United States and to a song by that master melodist Mr Stephen Foster, whose very name evokes the heart and spirit of the old South, and we have now one of his loveliest ballads, the last in fact that he ever wrote: Beautiful Dreamer. To sing it is an artiste long held in our highest esteem: Mr/Miss N.

(*See also* Alabama Jubilee *etc.*)

BECAUSE   1902
(Edward Teschemacher: Guy D'Hardelot)
Thorpe Bates, Enrico Caruso, John McCormack, Ernest Pike, Denham Price, Leonard Russell, Maggie Teyte

Our Mr N is the fortunate possessor of a superb tenor voice, heard at its best now in that grand old ballad: Because. Ladies and gentleman, Mr N.

BEDELIA 1903
(William Jerome: Jean Schwartz)
Emma Carus, Lloyd Morgan

(1) *From "The Jersey Lily", Victoria, New York*

Handsome is as handsome does, so they say, but what better way to continue our programme than with Mr N, who in No X hymns the praises of his beloved Bedelia. Ladies and gentlemen, that Hibernian Heart-throb, Mr N.

(*See* Band Played On, The *etc.*)

(2) *Interpolated into "The Orchid", Gaiety, and sung by George Grossmith jnr to his own lyrics*

Mr X now informs us about the object of his affections, Bedelia, a young lady passionately devoted to the theatre. The clever lyrics of this next song mention many stars of the British musical and dramatic stage as you will hear now in a characteristically sunny and subtle performance from Mr X. / I heard you down there, you low crowd. "Bedelia, I want to feel ya..."

(*See also* Fallen Star, If the Managers Only Thought the Same as Mother, I Want to Sing in Opera, Night I Appeared as Macbeth, Ring Down the Curtain, Sing Us One of the Old Songs)

BEER, GLORIOUS BEER *See* GLORIOUS BEER

BELGIUM PUT THE "KIBOSH" ON THE KAISER 1914
(Alf Ellerton)
Mark Sheridan

It's one of our allies whom we acknowledge now in No X, Belgium put the Kibosh on the Kaiser. Gallant little Belgium to be serenaded by a gallant little Britisher. Stand by your beds please please for Captain (*alter rank to suit costume*) N! / Mr/Miss N whose grandfather fell at Waterloo. Somebody pushed him off platform five...

(*See also* Army of Today's All Right, The *etc.*)

BELLA WAS A BARMAID 1902
(J. P. Harrington: George Le Brunn)

Now for a lady who is the embodiment of all that is finest in Music Hall, (*if well built*: and whose not inconsiderable body we now enjoy

Song Introductions   29

in the person of) Miss N. Miss N treats us to one of her very special characterisations: Bella, who was—a barmaid. For this item I would like you to imagine that you are now seated in what I believe is known as licensed premises. Nevertheless, every delicacy of taste and tone will I am sure be displayed by Miss N! / Thank you Miss N, the proud possessor of the finest set of pumps in the business ... oh, you noticed...?

BE MY LITTLE BABY BUMBLE BEE   1911
(Stanley Murphy: Henry I. Marshall)
Elizabeth Brice & Charles King, Ada Jones & Billy Murray, Elizabeth Spencer & Walter Van Blunt
From "Ziegfeld Follies of 1911", Jardin de Paris, also interpolated into "A Winsome Widow", Liberty (both New York). In London interpolated into "The Grass Widow", Apollo

Let us look forward to summer (alter to suit season—e.g. Here we are in the middle of summer) with cows softly lowing in the green pastures, larks singing in the blue sky and the bees a-buzzing. How doth the little busy bee improve each shining hour? One such will improve if not the next hour at least the next few coruscating minutes. Here she is, the Queen of the Hive, Miss N! / There's a honeypot if ever I saw one. (Others taking part can be referred to as her "attendant drones")

BESIDE THE SEASIDE See I DO LIKE TO BE BESIDE THE SEASIDE

BIGGEST ASPIDISTRA IN THE WORLD, THE   1938
(Tommie Connor & Will E. Haines & Jimmy Harper)
Gracie Fields

Music Hall songs deal with so many subjects that it isn't altogether surprising to find one on *Liliaceae* ... no gardeners among you? That perhaps gives you a clue. Yes, a horticultural h'aria from that hardy perennial, the evergreen Miss N. / Miss N, our own little bedding plant.

(*See also* Honeysuckle and the Bee, If I Should Plant a Tiny Seed of Love, Just Like the Ivy, Moonlight Blossoms, Only a Pansy Blossom, Pansy Faces, Sweet Little Rose of Persia, Tell Me Dear Flower)

BILL BAILEY, WON'T YOU PLEASE COME HOME?   1902
(Hughie Cannon)
Carroll Johnson, Victoria Monks, Eva Mudge

In our next aria—No X—the artiste pleads with one Mr Bill Bailey to please return to the domestic hearth. Let us rush to assure her that however recalcitrant Mr Bailey may be we shall respond with might and main. For the artiste in question is none other than the sulky and the sultry Miss N. / What could follow that other than the end of the world?

BILLY (FOR WHEN I WALK) 1911
(Joe Goodwin: James Kendis & Herman Paley)
Madge Temple, Beth Tate

The reigning beauty of (*name of company*) is of course Miss N... ah...! ... who now directs her formidable array of charms in the direction of any gentleman in the audience called Billy. Any Billies in? You, sir? Ah well, she'll have to make do. And to explain her emotional enslavement is the Aphrodite of the Halls, Miss N. / Miss N, walking ever in the path of virtue, bless her.

BILLY MUGGINS 1897
(Charles Ridgewell)
Charles R. Whittle

Now I have to say I'm not quite sure what our next artiste is going to do for us, but I suspect that by the time he's finished—we shall wish he hadn't bothered. He's the sort of chap who can light up a room just by leaving it, for he is Mr Billy Muggins! / Billy Muggins, bearing a close resemblance to our Mr N, who has been attending classes for physical jerks...

(*See also* Grass Widower, I'm Shy Mary Ellen I'm Shy, My Motter, Playing the Game in the West)

BILLY'S ROSE 1881
(George R. Sims)

The playwright and journalist Mr George R Sims has published a number of poems under the pen-name Dagonet, and it is the most celebrated of these "Dagonet Ballads", as he called them, that we are to hear this evening: Billy's Rose, a poem which draws our attention to the stark poverty which is still alas all too prevalent in our society. Billy's Rose, to be recited now by Mr N. / You'd need a heart of stone not to be moved. Mr N with Billy's Rose. And we continue with...

(*See also* Burglar Bill, Fallen Star, Green Eye of the Little Yellow God, I Ain't 'Arf a Lucky Kid, Pigtail of Li Fang Fu, Runcorn Ferry, Sailor's Farewell, Shooting of Dan McGrew, Tale of Ackmed Kurd, Yarn of the Nancy Bell)

Song Introductions

BIRD IN A GILDED CAGE, A 1899
(Arthur Lamb: Harry Von Tilzer)
May A. Bell, Florrie Forde, Marie Kendall, James Norrice

(*For comedy version*) Imagine a lady's boudoir in one of Britain's stateliest homes—you'll have to imagine it because we couldn't afford a set—where despite all the advantages of wealth and privilege, there writhe beneath the genteel surface much misery and frustration, for as you can see in No X, she was only A Bird in a Gilded Cage. Ladies and gentlemen, the Canary of (*local*), Miss N! / There you heard Miss N, singing not so much bel canto as bel panto.

(*For straight version*) We strike a more serious note now as we contemplate the eternal problems associated with love and marriage. Perhaps should I say love *or* marriage, for in No X our Miss N relates the sad tale of the woman who, alas, made the wrong choice and is now only a Bird in a Gilded Cage. A touching little ditty, touchingly performed by Miss N! / A fable for our times there from Miss N.

BIRD ON NELLIE'S HAT, THE 1906
(Arthur Lamb & Alfred Solman)
Janet Allen, Maidie Scott, May Ward

Miss N now trips daintily into view, dressed in the very height of fashion, to tell us the quaintest of stories and one that I know will be of especial interest to the ladies. So let her now expatiate upon her friend, Nellie, and upon Nellie's unusual headgear. Yes, a millinery item from that succulent songstress Miss N. / Thank you Miss N. With so large a bird on her hat she's sure to be spotted ... what do you want—wit?

BIRMINGHAM JAIL Early 19th cent.
(anon.)

A complete change for Miss N from her previous number as she gives us a folk ballad, Birmingham Jail, bringing to it all the intensity of feeling which characterises so much of her work for us here. Ladies and gentlemen, Birmingham Jail, sung by Miss N. / An immense performance there as we have come to expect from Miss N.

BLESS THIS HOUSE 1927
(Helen Taylor: May H. Brahe)
Peter Dawson, Gracie Fields, John McCormack

Our next song, I'm delighted to say, is that fine ballad Bless this

House, a sentiment I am sure we all share, especially when sung so superbly by N. / Does your heart good, does it not?, to hear those old songs again.

BLUE BELL 1898
(Edward Madden & Dolly Morse: Theodore Morse)
Hamilton Hill

Saying farewell to loved ones is a theme explored in many songs but rarely so poignantly as in No X, Blue Bell. This song comes from the United States and quickly became popular here during the Boer War. The parting of lovers who may never see one another again is most telling portrayed for us now by N.

(*See also* Army of Today's All Right *etc.*)

BOBBING UP AND DOWN LIKE THIS 1899
(Worton David: Norman Reave)
Austin Rudd

There's always an air of naughtiness, of barely-repressed licentiousness about the seaside, isn't there? I think it's to do with seeing all those people with nothing on under their swimming costumes. So now, direct from bathing machine number twenty-five, in an explicit, full-frontal performance is the unexpurgated Mr N! / Stretching the boundaries of the permissible there was Mr N.

(*See also* All the Girls are Lovely by the Seaside *etc.*)

BOERS HAVE GOT MY DADDY, THE 1900
(A. J. Mills & Harry Castling)
Tom Costello, Charles Foster, Arthur Reece

It is a melancholy fact that one of Her Majesty's possessions, namely South Africa, is currently in rebellion against the Crown. In the next item our Mr X meets a small boy whose soldier father has been taken captive by the Boer. No X: The Boers Have Got My Daddy, most evocatively sung for us now by Mr N. / Mr N—let's hope Daddy'll be home by Christmas...

> (*See also* Come Home Father, Daddy's on the Engine, Daddy Wouldn't Buy Me a Bow Wow, Father's Got the Sack from the Waterworks, Following in Father's Footsteps, Give Me a Ticket to Heaven, Has Anybody Seen My Tiddler?, If the Managers Only Thought the Same as Mother, I'm Glad I Took My Mother's Advice, I Want to Play with Little Dick, Johnny Morgan's Sister, Our Lodger's Such a Nice Young Man, Please Sell No More Drink to My Father, There They are the Two of Them on Their Own, They Always Pick on Me, What's that for Eh?)

Song Introductions   33

BOILED BEEF AND CARROTS   1909
(Charles Collins & Fred Murray)
Harry Champion

Those among us—there may be some here tonight—who have the misfortune to be foreigners tend to sneer at our British cuisine—damn cheek! What could be more palatable or nutritious than bangers and mash, tripe and onions, jellied eels... (*grasp table and swallow hard*)... or good old Boiled Beef and Carrots—No X? Here then is an artiste world famous in Willesden (*or local*) Mr N! / That's got the party going.

(*See also* Ca-bages Ca-beans and Car-rots, Come in and Cut Yourself a Piece of Cake, I Can't Do My Bally Bottom Button Up, I Do Like an Egg for My Tea, I Do Like a S'nice S'mince S'pie, It's a Pity to Waste the Cake, Little Bit of Cucumber, Marrow Song, Put a Bit of Treacle on My Pudden Mary Ann, That Gorgonzola Cheese, Yes We Have No Bananas)

BOND STREET TEA-WALK, THE   1902
(J. P. Harrington: George Le Brunn)
Marie Lloyd

What could be nicer than a little gossip in a fashionable refreshment in one of London's smartest thoroughfares? With Britain's answer to the cake-walk, we proudly present the infinitely more genteel Bond Street Tea-Walk, as demonstrated with the utmost point and piquancy by Miss N.

(*See page 201 for further songs of London*)

BOWERY, THE   1891
(Charles Hoyt: Percy Gaunt)
Harry Conor
From "A Trip to Chinatown", Madison Square and Hoyt's, New York. For UK version see Brighton). *Melody based on the Italian ballad* La Spagnola.

The Bowery is an American song with the same melody as a British song called "Brighton", but whether they pinched it from us or vice versa really matters not—it's a jolly good tune. The American version extols the dubious delights of life in down-town Manhattan, and so it is in this unsalubrious part of New York that we say Hi, There! to Mr N!

(*See also* Alabama Jubilee *etc.*)

BOY IN THE GALLERY, THE   c1881
(George Ware)
Dot Hetherington, Jenny Hill, Marie Lloyd, Louie Pounds, Nellie Power

We come now to one of the most elegiac songs of this Victorian age in which we are privileged to live: No X, The Boy in the Gallery. Hankies at the ready then, gentlemen, for the adorable, the angelic, the altogether alluring Miss N. / A most fetching performance there by Miss N. And thank you for your co-operation with the handkerchiefs—I'm glad I wasn't any closer.

BOYS OF THE CHELSEA SCHOOL 1902
(Frank W. Carter & R. P. Weston)
George Leyton

Opposite Chelsea Royal Hospital, home of those heroes of yesteryear the Chelsea Pensioners, lies the Chelsea School whose boys look forward to the day when they themselves can don the Queen's uniform and help to defend all that we hold dear and share in our island's glorious history. To extol this patriotic ambition is none other than Mr N!

BOYS OF THE OLD BRIGADE See OLD BRIGADE, THE

BRAHN BOOTS 1935
(R. P. Weston & Bert Lee: R. Harris Weston)
Stanley Holloway

We're all governed, are we not?, by laws and codes of conduct. To conform to accepted convention is no more than common politeness, for a breach of etiquette can cause confusion and embarrassment. As was recently witnessed by our next artiste at a sad family gathering, so let us heed the words of N. / N, with a sad story of a sartorial solecism ... a bit slurpy that, sorry.

BRIGHTON 1894
(Brit. lyrics Fred Gilbert: music arr. Richard Morton)
R. G. Knowles
From "A Trip to Chinatown", Toole's. See Bowery, The

Brighton is a seaside town of raffish if not downright salacious reputation, popular with working-class holiday-makers and professional co-respondents. Which of these two categories our next artiste falls into I leave you to judge. A guarded welcome therefore for Mr N!

(*See also* All the Girls are Lovely by the Seaside *etc.*)

BRIGHTON 1911
(Paul Rubens & Arthur Wimperis: Paul Rubens)
Connie Ediss

Song Introductions   35

aka Take Me on The Boat to Brighton. *From "The Sunshine Girl", Gaiety*
An animated aria follows—an investigation into the somewhat dubious attractions of Brighton—conducted by a lady anxious to experience Life with a capital L, the spectacularly-gowned and even more spectacularly-shaped Miss N.
(*See also* All the Girls are Lovely by the Seaside *etc.*)

BRINDISI   1856
(F. Mario Piave: Guiseppe Verdi)
Lizzie Pearce & Russell Grover, Maria Piccolomini & C. A. Zolari
From "La Traviata" (Fenice, Venice, 1853) based on the younger Dumas' novel and play "La Dame Aux Camélias". Note: Brindisi: a toast (It.). In opera the word has become a generic term for a drinking song and is found in sundry works. The "Traviata" Brindisi is often also sung as a soprano solo.

We enter the portals of grand opera with an aria from Verdi's La Traviata: Brindisi, a toast to life, love and laughter. A spirited—indeed spiritous—rendering of this scintillating aria now from Miss M and Mr N. / Brindisi from La Traviata, sung magnificently by Miss N and Mr N.
(*See also* And the Great Big Saw Came Nearer and Nearer *etc.*)

BROKEN DOLL, A   1915
(F. Clifford Harris: James W. Tate)
Al Jolson, Clarice Mayne, Ida Rene
From "Samples", Playhouse (briefly) moving in January 1916 to the Comedy and finishing its run at the Vaudeville.

We continue with a song entitled a Broken Doll, No X, in which the ravishing Miss N laments the inconstancy of her erstwhile admirer, though it is hard to see how any man could throw over the palpable charms of that pleasing personification of pulchritude N. / A performance of heart-breaking poignancy there from N.

BROWN BOOTS *See* BRAHN BOOTS

BURGLAR BILL   1887
(F. Anstey)
Note: This poem was never intended for actual performance, being written as a parody on contemporary drawing-room recitations. However I have seen it recited both as a burlesque and, most remarkably, as a successful straight item.

No Music Hall programme is complete without an emotion-charged recitation, and accordingly Mr N now demonstrates another facet of his miniscular talents with Burglar Bill, by Mr F Anstey. Our Mr N has been described as a very "committed" artiste as I'm sure we shall soon all agree with that judgement. Ladies and gentlemen, with Burglar Bill: Mr N. / Uncanny, isn't it, how he gets under the skin of the characters?

(*See also* Billy's Rose *etc.*)

BURLINGTON BERTIE FROM BOW 1914
(William Hargreaves)
Ella Shields

We come up a notch or two in the social scale as we proudly present a gentleman of quality, but one who has—how shall we say?—seen better days. A heavy swell down on his uppers, but nonetheless smiling in the face of adversity. Yes, Nil Desperandum is the motto of the one and only, the legendary Mr Burlington Bertie! / (*If a woman*) Our very own Miss N whose undoubted femininity will be revealed in all its glory later on in the programme. (*If a man*) That was of course Mr N, keeping his pecker up.

(*See page 201 for further songs of London*)

BUTTERCUP, THE 1867
(F. C. Burnand: Arthur Sullivan)
George Du Maurier & Quentin Twist
From "Cox and Box", a musical adaptation of J Maddison Morton's 1847 farce "Box and Cox". The first public performance (at the Adelphi) was a charity matinee only; for the first fully-fledged production (at the Gallery of Illustration, Regent Street, in 1869) the singers were Arthur Cecil & T German Reed.

Now for a duet for male voices from Sullivan & Burnand's one-act opera Cox and Box, sung by a baritone known and feared all along the Pennine Way (*or local*), and by a tenor who has been compared to Caruso, though not very often. So with The Buttercup, to be sung in B-flat or nearest offer, it's my doleful distinction to introduce Messrs M and N! / Thank you Messrs M and N, who have asked me to point out that they are just good friends.

Note: A version of this song for soprano and baritone is published by Cramer/Boosey & Hawkes under the title The Dicky Bird And The Owl *with lyrics by Margaret A Sinclair.*

(*For two-handers and/or possible concerted items see page 199*)

BY THE BEAUTIFUL SEA 1914
(Harold R. Atteridge: Harry Carroll)
Du Four Boys, Molly Wood Stanford

A trip to the briny, now, to the Beautiful Sea. Last time I saw my wife

Song Introductions   37

on the beach—I was so embarrassed. She had a hole in her bathing costume! Well, you could distinctly see her left knee! No embarrassments now, however—nothing but *wholesome* diversion from Miss/ Mr N!

(*See also* All the Girls are Lovely by the Seaside *etc*.)

BY THE LIGHT OF THE SILVERY MOON   1909
(Edward Madden: Gus Edwards)
Al Jolson, Lillian Lorraine, Georgie Price, Ella Retford

No X, By the Light of the Silvery Moon, is a song in which courtship is likened to the enactment of a play not in the theatre but in the park. Settle down then for Act One, as performed by the vital, vivacious and (*if appropriate*) voluptuous Miss N.

(*For duet version*) We now present two artistes—each of either gender! Ingenuity can surely go no further. A romantic item, as you may have surmised, in which courtship is likened to the enactment of a play—not in the theatre but in the park. No X, By the Light of the Silvery Moon, whose beams now shine down upon Miss M and Mr N. / Let's hope it all ends happily... I'm sure it will.

(*For other two-handers and/or possible concerted items see page 199*)

BY THE SEA (BY THE BEAUTIFUL SILVERY SEA)   c1910
(John A. Glover Kind)
Ada Reeve, Ernest Shand, Mark Sheridan

(*See also* All the Girls are Lovely by the Seaside *etc*.)

BY THE SIDE OF THE ZUYDER ZEE   1906
(A. J. Mills: Bennett Scott)
Maudie Darrell, May Moore-Duprez, Happy Fanny Fields, Albert Pearce, Annie Purcell

Now to a guest artiste from the Continent: Mr N who is of Dutch extraction—his father was a dentist from Rotterdam. But Mr N is not a happy Hollander, for he is parted alas from his Deitcher Girl, Gretchen. Foreigners have their romantic proclivities too, you know—that's why there's so many of them. A warm British welcome to Mr N. / While Mr N enjoys a swift livener—he loves his Bols—we continue with...

(*See also* Dutchman's Courtship, The)

CA-BAGES, CA-BEANS AND CAR-ROTS   1919
(Wynn Stanley & Andrew Allen)
George Bass

One of the advantages of being a Music Hall artiste is that one is free to air one's personal likes and dislikes, though I have to say I do think in this next somewhat bizarre song our Mr N does rather abuse the privilege. Nevertheless we're stuck with him so let's make the best of it as we give a cautiously qualified welcome to Mr N. / Ca-bages, Ca-beans and Car-rots from Mr Ca-N. Ca-thank you.

CALL ROUND ANY OLD TIME 1908
(E. W. Rogers: J. Charles Moore)
Victoria Monks

Now to the lady with a bevy, nay plethora of admirers, and quite right too, Miss N. Call Round Any Old Time she expostulates in No X, and I for one would be delighted to darken her doormat any time. A heart-warming song from that most heart-warming of artistes, Miss N. / Miss N in top form—wasn't that grand?

CAN-CAN, THE c1850
Colonna Troupe, Mlle Finette, Rigolboche, Mlle Sara (Sarah Wright)
The most celebrated music for the can-can is from Offenbach's "Orpheus in the Underworld", des Bouffes-Parisiens, Paris, 1858. A version was produced at Her Majesty's in 1865 though the scandalous dance as we know it today was not seen in London till 1870, when it lost the Alhambra its licence and made Leicester Square "a hideous, howling wilderness".

To France, to Paris, with a display which challenges not only the terpsichorean abilities of the ladies of the company but also the digital dexterity of the Maestro. For before your very glassy eyes, direct from the Moulin Rouge, Wapping (*or local*), we give you the vigorous, the volcanic—Can-Can! / I'm exhausted just watching it. The Ladies of the Company with the Can-Can! Personally I can't can't...

(*See also* Fiacre, Gendarmes Duet, I Like Your Old French Bonnet, Ta-ra-ra-boom-de-ay)

CAN LONDON DO WITHOUT ME? 1902
(William Hargreaves)
Tom E. Hughes

If Music Hall songs are sometimes accused of concentrating too much on London it must be remembered that it was in London that Music Hall began its glorious existence. I make no apology therefore for No X, in which our Mr N avers that though he can do without London,

Song Introductions

can London do without him? Such hubris. Nevertheless, here he is, Metropolitan Man incarnate, Mr N. / Mr N, and a safe journey to him, wherever he's going.

(*See page 201 for further songs of London*)

CAN'T STOP! CAN'T STOP!! CAN'T STOP!!! 1895
(Harry Wincott)
Harry Freeman

As you will have gathered every economy has been lavished on tonight's production, and here is one of the biggest: Mr N. With a song entitled Can't Stop! Can't Stop!! Can't Stop!!!—and I hope he keeps his word—is the man with the gimlet eye, the finely chiselled nostrils and the hammer toes, Mr N! / Mr N, who has been described as a finished artiste...

CAPTAIN CALLED THE MATE, THE 1888
(Arthur West)
Alexandra Dagmar, Harry Freeman, Arthur West

A piquant aria now from Miss N concerning an unmarried lady, a Miss Spriggings, who travelled on the high seas *unaccompanied!*, all the way to Australia with one very special object in view. And what is that object, I hear you ask? Go on then—ask ... all will be revealed by Scunthorpe's (*or local*) answer to Dame Nellie Melba, our very own Miss N. / Just fancy, ladies, waking up and finding yourself in bed next to—a cobber...!

CAPTAIN GINJAH, O.T. 1910
(Fred W. Leigh & George Bastow)
George Bastow

Mr N is celebrated in our community for his numerous meticulous characterisations, each of which features a careful selection of wigs, costumes, make-up, voice, movement, etc. And the strange thing about these characterisations is that in them Mr N is always exactly the same. Quite a feat. And in No X he again astounds us with his protean abilities as Captain Ginjah, O.T. Ladies and gentlemen, Mr N. / Thank you so much, Mr N—you wouldn't have known it was him unless I'd told you, would you?

(*See also* Army of Today's All Right, The *etc.*)

CAPTAIN WITH HIS WHISKERS, THE 1869
(Thomas Haynes Bayly: Alfred Mullen & Sidney Nelson)
Mrs W. J. Florence, Emma Nichols

Note: Haynes Bayly's poem was first set to music by Sidney Nelson in 1838 and sung by Lucy Vestris under the title "Oh! They March'd Thro' the Town". In his popular later version Mullen altered both words and music.

Now an item of incalculable delight to the legion of admirers of Miss N! The Captain with his Whiskers is a song which treats of that electrifying moment when the attraction between a man and a woman seems to enter into the realms of the metaphysical, indeed the mystical. This strange bond which, all unbidden, can so disturb our lives is now explored by the Sweetheart of (*local*) Miss N! / The Captain with his Whiskers, exquisitely delivered by Miss N.

CASEY JONES 1909
(T. Lawrence Seibert: Eddie Newton)
The Two Bobs, Albert Whelan
Note: This song was inspired by the real-life Casey Jones who died heroically at the controls of the Cannon Ball Express on 30 April 1900.

(*For ensemble version*) We trundle on with a locomotive aria. My uncle used to work on the LMS as a wheel-tapper. After three days he'd brought the whole network to a halt—then they found his hammer was cracked. We couldn't get the Orient Express on our stage but we have got the next best thing—the Leyton Orient Flyer (*or local*). Yes, our full technical resources are now pressed into service in order to recreate the last fatal journey of the late, lamented Casey Jones! / Now we can all take on coal and water because that brings us to the first interval!

(*See also* Charming Young Widow I Met in the Train, Daddy's on the Engine, I've Never Lost My Last Train Yet, Jessie the Belle at the (Railway) Bar, Mary's Ticket, Oh! Mr Porter, Riding Down to Bangor, Signalman on the Line, There's Danger on the Line, Watching the Trains Come in, What Did She Know About Railways? *Also see page 199 for other possible concerted items*)

CHALK FARM TO CAMBERWELL GREEN 1915
(Guy D'Hardelot: Lionel Monckton)
Gertie Millar
From "Bric-a-Brac", Palace

We now have the pleasure of accompanying the fragrant Miss N on a bus trip across London from north to south, yes from Chalk Farm to Camberwell Green. And an incident-packed journey this turned out to be as you shall hear from the ever-susceptible Miss N. / I'm sure we all enjoyed the ride there, in the company of the joyful Miss N.

(*See also* Riding on Top of the Car *for another bus song and page 201 for further songs of London*)

Song Introductions

CHAMPAGNE CHARLIE   1866
(George Leybourne: Alfred Lee)
George Leybourne
A ladies' version was sung by Louie Sherrington

Swaggering into view now comes the very epitome of the heavy swell, the fashionable card, oozing bonhomie and heartiness from every pore. With malice toward none and with charity for all it has to be Champagne Charlie in the redoubtable person of our own, our very own, Mr N. / There's a man who gets the most out of life. A gentleman and a boozer.

(*See* 'Arf A Pint of Ale *etc.*)

CHARLIE ON THE MASH   1898
(Fred Murray & Fred W. Leigh)
Florrie Forde

I'm not sure what our next artiste is going to regale us with though I suspect it is loosely connected with No X, a song entitled Charlie On The Mash, that is to say Charlie on the Prowl. No woman is safe—or would wish to be in the company of that Heart-throb of the Halls, Mr N! / Well done, sir. Mr N in his own inimitable style as Charlie on the Mash.

CHARMING YOUNG WIDOW I MET IN THE TRAIN, THE   c1878
(W. H. Cove)
Fred Albert, W. Randall

Mr N follows apace with No X, Waiting for the Train, a song outlining the hazards which may befall the unwary gentleman traveller on that particular mode of transport. An admonitory aria then, impeccably delivered by the impeccably attired Mr N. / Mr N, warning us of women's wiles.

(*See also* Casey Jones *etc.*)

CLICQUOT!   1870
(F. W. Green: J. Riviére)
Alfred Vance

One thing Mr N likes above all is a really good wet, for as he now roundly declares in No X Cliquot! Cliquot! That's the wine for me. And who would argue with the bibulous and Bacchanalian bon viveur, Mr N! / Amazing how cheerful he keeps. D'you know he's got a wife and two kidneys to support?

(*See* 'Arf A Pint of Ale *etc.*)

COCKLES AND MUSSELS 1884
(James Yorkston)
Possibly based on a folk-song.

Prepare now to be harrowed to the core—how long is it since you were harrowed, missus? Far too long, yes ... as we bring you that real Irish tear-jerker: Cockles and Mussels, a song which traces the life and works of poor Molly Malone, a citizeness of Dublin. So ladies take hold of your hankies, and gentlemen take hold of your ladies, as we...

(For girl) ... positively melt before the charms of Miss N.

(For boy) ... meet the man who made Macgillycuddy Reek, Mr N.

When we met at rehearsals N said "would you like me to sing this song in Erse?" I said, "No, here in *(local)*'ll be fine."

(See also Band Played On, The *etc.)*

COFFEE SHOP AT PIMLICO, THE 1864
(Frank Bell)
Frank Bell

On with the tale of a punctured romance and of the strange events which befell when Mr N was lured by a pair of roguish eyes into a Coffee Shop in Pimlico, a song with an unusual and interesting rhyme scheme. So let us now share in the agony of blighted affection as suffered by Mr N.

(See page 201 for further songs of London)

COME AND PUT YOUR ARMS AROUND ME, GEORGIE DO 1909
(A. J. Mills: Bennett Scott)

That enchanting artiste Miss N now brings us all the elegance, grace and sophistication of a high society ball. Sweet music, romance, gaiety—rather like Berwick St Market (*or local*) on a Saturday afternoon. No X on your songsheets: Come and Put Your Arms Around Me, Georgie Do. Any Georges in the house? This could be your lucky night! ... as we shall discover from the gorgeous, the glamorous, the glittering Miss N.

COME, COME, I LOVE YOU ONLY *See* MY HERO

COME DOWN AND OPEN THE DOOR 1898
(C. G. Cotes: Bennett Scott)
Sisters Wood

Song Introductions   43

Note: This is a re-working of an 1884 song called Come Down and Open the Door, Love *(A. Sutherd & Slade Murray, arr. Edmund Forman) and sung by Slade Murray.*

We now present Mr N, a man who can sing like a mermaid can do the splits. He tells us of the marital problems of one Mr Bill Johnson, though I can't think for the life of me why the management is so obsessed with these squalid little lower-class dramas. Nevertheless here for the first and with any luck last time this evening, is Mr N! / Thank you, Mr N—trying for a comeback yet again.

COME DOWN, MA EVENING STAR   1902
(Robert H. Smith: John Stromberg)
Lillian Russell
From "Hokey Pokey", Weber & Fields' Music Hall, New York, and interpolated into "Twirly Whirly" at the same theatre 1912.

From Broadway comes news of a new musical show featuring a song of great lyrical and emotional power: Come Down, Ma Evening Star, to be given a full-bloodied performance by a lady whom we consider to be a star at any time of the day or night, that firm favourite Miss N.

COME HOME, FATHER   1858
(Henry Russell: Henry Clay Work)
Alabama Barnstormers, Horace Norman (Christy Minstrels)
Featured in the legendary American prohibitionist drama "Ten Nights in a Bar-Room" by William W Pratt, first performed at the National Theatre, Washington DC, on 23 August 1858

Now for an intensely dramatic item. Picture a poor little girl on the— in the streets. It is midwinter, the piercing snow is blowing through her thin shabby garments... (*ah!*) ... the driving snow is swirling round her frail form... (*aaah!!*) ... she is ill, starving... (*aaaahhh!!!*) ... but still she pleads with her scapegrace father to come home. An agonised plea indeed from that most miserable of pleaders, Miss N! / How unkind of you to laugh. That was supposed to be pathetic...

(*See also* Boers Have Got My Daddy, The *etc for Child Songs and* 'Arf a Pint of Ale *etc. for drink songs*)

COME IN AND CUT YOURSELF A PIECE OF CAKE   1911
(Alec Kendal)
Jack Pleasants

Bursting upon our astonished gaze shortly will be Mr N with a simple domestic number, I understand, with none of that tendency to coarseness which mars so many Music Hall songs and which I know you dislike so much ... don't you? Yes ... so with Come In and Cut Yourself a Piece of Cake, and *rising* to the occasion with a slice of life, is Mr N. / Mr N ... that used to be a good number.

(*See also* Boiled Beef and Carrots *etc.*)

COME INTO THE GARDEN, MAUD 1856
(Alfred Tennyson: Michael W. Balfe)
Joseph Cheetham, John Coates, John McCormack, Sims Reeves

Mr Michael Balfe is the composer of such well-loved ballads as Excelsior, I Dreamt That I Dwelt In Marble Halls, and Killarney, but tonight we hear his immortal setting of Tennyson's poem Come Into The Garden, Maud. A few moments of unalloyed delight now from Mr N.

COME OVER THE GARDEN WALL 1920
(Ballard MacDonald: James W. Tate)
Clarice Mayne

Mr James W Tate wrote any number of songs for his wife, Miss Clarice Mayne, such as Ev'ry Little While, A Broken Doll, I Was A Good Little Girl Till I Met You, and also No X, Come Over the Garden Wall, a song which like so much of Mr Tate's work has a cutely engaging verse and a very singable chorus. And to sing it we have the cutely engaging— and engagingly cute Miss N.

COMRADES 1887
(Felix McGlennon)
Tom Costello

It may be a surprise to many of you to learn that our next song was first performed on the Halls as early as 1887. I refer to No X, Comrades, first sung by Mr Tom Costello, a popular star of the day who most unusually included both comic and strongly sentimental songs in his repertoire. We hear this song of friendship, loyalty and sacrifice now from a gentleman whose many previous appearances on this stage have I know earned your respect and admiration: Mr N.

(*For other two-handers and/or possible concerted items see page 199*)

COSTER GIRL IN PARIS, THE 1912
(Fred W. Leigh: Orlando Powell)
Marie Lloyd

Song Introductions   45

Our Miss N has recently got herself married, and as if that weren't excitement enough she spent her honeymoon in Paris. So here to tell us of this momentous trip, direct from the Hackney Road Montmartre, is that celebrated Cosmopolitan Cockney Miss N! / Well done, Miss N. I love being abroad—only tonight I'm a chap ... don't you think I'm funny? (*No!*)... I laughed when *you* came in...

(*See page 201 for further songs of London*)

COSTER'S SERENADE, THE   1890
(Albert Chevalier: John Crook)
Albert Chevalier

Some things may change in this wicked world but never our affection and admiration for Mr N, who now raises the emotional temperature as only he can with the Coster's Serenade, written by Mr Albert Chevalier—it was this song that made Chevalier's reputation on the Halls, now to be rendered to perfection by Mr N. / A most tender performance from Mr N.

(*See page 201 for further songs of London*)

COULD YOU BE TRUE TO EYES OF BLUE?   1901
(Will D. Cobb: Gus Edwards)
Lilian Doreen, Hamilton Hill, Hilda Trevelyan
From "A Chinese Honeymoon", Theatre Royal, Hanley, (Strand 1901)

Could You Be True To Eyes Of Blue? implores our next artiste. There can only be one answer, gentlemen, when such a question is posed by that dainty and decorous damsel Miss N! / A delightful little number, and a delightful little number singing it.

(*See* Algy *etc*)

COVER IT OVER QUICK JEMIMA   1911
(Charles Collins & E. A. Sheppard)
Harry Champion

Another of our most popular artistes is Mr N who is now going to give us a specimen ... of his powers, by telling us a little about his home life—and believe me, a little goes a long way. His song is entitled Cover it over Quick, Jemima, so let's hope he gets it over quick—Mr N! / Thank you, Mr N, a fine artiste and a keen sportsman. Oh yes—he's just bought himself a second racing-pigeon!

COWSLIP AND THE COW, THE   1905
(Frank Leo)
Wilkie Bard, Albert Whelan

A rural tale now from our Mr N, who is a keen countryman as well as a noted Music Hall artiste, having just completed a very successful tour as principal vocalist with Lockhart's Elephants. But now in No X he sings of less exotic fauna in The Cowslip and the Cow. A warm welcome for that jovial gentleman farmer Mr N! / I said to him would I do any good on the farm? He said no, we've got special stuff for that...

> (*See also* Down at the Farm-yard Gate, How Ya Gonna Keep 'Em Down on the Farm?, I'm Ninety-Four This Mornin', I'm Waiting Here for Kate, K-k-k-katy, Rest of the Day's Your Own, Riley's Cowshed, She's Proud and She's Beautiful, Shine on Harvest Moon, Varmer Giles)

CRUEL MARY HOLDER   1866
(Arthur Lloyd: arr. G. Bicknell)
Arthur Lloyd

Mr N reappears in very different mood from his first offering as he tells us of Cruel Mary Holder who spurned Joe Molder, because he wouldn't be a soldier, a tale told in a fascinating rhyming pattern worthy of the Bard of Avon himself. And to attempt it: the downright doomy and garrulously gloomy Mr N. / I think he's better off without her, don't you? Certainly...

CURSE OF AN ACHING HEART, THE   1913
(Harry Fink: Al Piantadosi)
Joe Burns, Emma Carus, Will Oakland, Manuel Romain

Something we have all experienced, I imagine, at some time in our lives is the Curse of the Aching Heart, the title of No X. Stepping into the limelight now, and singing from the depths of anguished loneliness, is the opulently ornate Miss N.

CUSHIE BUTTERFIELD   1863
(George Ridley)
George Ridley

See Polly Perkins Of Paddington Green

Mr George Ridley was a renowned singer and songwriter around Tyneside and Wearside, being best remembered for The Blaydon Races and the song we are about to hear now: Cushie Butterfield, a vivid and vigorous evocation of working-class life in the north-east. With the story of Miss Butterfield, a seller of yellow clay, please welcome all the way from Gateshead the king of the keelmen, Mr N. / Mr N with Cushie Butterfield—I still don't know whether

Song Introductions 47

she married him or not. (*Shout off*) Did she marry you? (*"Yes!"*) Thank God for that...

CZARDAS 1876
(Eng w Hamilton Aïdé: Johann Strauss II)
Mlle C. Cabella, Marie Geistinger
From "Die Fledermaus", an der Wien, Vienna 1874. London: Alhambra

Undoubtedly the most popular of the sixteen operettas by the younger Strauss must be Die Fledermaus, and from this lively work Miss N now gives us Rosalind's spectacular Czardas aria. My delight to introduce the coruscating charms and talents of Miss N! / There she goes, taking her top B flat with her...

DADDY'S ON THE ENGINE 1895
(P. H. Snape & Arthur Albert: Sam Potter)
Arthur Albert

Mr N now thrills us to the core with an exciting railway ballad in which his paterfamilias performs prodigally on the footplate: No X, Daddy's On The Engine, and my copy of Bradshaw informs me that on platform one in about three seconds will arrive Mr N! / I think his voice was not so much trained as shunted.

(*See also* Boers Have Got My Daddy, The *etc for Child Songs*; Casey Jones *etc. for railway songs*)

DADDY WOULDN'T BUY ME A BOW WOW 1892
(Joseph Tabrar)
Arthur Roberts, Vesta Victoria

I am honoured now to introduce a very young lady who is in fact this year's winner of the National Talent Competition for the Daughters of Deserving Spinsters. Daddy Wouldn't Buy Me a Bow Wow she pleads in No X, and who could refuse anything of that pert parcel of predatory pubescence, Miss N! / I'm asked to tell you that the cat used by Miss N in that item is in fact—stuffed...

(*See also* Boers Have Got My Daddy, The *etc.*)

DAISY BELL 1892
(Harry Dacre)
Florrie Forde, Katie Lawrence

In 1833 a blacksmith from Dumfriesshire came up with an invention that was to revolutionise travel for the masses. This device soon inspired to any number of popular songs and we now proudly present the most popular of them all. So, sending us now into transports of delight is Miss N. / Our thanks to Miss N who you may recall was voted Miss Back-Pedal for 1897. The first bicycle I ever saw was a penny-farthing being ridden by a nun. Virgin on the ridiculous...

 (*See also* Salute My Bicycle)

DANCE OF THE GRIZZLY BEAR, THE   1910
(Irving Berlin)
Irene Castle & Vernon Blyth, Sophie Tucker
From *"Ziegfeld Follies of 1910", Jardin de Paris, New York*

America has given us the Pussy Foot, the Turkey Trot, the Bunny Hug, but now with the latest dance craze The Grizzly Bear we proudly present two artistes whose stylish and sophisticated performances have put them very much in a class of their own. Yes, with The Grizzly Bear, it's that dashing duo, the Dandy Doodles! / (*Give names*) Miss N was the one in the dress.

 (*For other two-handers and/or possible concerted items see page 199*)

DANCE WITH YOUR UNCLE JOSEPH   1915
(William Hargreaves & Dan Lipton)
Charles R. Whittle

Mr N now craves your indulgence with a song of terpsichorean avuncularity! Dance with your Uncle Joseph is the title of No X on your songsheets, though, children, under no circumstances should you accept sweets from that dirty old—grand old man of the Halls, Mr N. / Mr N (*If a maniacally energetic performance say to pianist*) It's not a full moon tonight, is it...?

DANCING ON THE STREETS   1894
(James W. Blake & Charles B. Lawlor)
Kate Carney
British version of Sidewalks of New York *qv*

No X, Dancing on the Streets, is an American song first aired in Britain by that great star of the Halls Miss Kate Carney. It has a rousing 3/4 tempo so may I ask you all please to refrain from refraining from the refrain. To be sustained for us now in stimulating style by Miss N. / I'm exhausted just watching that, aren't you? Well done, Miss N— you'd better go and have a lie down—I'll join you later.

 (*See also* Alabama Jubilee *etc. for American songs and page 201 for further songs of London*)

Song Introductions   49

DANNY BOY   1912
(F. E. Weatherly: trad)
John McHugh, Edna Thornton

Mr FE Weatherly has in his poetic career provided the words to some fifteen hundred songs, including The Holy City and Roses of Picardy. We hear now his lyrics to a traditional tune, the haunting Londonderry Air. This is of course Danny Boy, and to sing it for us, who better than Mr N. / There have been many attempts to put words to that wonderful melody, but I'm sure you would agree that Mr FE Weatherly's lyrics outclass all others. Danny Boy, sung by Mr N.

(*See also* Band Played On, The *etc.*)

DARK GIRL DRESS'D IN BLUE, THE   1862
(Harry Clifton)
Harry Clifton, George Leybourne

We have now an item which highlights the dangers of putting your trust in strange women, and especially, gentlemen, should you beware The Dark Girl Dress'd in Blue. One who particularly regretted meeting this mysterious charmer is our very own Mr N. / Thank you Mr N, for that timely warning. Watch out for strange women. And as far as I'm concerned the stranger the better.

DARLING MABEL   1896
(A. J. Mills: Bennett Scott)
Leonard Barry

The ever-fascinating subject of courtship is the burden of No X, Darling Mabel, to be performed by a perpetual favourite here in (*local*), that steadfast stalwart of our company, Mr N. / Isn't that a really sweet song? Darling Mabel, from Mr N.

DEAR LITTLE SHAMROCK, THE   1806
(Andrew Cherry: William Jackson)
Note: It would appear that this song was substantially revised some time in the mid 19th century, probably by a descendant of Andrew Cherry.

(*For Comedy version*) Our company includes Mr N who comes from Dublin. In his youth he decided to obey Mr Horace Greeley's injunction to Go West Young Man (*indicate West*) ... which was how he finished up here (*indicate east*) ... howsoever, he now presents a song of such glutinous sentimentality as to put your fillings in deep jeopardy. The Dear Little Shamrock, which will now be purveyed to us by Mr N. / Mr N had intended to sing that for St Patrick's Day but he got the date wrong.

(*See also* Band Played On, The *etc.*)

DEAR OLD SHEPHERD'S BUSH 1916
(F. Clifford Grey: Nat D. Ayer)
Frank Lester
From *"The Bing Boys Are Here"*, *Alhambra*

Next, one of those songs so popular on the Halls in which the singer, exiled from hearth and home, longs to return to his origins—songs like The Miner's Dream of Home, Carry Me Back To Old Virginny, I Want To Go Back To Michigan, and so on. Here then in nostalgic mood is Mr N. / Dear old Shepherd's Bush, eh? I hear things are looking up in Shepherd's Bush—they're sending missionaries from Deptford.

(*See page 201 for further songs of London*)

DID YOUR FIRST WIFE EVER DO THAT? 1932
(Harry Castling)
Marie Kendall
Note: *Originally sung by Marie Kendall in the film "Say It With Flowers" this song was not published until 1987, in EMI's "Great Comedy Songs" Book 2.*

Our Miss N, a lady of acute delicacy and refinement, has recently taken the plunge and married a widower, a gentleman somewhat lacking in sensitivity. What a predicament for an inexperienced young female to find herself in! Let us offer succour and support then for this tortured, vulnerable, wilting little flower: Miss N. / Some marry for love, some for money—I think Miss N married for spite.

DOES THIS SHOP STOCK SHOT SOCKS? 1912
(Herbert De Pinna)
George Graves, Archie Pitt

(*For "nervous" performance*) For the next diversion we have bright lights! Scarlet drapes! A comical costume! But then Mr N needs all the help he can get, especially as he only seems to have a passing acquaintance with the chorus. However, we do have the advantage of finding the words at No X—Does this Shop Stock Shot Socks with Spots? Sheer poetry ... here then is the Draper's Nightmare himself: Mr N. / (*If in eccentric costume*) Thank you, Mr N, and our wardrobe mistress has asked me to point out that the costume worn by Mr N for that is, in fact, his own...

Song Introductions   51

DO IT AGAIN   1917
(Mason Dixon: A. Grock & L. Silberman & T. W. Thurban)
Fred Barnes, Irene Bordini

Mr N now makes his first solo appearance, and if last night's outrage (*or rehearsal*) is anything to go by it'll be his last. Mind you, we should have known better than to let him loose on a song called Do It Again. But it does have a tricky chorus at No X so may I ask you to pay the closest attention to the frenetic and feckless Mr N. / I'll have to have a word with that young man's vicar, next visiting day at the Scrubs (*or local prison*).

DON'T BE CROSS *See* MILLER'S DAUGHTER, THE

DON'T DILLY DALLY   1919
(Charles Collins & Fred W. Leigh)
Marie Lloyd

"We had to move away, 'cos the rent we couldn't pay..." A rhyming couplet worthy of the Bard himself. Aficionados of the Music Hall will immediately have recognised the opening lines of the first verse of perhaps the most popular chorus song of them all. To sing it needs a very special artiste indeed, and we are fortunate enough to have secured the services of the Queen of the Halls herself, in the proud plenitude of her powers, Miss N. / Miss N in top form as ever with her unique interpretation of Don't Dilly Dally. Wonderful.

DON'T GIVE ME DIAMONDS, ALL I WANT IS YOU   1910
(Charles K. Harris)
Gertie Gitana

It's nice to hear in these increasingly materialistic times that our Miss N has her priorities right. Don't Give Me Diamonds, she insists, 'Cos All I Want Is You. And all we want now is the dazzling and dynamic Miss N. / Just a touch of cynicism creeping in there, would you say...?

DON'T HAVE ANY MORE, MRS MOORE   1926
(Harry Castling & James Walsh)
Lily Morris

Miss N now delivers herself of a piquant little tale concerning her next door neighbour, one Mrs Moore to whom in No X she offers some sage advice, to whit, not to have any more. Quite what it was that Mrs

Moore had a surfeit of will now be revealed by the ripe and fruity Miss N!

DON'T STOP MY 'ARF A PINT O' BEER 1907
(Cornelius Pratt: J. Charles Moore)
Gus Elen

Mr N now graciously consents—graciously consents?! You try and stop him—to harrow us with an impassioned plea, No X, Don't Stop My 'Arf a Pint o' Beer. Here then, direct from Burridge's Cocoa Rooms in the Balls Pond Road (*or local*) is Mr N. / Mr N is a light drinker these days—he only drinks when it's light.

(*See* 'Arf A Pint of Ale *etc.*)

DOWN AT THE FARM-YARD GATE 1893
(Felix McGlennon)
Katie Lawrence

As you will see our next turn features the use of a stage property, one which our scenic designer fondly imagines to be a farmyard gate, and upon which we find seated Mr N, the better to outline a bucolic tale of ecstatic expectation. It's that blithe and blissful bumpkin: Mr N! / Rustic roguishness there from Mr N.

(*See also* Cowslip and the Cow, The *etc.*)

DOWN AT THE OLD BULL AND BUSH 1903
(Percy Krone & Russell Hunting & Andrew B. Sterling: Harry Von Tilzer)
Florrie Forde
Adapted from Under the Anheuser Bush (*Andrew B Sterling: Harry Von Tilzer*)

Miss N now offers a song with the most distinguished provenance—music by Sir Arthur Sullivan and the lyrics by Alfred Lord Tennyson. No X on your songsheets Down at the Old Bull and Bush. So let us revel in the cheery disposition and big brown eyes (*alter to suit*) of that most appetising of artistes, Miss N! / A song and a half given a performance and a half by Miss N.

(*See* 'Arf A Pint of Ale *etc.*)

DOWN AT THE WELSH HARP WHICH IS HENDON WAY *See* COSTER'S SERENADE, THE

DOWN THE DIALS 1893
(Harry Wincott: Gus Elen)
Gus Elen

Song Introductions　　　　　　　　　　　　　　　　　　53

It is some years since Mr Charles Dickens shocked the nation by revealing the sordid and disgraceful conditions prevailing in that part of London known as the Seven Dials. Do you know it? ... perhaps some of you live there—just behind Cambridge Circus—an area where cutpurses and blackguards of every description abound, as we shall now discover in the unsavoury company of a desperate and dissolute Denizen of the Dials! / That was our Mr N whose next appearance will feature a complete change of clothes—which'll be a great relief to everyone in the dressing-room.

DOWN THE ROAD　　　　　　　　　　　　　　　　　　1893
(Fred Gilbert)
Gus Elen

Our next song celebrates the strong bond of affection which grows almost unconsciously, I suppose, over the years between the costermonger and his constant partner on the road—his horse. And earning his little bit of corn now is the Pearly King of (*local*) Mr N! / Down the Road, most affectingly sung for us by Mr N.

DOWN WENT THE CAPTAIN　　　　　　　　　　　　　1887
(Fred Bowyer: Kate Royle, arr. George Ison)
G. H. Macdermott, Kate Royle

(*For large lady*) Few personalities fill our stage more amply than Miss N, now seen in a naughty nautical number. Miss N recently took ship for a cruise and as you might expect the captain, the officers and the crew all went down like ninepins before the exuberant and effervescent charms of Miss N. / There—that'll teach her to catch a packet.
　　　(*See also* All Hands on Deck *etc*.)

DUTCHMAN'S COURTSHIP, THE　　　　　　　　　　　c1875
(Harry Clifton)
Harry Clifton

For our next item we welcome an artiste from the continent in the person of Mynheer Rip Van Groggenheim, from Holland—one of the Low Countries ... he should feel at home here ... But it would seem that for this particular Nederlander the course of true love does not run smooth. A friendly British welcome then—not too friendly or he might not go back—for Mynheer Rip Van Groggenheim. / Mynheer Groggenheim bore a marked resemblance to our Mr N, didn't you think? Perhaps his father worked on the ferries.

Mynheer, the Dutch equivalent of Mister, is pronounced Min-eer.
(*See also* By the Side of the Zuyder Zee)

'E DUNNO WHERE 'E ARE 1898
(Harry Wright: Fred Eplett)
Gus Elen

Mr N next claims our attention; his last appearance caused a great deal of alarm and despondency due to the grim and uncompromising reality of his performance. Now he inveighs against the evils of inherited wealth, especially when it's inherited by someone else. A dour dissertation from the somewhat surly Mr N.
(*See also* Any Old Iron? *etc.*)

END OF MY OLD CIGAR, THE 1914
(R. P. Weston & Worton David)
Harry Champion

Last time Mr N bestrode this stage there were extraordinary scenes of riotous enthusiasm, and I see no reason why history should not repeat itself as we welcome, with the End of his Old Cigar, the entire and ever-welcome Mr N. / He did that act last time he was here and tonight—he's just done it again.

ESAU TAKE ME ON THE SEESAW 1908
(C. W. Murphy & Dan Lipton)
Madge Temple

Miss N now delights us with No X, a song with a Biblical resonance: Esau, Esau, Take Me On The Seesaw... Esau as we know was an hairy man... (*to bald man: No relation to you, sir*) ... the only thing I know about him is that he sold his birthright for a mess of pottage—which incidentally is available at the snack bar during the interval. Let's exult now in the silvery tones of the tasty and tantalising Miss X.

EVERYBODY'S DOIN' IT NOW 1911
(Irving Berlin)
Ida Barr, Lydia Barry, Ethel Levey, Ruby Raymond, Maud Tiffany
Included in "Everybody's Doing It", the Empire revue of 1912.

Onward and upward with an American song—and an American dance, I shouldn't wonder—by Mr Irving Berlin, who is making quite a name for himself in the world of popular song. His latest effort is called Everybody's Doin' It Now, a title susceptible to any number of dubious interpretations. But here now with a clean mind and an open heart is Mr N! / Everybody's Doin' It Now, from Mr N. (*If after very energetic dance*) He certainly did it—I don't think I'll bother...

(*See* Alabama Jubilee *etc*.)

EVERY LITTLE MOVEMENT HAS A MEANING OF ITS OWN
1910
(Fred Cliffe: J. Charles Moore)
Marie Lloyd

(*Not the Harbach: Hoscha song of the same name from "Madame Sherry", New Amsterdam, New York*)

Every Little Movement, trills the lady you are about to see, has a Meaning of its Own. I refer to that gloriously gladsome past-mistress of the significant gesture: Miss N! / (*If busty*) There's a lady who hasn't just got *it*, she's got two of 'em...

EVERYTHING IN THE GARDEN'S LOVELY   1898
(J. P. Harrington: George Le Brunn)
Marie Lloyd

Our scenic designer now offers a setting fit for a queen, or at least for the queen of all our hearts, for here now—assuring us that Everything in the Garden's Lovely—is that blissfully blushing blossom: Miss N. / Everything in the Garden's Lovely from Miss N. In my garden I sprinkle whisky on the lawn. Whisky, yes ... saves a lot of trouble. The grass comes up half cut.

EVERYTHING IS PEACHES DOWN IN GEORGIA   1918
(Grant Clarke: Milton Ager & George W. Meyer)
American Quartet, Farber Sisters, Al Jolson

With No X, Everything is Peaches Down in Georgia, we got over to the United States for a sample of that easy-going syncopated rhythm so characteristic of American popular song and which lends itself so well to the type of dance known as soft-shoe. As demonstrated by the very soft-footed and suavely stylish Mr N. / A peach of a performance there from Mr N. Well done, sir.

(*See also* Alabama Jubilee *etc*.)

EV'RYBODY KNOWS ME IN MY OLD BROWN HAT   1920
(Charles Collins & Fred W. Leigh)
Harry Champion

A millinery motet now in which Mr N will, if I'm not mistaken, expound the curious effect upon the general populace of his cady, his lid, tile, titfer, in other words his Old Brown Hat. To be delivered prestissimo by the chap with the chapeau extraordinaire, Mr N. / Mr N singing there in a personal best time of three minutes, forty-five seconds.

EV'RY LITTLE WHILE 1916
(F. Clifford Harris: James W. Tate)
Clarice Mayne, Lee White
From "Some", Vaudeville

A bitter-sweet ballad now as Miss N years for the speedy return of the man in her life. Ev'ry Little While, she sighs, and *for* a little while let us rejoice in the palpitating presence and the wistful tones of Miss N. / Miss N, for whom the word charm might have been invented.

EXCELSIOR 1850
(Henry W. Longfellow: Michael W. Balfe)
Hubert Eisdell & Norman Allin, John Harrison & Robert Radford, Ernest Pike & Peter Dawson, Herbert Thorpe & Foster Richardson

We continue with not one artiste, but with two artistes—together, simultaneously and at one and the same time! And with any luck—singing the same song! This is a setting for two male voices by Mr Michael Balfe of Longfellow's celebrated poem Excelsior, to be sung now in suffocatingly close harmony by Messrs M & N! / Thank you Messrs M & N—and don't give up the day jobs.

(*For other two-handers and/or possible concerted items see page 199*)

FALLEN STAR, A 1898
(Albert Chevalier: Alfred H. West)
Albert Chevalier

Mr N, that fine actor whose performances we have admired in so many of our productions now depicts an old actor who once basked in public adulation but has quite fallen out of favour. He has taken a job as a waiter (*alter to suit*) and we see him now, clearing up after a hard evening's work, reminiscing upon the glories that are past, and will never be again. Ladies and gentlemen, that Fallen Star, Mr N. / Mr N there in a fine portrayal indeed—A Fallen Star.

(*See also* Billy's Rose *etc. for monologues. For stage songs see* Bedelia (2) *etc.*)

FALL IN AND FOLLOW ME 1910
(A. J. Mills: Bennett Scott)
Whit Cunliffe, Charles R. Whittle

Song Introductions 57

We continue in jaunty tempo as we greet one of our regular favourites Mr N who is about to strut his stuff with No X, Fall In and Follow Me—No X. A Mr Gibson, it seems, once a military man, is up West on the spree with some friends, included amongst whose number is the indefatigable, the incorrigible, Mr N! / (*If in uniform*) There you saw the Army's secret weapon Mr N.

FARMER GILES See **VARMER GILES**

FATAL WEDDING, THE See **THOSE WEDDING BELLS SHALL NOT RING OUT**

FATHER DEAR FATHER See **COME HOME, FATHER**

FATHER'S GOT THE SACK FROM THE WATERWORKS   1915
(Charles Collins: Terry Sullivan)
Maidie Scott

Some families suffer more than their fair share of misfortune, and our next artiste has the misfortune to be a member of just such a family. A consolatory welcome therefore, for that pain-wracked, pale, pathetic, pallid—I've run out of p's—person, little Miss N! / Miss N. Small in stature but immense in talent.
    (*See also* Boers Have Got My Daddy, The *etc.*)

FIACRE, LE   1892
(L. Xanrof. English lyrics by Barry Gray)
Yvette Guilbert, Jean Sablon

Now to a French song ... to be sung *in French!* It is entitled Le Fiacre, which roughly translated into English means "the—fiacre". To be sung by a lady known the length and breadth of the Champs Elysées as Pattie de Faux Pas: Mademoiselle N. (*If a male*) To be sung by that well-known Gallic symbol, Monsieur N. / Le Fiacre from Mr/Miss N, who acquired that accent from a Johnny Onion man in Dover.
    (*See also* Can Can *etc.*)

FISHERMEN OF ENGLAND, THE   1921
(Gerald Dodson: Montague F. Philips)
Thorpe Bates, Peter Dawson

What a romantic sight it is at the seaside to see the fishermen mending their nets and painting their boats. But the fisherman's life is one of unremitting toil and danger, and we pay tribute to these hardy folk with The Fishermen of England, robustly sung for us now by Mr N.

FLANAGAN 1910
(C. W. Murphy & Will Letters)
Florrie Forde

Miss N asks us to turn our attention to one Mary Ann, a lady with an admirer who she urgently hopes will take her to the Isle of Man—again. His name is, of course, Flana—oh, you know him, do you, girls? Yes, he certainly gets around... So, to tell us more, please give an encouraging welcome to the pungently persuasive Miss N.

(FLOATING WITH) MY BOATING GIRL 1911
(Terry Sullivan)
Fred Barnes

What could be nicer, gentlemen, than taking your sweetheart on the river for a leisurely boat trip?—so in No X let us enjoy a little riverine romance with the exultant and exhilarating Mr N. / I'm very fond of boating myself—there's nothing I like better than an oar in each hand.

(*See also* Row Row Row)

FLORAL DANCE, THE 1911
(Katie Moss: air trad Cornish arr. Katie Moss)
Peter Dawson

It was the musician-poetess Miss Katie Moss who took a traditional air from her native Cornwall and fashioned it into that most splendid of ballads: The Floral Dance. Most splendidly and persuasively sung for us this evening by Mr N.

FLOWER SONG 1875
(Henry Hersee: Georges Bizet)
Italo Campanini, Paul Lhérie
From "Carmen", Opéra-Comique, Paris. London: Her Majesty's, 1878

We always like to include an operatic item in our programme and it is that fine tenor Mr N who favours us with an aria from Monsieur Bizet's "Carmen". Don José is in prison for dereliction of duty, having allowed Carmen to escape. His only consolation is the rose which the bewitching enchantress has left behind. Ladies and gentlemen, The Flower Song, superbly delivered by Mr N. / Well done, sir. Mr N with the Flower Song from Carmen.

Song Introductions   59

FLYING TRAPEZE, THE (THE DARING YOUNG MAN ON)
c1868
(George Leybourne: Alfred Lee)
George Leybourne

Now to one of the finest artistes ever to entertain a queue, Mr N, who introduces us to the Man on the Flying Trapeze, a howling cad if ever there was one. For he has cut out poor Mr N from the affections of his lady love ... aaah. Here now then, throwing himself on your mercy, is the love-lorn and lachrymose Mr N. / Mr N has never had much success with the fair sex. He did have a woman once—just the once— she was a suffragette ... mind you, she was chained to the railings at the time.

FOLKESTONE FOR THE DAY   1900
(Edgar Bateman: George Le Brunn)
Marie Lloyd

(*For two-hander*) Recently a summer day-trip was undertaken by a group of local ladies—twenty in all, with their chaps. Off they went to the seaside, bursting with excitement, and as you will gather from No X Folkestone will never be the same again. Here then with a whiff of the briny and a magnum of joie de vivre are two survivors of that expedition, the Misses M & N! / Those were the Misses M and N. I don't know which is which but I'm sure they do.

(*For other two-handers and/or possible concerted items see page 199*)

FOLLOWING IN FATHER'S FOOTSTEPS   1892
(E. W. Rogers)
Vesta Tilley

It is surely the hope of every British father to see his son following in his footsteps. So now, following his dear old dad down the straight and narrow path of righteousness, is that epitome of elegance and egregious effervescence Mr N! / Thank you Mr N—did you know his father had a very distinguished career? He was with the dipsomatic corps.

(*See also* Boers Have Got My Daddy, The *etc.*)

FOR ME! FOR ME!   1895
(Harry Wincott)
Fred Earle

Our next artiste, Mr N, is a wise old bird, as well as being a personal friend of long standing. In fact I often wheel him to the Post Office for his pension. But if anybody knows a thing or two it's him, it's him, it's him! as we are about to discover. So here he is now—the only one in captivity—Mr N! / That song has been passed by the Lord Chamberlain and a number 43 bus.

FOR MONTHS AND MONTHS AND MONTHS 1909
(Joseph Tabrar)
Jack Norworth, Jack Smiles

Now for the prime favourite Mr N, who is going to sing for months and months and months. No, that's the title—it'll only seem like it. But here he is in one of those breakneck performances of which he is an acknowledged past-master: streaking into view, it's the dynamic and dauntless Mr N. / Strange—he normally sings that quite fast.

FOR OLD TIMES' SAKE 1898
(Charles Osborne)
Florrie Forde, Al Jolson, Millie Lindon, Harry Taylor

A good old sentimental wallow now, as Miss N takes us down memory lane with that lifting if lachrymose lay, No X, For Old Times' Sake. Let us greet once again then the lady whose talents we prize above rubies, gliding seductively from up left to down centre: Miss N.

FOR TONIGHT See WALTZ SONG

FOR YOU ALONE 1909
(P. J. O'Reilly: Henry E. Gheel)
Enrico Caruso

A nice drawing-room ballad now. Funny how genteel families sing in their drawing-rooms. In my house we not only sing in the drawing-room we draw in the singing-room, and you have to be ever so refined to do that. I'm just filling in time here, you understand, to enable the maestro to arrange his music and take a deep breath before plunging into For You Alone. Also taking a deep breath, I've no doubt, is the singer: Mr N. / For You Alone, but sung for us all by Mr N.

FOUR-AND-NINE 1915
(Worton David: Bert Lee & The Two Bobs)
The Two Bobs

Mr N is one of those who likes to flash his money about, when he has

Song Introductions 61

it, that is. So here now coming into his own, which is a good trick if you can do it, is the last of the big-time losers, Mr N. / Thank you, Mr N. We'll let you know.

FOUR-'OSS SHARRYBANG, THE c1890
(Corney Grain)
Corney Grain

Two artistes now—Miss N and Mr N—tell us their adventures aboard a Four'oss Sharrybang, this being an omnibus of peculiarly French design... nevertheless I am sure the doings aboard will be entirely free from the slightest taint of vulgarity or impropriety. So, having killed the act stone dead, it's *en voiture* for Miss N and Mr N!

(*For other two-handers and/or possible concerted items see page 199*)

FRANKIE AND JOHNNY c1860
(anon.)
Frank Crumit, Leighton Brothers

Variety is what we aim for in our productions, and there could scarce be any greater contrast between (*previous number*) and the song of passion and tragedy you are about to witness. This is the American legend of those two ill-starred and ill-requited lovers Frankie and Johnny, related in a voice that thrills and moves as very few can: ladies and gentlemen—Miss N. / Miss N in magnificent form with the story of Frankie and Johnny—and let that be a terrible lesson to you all.

(*See also* Alabama Jubilee *etc.*)

FRIEND O' MINE 1913
(F. E. Weatherly: Wilfrid Sanderson)
Norman Williams

Our next ballad celebrates friendship, with music by Mr Wilfred Sanderson, who composed such well-loved songs as Captain Mac', Drake Goes West and Up From Somerset. The words are from the pen of Mr FE Weatherly who gave us The Holy City, Danny Boy, Roses of Picardy and so many more memorable lyrics. These two gentlemen's talents are combined in Friend O' Mine, and to sing it, our good friend Mr N.

FROM MARBLE ARCH TO LEICESTER SQUARE 1914
(Charles Knight: Kenneth Lyle)
Vesta Tilley

We return to the Metropolis, to London, with a tour of the West End, the very heart of Empire, where our knowledgeable guide is none other than that celebrated man-about-town and deb's delight, Mr N. / Well done, Mr N. What a gentleman. I know he's a gentleman, it says so on his dressing-room door. (*If a male impersonation*) There we saw Miss N in a male impersonation correct down to the smallest detail. Or so I'm told.

(*See page 201 for further songs of London*)

FROM POVERTY STREET TO GOLDEN SQUARE 1908
(Paul Pelham & Herbert Rule: Herbert Rule)
Kate Carney, Florrie Forde

We are all at the mercy of Dame Fortune, that fickle jade, who sometimes smiles upon us and sometimes withholds her favours. But here is a lady who I am pleased to say will bestow her favours upon us most bountifully, so let us give an equally bounteous welcome to Miss N. / Miss N like all of us has had her ups and downs, though in her case not for some considerable time.

FUTURE MRS 'AWKINS, THE 1892
(Albert Chevalier)
Albert Chevalier

A name hallowed in the Pantheon of the Halls is that of Mr Albert Chevalier, who has given us so many memorable songs—My Old Dutch, Knocked 'Em in the Old Kent Road, The Coster's Serenade and so on. Another of Mr Chevalier's keenly observed songs of Cockney life we are about to hear now: The Future Mrs 'Awkins, most effectively and affectingly sung by our very own Mr N.

GALLOPING MAJOR, THE 1906
(Fred W. Leigh: George Bastow)
George Bastow

I'm proud to announce that our next artiste is an ex-Serviceman who served for many years with conspicuous lack of gallantry in the Queen's Own Straitjackets. Like so many of our gallant officers he has a keen eye for the gals, so here now thundering into view is our very own Galloping Major N! / Mr N, who fought with Gordon at Khartoum, he fought with Baden-Powell at Mafeking, he fought with Kitchener—he couldn't get on with anyone.

(*See also* Army of Today's All Right, The *etc.*)

Song Introductions 63

GAY BOHEMIA 1895
(Harry H. Greenbank: Sidney Jones)
Maurice Farkoa
From "An Artist's Model", Daly's

Miss N now invites us to experience the hedonistic, pleasure-seeking world of Gay Bohemia. Is (*local*) ready for this, you may well ask. Go on then—ask. (*Audience: "IS (local) READY FOR THIS?"*) Yes, I think we are. so it gives me great pleasure to present to you a lady uniquely qualified to tell us all about the Balkan position, the categorically cosmopolitan Miss N! / Miss N, raising the temperature as only she can.

GENDARMES' DUET 1871
(H. B. Farnie: Jacques Offenbach)
Felix Bury & Edward Marshall
Paris: des Bouffes-Parisiens 1859. London: Philharmonic, Islington

Now to an item extracted kicking and screaming from Monsieur Jacques Offenbach's "Genevieve de Brabant", a style of presentation known as opera pouffe—bouffe. Whatever it's called, this is the celebrated duet featuring two of the French boys in blue—or should I say "deux garcons en bleu". Yes, you've guessed it. It's The Bold Gendarmes! / An arresting performance there from Messrs M & N.
   (*See also* Can-Can *etc. for French songs. See* Ask a P'liceman *and* P.C. 49 *for police songs*)

GENEVIEVE *See* SWEET GENEVIEVE

GEORGIE TOOK ME WALKING IN THE PARK 1908
(Ballard MacDonald: Donovan Meher & James W. Tate)
Clarice Mayne

No X as you can see is entitled Georgie Took Me Walking in the Park and it wasn't just to watch the ducks, I'll be bound. With full details of this romantic rendezvous is a young lady who in this programme is making her maiden appearance—something that only happens once so watch very closely. May I ask you for your customary warmth of welcome for the newest of our newcomers, Miss N. / Miss N's first but I'm sure by no means her last appearance with us.

GET OUT AND GET UNDER *See* HE'D HAVE TO GET UNDER (GET OUT AND GET UNDER)

GET YOUR HAIR CUT 1892
(George Beauchamp & Charles Osborne: Fred Eplett)
George Beauchamp

No X, for those of you too mean to buy a songsheet, is entitled Get Your Hair Cut, a song which can only mean an appearance by the Samson of the Halls—he always brings the house down—that well-known tonsorial tenor and phrenologist to the gentry, Mr N. / A truly barberous performance there from Mr N, who in the interval will be coming round to sell you anything you might need for the week-end.

(*See also* Little Bit off the Top, A)

GHOST OF BENJAMIN BINNS, THE 1884
(Harry Dacre)
Harry Randall

Every self-respecting theatre has its ghost, and the (*local*) is no exception. So, ladies and gentlemen, quiver and quake now in the presence of that ectoplasmic emanation, our very own Phantom of the Uproar: the Ghost of Benjamin Binns! / That apparition was better known to his nearest and dearest as Mr N.

GHOST OF SHERLOCK HOLMES, THE 1894
(Richard Morton: H. C. Barry)
H. C. Barry

This nineteenth-century has seen a tremendous advance in scientific methods of detecting crime, pioneered by that superlative sleuth, the late lamented Mr Sherlock Holmes. We now present to you his shade, so direct from making a big splash at the Reichenbach Falls is the Ghost of Sherlock Holmes! / Come back Moriarty, all is forgiven. Mr N was accompanied in that haunting refrain ... by the Speckled Band.

GIDDY LITTLE GIRL SAID "NO!", THE 1894
(J. P. Harrington: Orlando Powell)
Harry Freeman

From what one reads in the popular prints one might be forgiven for thinking the moral fibre of the nation is in serious decline. How reassuring then to hear of the Giddy Little Girl who said No. But if anyone can make her change her mind it is that louche and libidinous lounge-lizard Mr N. / Thank you Mr N. Never trust a man who wears yellow spats (*alter to suit the costume*) that's what I always say. What do you always say? ... Get on with it, oh all right ...

Song Introductions   65

GILBERT, THE FILBERT   1914
(Arthur Wimperis: Herman Finck)
Basil Hallam
From "The Passing Show", Palace

Music Hall generally depicts the seamier side of life, with its characters drawn from the lower ranks of society. The next artiste to step into view, however, as No X informs us, is most decidedly not your average geezer but is none other than the Pride of Piccadilly, the colonel of the knuts himself: yes, it's Gilbert—The Filbert! / Mr N as Gilbert, The Filbert. No flies on him... which can be very inconvenient...

GINGER, YOU'RE BALMY   1910
(Fred Murray)
Harry Champion

Catch-phrases are often so silly you wonder how they ever caught on, and quite the barmiest of them all must be No X: Ginger, You're Balmy. This song was first made famous by Mr Harry Champion who no longers works at our salary level so doing his level best is our very own Mr N. / Thank you for that, whatever it was. Mr N, full of himself as usual.

GIPSY'S WARNING, THE   1874
(Henry A. Goard)
Christy Minstrels, Ernest Pike

We carry on with No X on your songsheets, a song explicitly directed to any innocent inexperienced young maiden in the audience... not very likely but you never know. We do have one about to mount the podium however, so to relay to us the Gipsy's Warning is the Darling of the Halls, Miss N. / (*If sung by an older woman*) Miss N as the vulnerable virgin—a most testing character study for her.

(*See also* Gypsy Warned Me, Only a Glass of Champagne, She Was Poor But She Was Honest)

GIRL THAT I M.A.R.R.Y... THE   1902
(Arthur Trevelyan)
James Norrie

And now Mr N shows us how even people in *trade* have their finer feelings like all of us... well, some of us. In No X he presents a humble grocer who confides to us his feminine ideal. So welcome now that would-be Casanova of the Cooked Meat Counter, Mr N. / There he goes, back to the bacon slicer ... mind you, she's not bad-looking either.

(*See also* Somebody Would Shout Out "Shop" *also* Yes We Have No Bananas)

GIRLS, STUDY YOUR COOKERY BOOK 1908
(Joe Burley: Maurice Scott)
Florrie Forde

No X indicates an item of special interest to the ladies for it is to do with cookery, and will be performed by a lady who is not so much cordon bleu as cordoned off. Ladies and gentlemen, the Mrs Beeton of (*local*): Miss N! / She's spent all day slaving over a hot sofa.

GIVE ME A LITTLE COSY CORNER 1918
(F. Clifford Harris: James W. Tate)
Clarice Mayne

In No X Miss N now sighs for a Little Cosy Corner, a song which celebrated the truism that home is where the heart is. A gentle and sentimental number, none the worse for that, imbued with her own particular brand of distinctive charm by Miss N. / Miss N, desirous of a little cosy corner. I'd be there, I can tell you...

GIVE ME A TICKET TO HEAVEN 1902
(E. Denham Harrison & Richard Elton)
Denham Harrison, Herbert Payne

Those of us who have experienced the pleasures and pains of parenthood will be aware how infinitely touching children can be when they try to grapple with the great mysteries of our existence. In No X Mr / Miss N sings of how one small girl attempted to cope with the most acute loss a child can suffer: that of her mother. Give Me A Ticket To Heaven is the title, and the singer is Mr /Miss N.

(*See also* Boers Have Got My Daddy, The *etc.*)

GIVE ME THE MOONLIGHT 1917
(Lew Brown: Albert Von Tilzer)
Fred Barnes, Elsie Janis, Clarice Mayne, Randolph Sutton
Included in "Hullo! America", Palace 1918

For the first time tonight, ladies and gentlemen, we feature—a prop! To whit, a bench for two where one can bill and coo—words taken from No X, Give Me the Moonlight. And which lady would not wish to indulge in an assignation with the Lothario of Leytonstone (*or*

Song Introductions   67

local), Mr N. / Mr N—a man who could charm the birds—and frequently does.

GIVE MY REGARDS TO LEICESTER SQUARE   1905
(William Hargreaves)
Victoria Monks

Many Music Hall songs as we know celebrate the charms of London and the love and loyalty which the smoky old Town inspires in its people. In No X we find Mr N about to experience the emotional turmoil of leaving not only London but England herself. To ease the pain of parting, a soothing welcome if you please for Mr N. / I was very homesick as a lad—that's *why* I left. I was sick of it.

(See page 201 for further songs of London)

GLORIOUS BEER   1895
(Steve Leggett: Will J. Godwin)
Harry Anderson

Now to an artiste who for many years alas has suffered from that rare complaint: alcoholic constipation. Yes, alcoholic constipation ... he can't pass a pub. Nevertheless with No X, as cheery and beery as ever, is Mr M "Mine's a pint" N! / Mr N, a man who is to teetotalism what Florence Nightingale is to all-in wrestling. (*If a woman*) Thank you Miss N, known to her many friends as the Sweet Smell of old Brewery.

(See 'Arf A Pint of Ale *etc.)*

GOLDEN DUSTMAN, THE   1902
(J. P. Harrington: George Le Brunn)
Gus Elen

Mr N is desirous of bettering himself—let's face it, there's plenty of scope—and although only a humble dustman he's found a novel way of improving his circumstances—see No X. I suppose we should applaud initiative wherever we find it, and so it is with modified rapture that I introduce the Golden Dustman himself, Mr N. / Mr N, our Golden Dustman, currently earning thirty bob a week and as much as he can eat.

(See also What D'yer Think of that?*)*

GOLDEN WEDDING, THE   1886
(Harry Adams: Charles Godfrey)
Charles Godfrey

So often marriage is seen as little more than a battleground between the sexes, but surely the reality is that all those gibes and cheap jokes hide our deep longing for a congenial partner through life, and in No X, Mr N celebrates the holy estate of marriage with that wonderful song The Golden Wedding. A story of wedded bliss now from Mr N. / A marvellous character study for Mr N with The Golden Wedding.

GOOD-BYE! 1903
(G. J. Whyte-Melville: F. Paolo Tosti)
Violet Cameron, Enrico Caruso, Kate Cove

Signor Francesco Paolo Tosti, singing master to both the Italian Royal family and our own, has since settling here produced any number of graceful and popular ballads. We now offer undoubtedly his most celebrated: yes, Tosti's Good-bye. But let us bid the warmest of welcomes to Mr/Miss N! / Tosti's Good-bye. But it's not goodbye to Mr/Miss N, I'm happy to say, who will be singing for us again later on.

GOOD-BYE, DOLLY GRAY 1898
(Will D. Cobb: Paul Barnes)
Tom Costello, Harry Ellis (Primrose & Dockstader Minstrels), Hamilton Hill, Harry MacDonough
Inspired by the Spanish-American War February-August 1898

All conflicts produce their characteristic songs and No X, Good-Bye Dolly Gray, expresses sentiments universally appropriate to the enforced parting of loved ones in time of war. It's a rattling good tune especially when delivered by that fine upstanding figure of a man, Mr N! / (*After comedy version*) Mr N, to whom the Prince of Wales once said "Where's the gents?"

(*See also* Army of Today's All Right *etc.*)

GOOD-BYE-EE 1917
(R. P. Weston & Bert Lee)
Florrie Forde, Daisy Wood, Harry Tate, Charles R. Whittle

In time of need our country's young men do not hesitate to flock to the colours, and our Miss N is so proud of her brother that her cups runneth over. In No X we find her recalling how only the other day she saw him off to do his bit. I hope he enjoys it. But now here is that solicitous sister: Miss N. / Miss N, who used to have an hour-glass figure but time marches on .

(*See also* Army of Today's All Right *etc.*)

Song Introductions

GOODBYE, LITTLE YELLOW BIRD See LITTLE YELLOW BIRD

GOOD MAN IS HARD TO FIND, A 1918
(Eddie Green)
Jack Norworth, Sophie Tucker, Lee White

Now we come to a lady whose uplift has lead to many a downfall, so ladies take hold of your menfolks, and gentlemen take hold of yourselves—please—for the Siren of (*local*) ... carrying all before her: Miss N! / Miss N there, sorting out the men from the boys.

GOOD MORNING, MR POSTMAN 1908
(Paul Pelham & Herbert Rule)
Kate Carney

Our Miss N is teetering on the very edge of the matrimonial abyss, a fate which in no wise seems to dampened her spirits. Indeed even as we speak she awaits with the liveliest of anticipation a postal missive from her intended. So with No X Good Morning Mr Postman let us wait no longer for the pulsating and palpitating Miss N.

GORGONZOLA CHEESE See THAT GORGONZOLA CHEESE

GRANDFATHER'S CLOCK 1876
(Henry Clay Work)
All Minstrel Companies, John Read, Henry Russell

A time-honoured ballad now from the American composer Mr Henry Clay Work, whose output includes the rousing Marching Through Georgia. But now we hear his Grandfather's Clock. Well, not the actual clock but the song of that name. Ladies and gentlemen, Mr N.

GRASS WIDOWER, THE 1891
(J. H. Woodhouse)
Dan Leno

We haven't seen our next artiste for—oh, it must be at least half an hour. Some performers bring with them an extra spark of excitement, the heady whiff of danger. So stand well back, gentlemen, and ladies hang on to your hats as I introduce that veritable whirlwind, storming into view, Mr N! / There he goes, Mr P universe himself.

(*See also* Billy Muggins *etc.*)

GREAT EXPECTATIONS See IT'S ONLY A FALSE ALARM

GREEN EYE OF THE LITTLE YELLOW GOD, THE 1911
(J. Milton Hayes: Cuthbert Clarke)
Milton Hayes, Bransby Williams
Parodied by Billy Bennett as The Green Tie on The Little Yellow Dog, *also by Reginald Purdell in his 1940 sketch* Pukka Sahib *(Reynolds/EMI) from "Up and Doing" at the Saville starring Stanley Holloway as the reciter and Leslie Henson and Cyril Ritchard as the disrupting Indian Army Officers. A two-handed version by the present writer (the reciter sabotaged by an "assistant" standing close behind him and illustrating the story with inappropriate gestures) is published in "Make 'Em Roar" Vol 1 (Samuel French 1980).*

I now have the honour of welcoming to our stage the distinguished Shakespearean actor Mr N Parts One and Two who will deliver himself of one of the most celebrated poems in the language: The Green Eye of the Little Yellow God, a tale throbbing with romance, drama, and horrifying revenge. Thrill and gasp now to the elocutionary excellence of Mr N. / Wasn't that truly terrible?

(*See also* Billy's Rose *etc. for monologues and page 199 for further two-handed and/or possible concerted items. For further "eye" songs see* Algy *etc.*)

GYPSY WARNED ME, THE 1920
(R. P. Weston & Bert Lee)
Violet Loraine
Interpolated into "The Whirligig", Palace

It is said that Romany women are blessed with the gift of second sight, and to pass on her own Gypsy's Warning—No X—we now welcome a lady endowed with so many fetching parts it's difficult to know where to begin. So I shall simply give you her name: the supernaturally bewitching Miss N. / My grand-dad was a fortune-teller. He was a bit fey—funny old chap—he had a glass eye and a crystal ball.

(*See also* Gipsy's Warning, The *etc.*)

HAMPSTEAD IS THE PLACE TO RURALIZE 1861
(Watkyn Williams: arr. G. Holmans)
Annie Adams, Albert Steele

There is nothing your average cockney likes better on a Sunday or a Bank Holiday than to commune with nature, to enjoy the delights of the countryside. If a bit of countryside can be found close to home, all the better—and to prove it we've put it on the song-sheet at No X. Yes, for our next artiste there is no doubt that Hampstead is the Place to Ruralize, so here he/she is, our very own elf/nymph of the woods Mr/Miss N! / Bringing us a breath of fresh air—Mr/Miss N.

(*See page 201 for further songs of London*)

Song Introductions

HAPPY ELIZA AND CONVERTED JANE 1881
(Will Oliver: arr. L. Field)
Sisters Cuthburt

(*For two women in Salvation Army costume*) Sitting here as we do, safe and sound in the heart of Empire, we never cease to recognise our debt to Her Majesty's Armed Forces. In our last programme we saluted the Royal Navy, so now we lash ourselves into a patriotic paroxysm in order to pay tribute to: The Army! / There you saw the Misses M and N. They tell me they save fallen women so I've asked them to save one for me.

(*See also* Lost Stolen or Strayed *and* Sister 'Ria, *also page 199 for other two-handers and/or possible concerted items.*)

HARD TIMES COME AGAIN NO MORE 1888
(Joseph Tabrar)
Johnny Danvers, Harry Rickards
Note: This is not for Stephen Foster's 1854 song of the same title

Again not one artiste but two artistes, two gentlemen who have seen better days, who are down on their luck. It could happen to any of us— well, to you anyway. Nevertheless these two coves can still smile in the face of adversity, so to describe their Hard Times for us now are the Gruesome Twosome! / That was Messrs M & N giving us a Hard Time. Thank you, gentlemen, for letting us share your misery. But cajoling us all into a happier mood comes...

(*For other two-handers and/or possible concerted items see page 199*)

HAS ANYBODY HERE SEEN KELLY? 1909
(C. W. Murphy & Will Letters)
Nora Bayes, Emma Carus, Florrie Forde, Charles R. Whittle

No X concerns the efforts of an Irish girl to establish the whereabouts of her missing sweetheart, a Mr Kelly who hails from the Isle of Man. Has anybody here seen Kelly? No? Well, let us do our best to assist in the search, as we enjoy an ever-popular song by an ever-popular singer Miss N. / Has Anybody Here Seen Kelly? first sung by the great Miss Florrie Forde, and given a grand performance for us tonight by our Miss N.

(*See also* Band Played On, The *etc.*)

HAS ANYBODY SEEN MY TIDDLER? 1910
(Frank W. Carter & A. J. Mills)
Millie Payne

Has anybody seen my tiddler? asks Miss N in No X. *Has* anybody seen her tiddler? Does anybody care? Yes, of course they do, as we hear a plaintive plea from the tiny but tantalising Miss N! / I'm not at all sure that song was entirely proper ... still, *you* seemed to enjoy it.

(*See also* Boers Have Got My Daddy, The *etc.*)

HAS ANYBODY SEEN A GERMAN BAND? 1907
(A. J. Mills: Bennett Scott)
Florrie Forde, Ella Retford

Miss N now depicts a young Fraulein who has mislaid her Teutonic admirer, a trombonist with one of these German Bands so popular in the streets of Britain nowadays. Careless of her, you might think, but then as you will discover in No X he is rather a furtive Frankfurter. A sympathetic welcome therefore for the Belle of Bavaria: Fraulein N. / Miss N is now ready to receive a limited number of pupils for her German lessons, which are much the same as her French lessons but the discipline's much stricter...

HE CALLS ME HIS OWN GRACE DARLING 1898
(Lawrence Barclay)
Vesta Victoria

Our next song presents a girl from a little fishing village down in Dorset. She has fallen in love with a local lad, a fisherboy, and I am delighted to report that her affections are reciprocated. Here she is in the first heady flush of womanhood: Miss Grace Darling! / Nice to know that romance is not yet dead... that was, of course, our very own Miss N.

HE'D HAVE TO GET UNDER (GET OUT AND GET UNDER) 1913
(Grant Clarke & Edgar Leslie: Maurice Abrahams)
Percy Bronson & Minnie Baldwin, Gerald Kirby, Bobby North, The Three Rascals
Interpolated into "Hullo, Tango!", Hippodrome

As you can see No X is all to do with that new-fangled invention the motor-car. Noisy, smelly things—and they're so unreliable. I had one once—never again. The starter wouldn't start ... the battery wouldn't bat ... the carburettor wouldn't carb ... and the pistons—they didn't work either. Nevertheless to share with us the adventures on the Queen's highway of one Johnny O'Connor is that blonde and blithely bonny balladeer Miss N! / Miss N, a lady with the finest chassis in the parish.

(*See also* Oh Flo! (Why Do You Go?))

Song Introductions   73

HE LED ME UP THE GARDEN   1929
(Fred Gibson: E. A. Searson)
Edith Faulkner

Miss N has been led well and truly Up The Garden as we hear now in a steamy saga of romance among the radishes, cuddles among the cabbages, and kisses among the cucumbers. A vegetarian vignette perhaps, but the red heat of primeval passion in tooth and claw will now be expressed by Miss N! / Miss N has another vegetable song: something about She Sits Among The Cabbages and Peas ... or was it She Sits Among the Lettuces and Leeks...?

HELLO! HELLO! HELLO! See IT'S A DIFFERENT GIRL AGAIN!

HELLO! HELLO! WHO'S YOUR LADY FRIEND?   1913
(Worton David & Bert Lee: Harry Fragson)
Harry Fragson, Mark Sheridan

In No X our Mr N narrates the deplorable behaviour of one Jeremiah Jones who has been kicking over the traces with embarrassing consequences. So to any married man here thinking of straying off the primrose path let this act be a salutary warning as we greet the bright and breezy Mr N. / (*To man in audience*) Are you married, sir? Or have you always had round shoulders?

HELLO! MA BABY   1899
(Ida Emerson: Joseph E. Howard)
Marguerite Cornille, Ida Emerson & Joe Howard, Millie Legarde, Julie Mackay

We proceed with a song concerned with the telephone, a modern device eminently suited—so lovers swiftly have realised—to the exchange of sweet nothings ... as we shall hear from the saucy and scintillating Miss N. / A telephone song from Miss N. What an operator...!

>   (*See also* Hello! Susie Green, Kitty the Telephone Girl, Nora Malone (Call Me by Phone), Which Switch is the Switch Miss for Ipswich?)

HELLO, SUSIE GREEN   1911
(Lester Barrett: Herman Darewski)
G. H. Elliott, Ella Retford

A new aid to courtship is enlivening the social scene: Mr Alexander Graham Bell's latest invention the telephone, a device by which a boy can murmur soft sentiments to his sweetheart in close intimacy without having to clean his teeth. What a boon to today's young lovers, and what a boon to our programme tonight is Mr N.

(*See also* Hello! Ma Baby *etc*.)

HERE'S TO LOVE AND LAUGHTER 1912
(Arthur Wimperis: Paul Rubens)
Violet Essex
From "The Sunshine Girl", Gaiety

A song from the fertile pen of Mr Paul Rubens entitled Here's To Love and Laughter, sentiments we all surely echo without reservation. And who better to express these robustly romantic sentiments than the ever-welcome Diva of (*local*), Miss N.

HERE WE ARE! HERE WE ARE!! HERE WE ARE AGAIN!!! 1914
(Charles Knight & Kenneth Lyle)
Mark Sheridan

A famous chorus now—No X—Here We Are! Here We Are!! Here We Are Again!!! but like so many Music Hall songs the verses are less well known. So what is the message the song is intended to convey? To enlighten us, here he is, here he is, here he is again, Mr N. / (*If in uniform*) Mr N, demonstrating his martial parts.

(*See also* Army of Today's All Right *etc*.)

HE'S GOING THERE EVERY NIGHT 1898
(Fred Murray & Fred W. Leigh: George Le Brunn)
Marie Loftus

(*For two women*) From time to time we like to offer the stage over to the members of our staff, and tonight it is the turn of our two dedicated and hard-working cleaning ladies. "Cleanliness", said John Wesley, "is indeed next to godliness", but then he never visited the (*name of theatre*). A patronising welcome therefore, if you please, for Nellie and Daisy! / There you saw the Misses M and N, two of the most enthusiastic scrubbers in the business.

(*For other two-handers and/or possible concerted items see page 199*)

HE'S GOING TO MARRY MARY ANN 1885
(Joseph Tabrar)
Bessie Bellwood

It is of course the goal of every right-thinking young woman to marry a good man, someone handsome and intelligent—like me, for in-

Song Introductions 75

stance—I see ... and we meet now a lady who tomorrow morning will be nervously plighting her troth. The name of this tremulous maiden is Mary Ann, better known to us as the ineffably ecstatic Miss N! / An excitably anticipatory Miss N. (*To man or woman in audience*) Are you married? You don't mind being tied down then...?... That's not what I've heard...

HE'S ONLY A WORKING MAN See ONLY A WORKING MAN

HIS LORDSHIP WINKED AT THE COUNSEL 1887
(George Dance: Peter Conroy)
Harry Rickards

Onward and upward with Mr N, who comes from a very good family—he's twice been presented at Court ... only minor charges ... nothing to stop him becoming a bishop (*or current scandal*) and he takes us over to Chancery Lane (*or local*), to the Law Courts for No X on your song-sheets: His Lordship winked at the Counsel. What is not on your songsheets is the subtitle of this song: A Breach of Promise, which will give you an idea of the general tenor of the next offering from Mr N! / Some forensic fun there from Mr N.

HITCHY-KOO 1912
(L. Wolfe Gilbert: Maurice Abrahams & Lewis F. Muir)
American Ragtime Octette, Lew Hearn & Bonita, The Three Rascals
Interpolated into "Hullo, Ragtime!", Hippodrome

It has been observed that Britain and America are two countries separated by a common language. And certainly some expressions coined by our cousins across the old herring-pond are quite baffling. What, for instance, are we to make of the title of our next song: Hitchy Koo? A translation will now be attempted by the multi-lingual and multi-talented Mr N. / Well done, Mr N. Dancing and singing the Hitchy Koo. So now we know.

(*See also* Alabama Jubilee *etc.*)

HOLD YOUR HAND OUT, NAUGHTY BOY 1913
(C. W. Murphy & Worton David)
Ella Retford

(*For busty girl*) Hold Your Hand Out, Naughty Boy cries Miss N, and with any luck—she might put something in it. Here now then, with No X—a stern lesson to all you married men never to stray—is that ever so stern and strict disciplinarian, Miss N! / Miss N, reminding you gentlemen that extra-marital activity is frowned upon in (*local*). Curious how things change—it used to be compulsory.

HOLY CITY, THE   1892
(F. E. Weatherly: Stephen Adams)
Herbert Cave, Peter Dawson, Edward Lloyd, Michael Maybrick
Note: "Stephen Adams" was a pseudonym of the singer Michael Maybrick.

We continue in very different vein with a classic ballad as popular now as the day it was written. Music by Mr Stephen Adams—himself a fine concert singer—and lyrics by Mr FE Weatherly: The Holy City, matchlessly sung for us by Mr N. / A most inspiring and uplifting performance by Mr N.

HOME! SWEET HOME!   1823
(John Howard Payne: Henry R. Bishop)
Maria Tree (first)
First published as a "Sicilian Air" and later used as a theme song in "Clari, or The Maid of Milan" (Covent Garden). Notoriously a favourite song of Adelina Patti who would interpolate it into whatever opera she happened to be gracing at the time.

Now for one of the few remotely serious moments in our programme—an aria from Sir Henry Bishop's 1823 opera "Clari, or The Maid of Milan", a work forgotten now except for the one imperishable ballad we are to hear now: Home! Sweet Home! And to do the honours: Miss N. / There's certainly no place like home, not when it's sung as superbly as that.

HONEYSUCKLE AND THE BEE, THE   1901
(Albert H. Fitz & William H. Penn)
Maud Courtney, Clifford Essex, Lulu Glaser, Ellaline Terriss
From "Prima Donna", Herald Square, NY. In London interpolated into "Bluebell In Fairyland", Vaudeville

"You are my honeysuckle, I am the bee", an expressive sentiment requiring beauty, youth, charm and vocal excellence to do it justice. But I decided to give someone else a chance, and that someone is none other than the (*lady/gentleman who was last seen etc ... etc.*) ... the roguishly ravishing/that rascally rapscallion Miss/Mr N!

(*See also* Biggest Aspidistra in the World, The *etc.*)

HOW CAN A LITTLE GIRL BE GOOD?   1919
(Bay: Reginald Tabbush)
Maidie Scott

Song Introductions   77

Now for a lady whose appearances regularly cause conniptions and palpitations amongst the gentlemen of our audiences. How Can A Little Girl Be Good? she wonders. How indeed in this wicked world, especially when endowed with such an abundance of feminine wiles as the small but supremely significant Miss N! / Every time I see Miss N the water on my knee bubbles.

HOW'D'YA LIKE TO SPOON WITH ME?   1905
(Edward Laska: Jerome Kern)
Georgia Caine & Victor Morley, Millie Legarde
Interpolated into "The Earl and the Girl" (Casino New York version) and into the 1914 London revival (Aldwych). Also interpolated into "The Rich Mr Hoggenheimer", Wallack's, New York.

Miss N returns to distract us as only she can with an invitation for the gentlemen, to whit, How'd'ya Like to Spoon with Me? Who could refuse so delectable a request especially when offered by that demure and dimpling damsel, Miss N! / Miss N, asking whether we'd like to spoon with her—silly question... (*If she has picked out a man in the audience*) You got more than you bargained for there, didn't you?

HOW'YA GONNA KEEP 'EM DOWN ON THE FARM?   1919
(Sam M. Lewis & Joe Young: Walter Donaldson)
Jacques Jacks, Dorothy Ward

Let us now pause to consider some of the deeper issues of life which so concern each and every one of us. Why are we here? What's it all about? Where are we all going? And above all: How'ya gonna keep 'em down on the farm, after they've seen Paree? A philosophical question of the greatest significance, posed now by Professor N. / A cosmic performance there from Mr N.

> (*See also* Cowslip and the Cow, The *etc. for countryside songs*, Army of Today's All Right, The *etc. for Great War songs and* Alabama Jubilee *etc. for American songs.*)

HULLO! TU-TU   1909
(Muriel Scott-Gatty: Charles Scott-Gatty)
Margaret Cooper

We salute the art of the dance with a lady who has danced her way into all our hearts. She has danced from Omsk to Tomsk; she has danced in every capital of Europe and she is here tonight—to sing for us. Known to her many friends as Tu-Tu, but more formally to her legion of admirers as Madame (*cod-Russian version of artiste's name*)! / Next week she'll be at (*local*) with the Bolshy Ballet giving excerpts from Swan Pond.

I AIN'T 'ARF A LUCKY KID   1914
(Charles Hayes: Billie Hayes)
Kathleen Burchell

For many young girls the only employment open to them is to go into service. They may be fortunate enough to be placed with a kindly and considerate family, but for some their lives are wretched indeed. I Ain't 'Arf a Lucky Kid, a bitter tale from Miss N. / Poor Miss N—let's hope she soon finds a more congenial situation.

(*See also* I Might Learn to Love Him Later on, Ooh! 'Er!, She's Only a Working Girl *for servant songs and* Billy's Rose *etc. for monologues*)

I AIN'T NOBODY IN PERTICULAR   1907
(Scott MacKenzie: Fred W. Leigh)
Alec Hurley

In private life some Music Hall performers can be rather bumptious, with over-inflated opinions of themselves, but our Mr N is of a more modest disposition for as he tells us now: he Ain't Nobody In Perticular. We might well disagree however as we enjoy the confidences of that King of Cockney Charmers, Mr N. / Mr N, proving the truth of the old saying that less is more.

I 'AVEN'T TOLD HIM NOT UP TO NOW   1898
(Fred Murray & Fred W. Leigh)
Alec Hurley

What we don't know can't hurt us, an interesting observation endlessly debated by moral philosophers down the ages, and now brought to an unarguable conclusion by the Aristotle of 'Ackney: Mr N. / Mr N, who next week will be appearing at the Abattoir, Aberystwyth (*or local*) where I'm sure he'll slay 'em…

I BELONG TO GLASGOW   c1920
(Will Fyffe)
Will Fyffe

Our Mr N is a Scot—did you know that? Yes, he comes not from the Highlands but from the Lowlands. Well, actually he's from (*local*) and you can't get much lower than that. But he claims to belong to Glasgow—which must be a big relief to (*local*) Council—so a warm Sassenach welcome to the man with the hairiest sporran this side of

Song Introductions   79

the Trossachs, Mr N. / Thank you, Mr N. You can tell he's a
genuine Scot—there's dandruff on his shoes...
   (See also Annie Laurie etc.)

I CAN SAY "TRULY RURAL"   1909
(Worton David & George Arthurs)
Wilkie Bard, Lily Morris, Herbert Rule

Mr N now offers a word of advice to any married man whose
domestic bliss is marred by his tendency to come home rather later
than is commensurate with domestic harmony. An interesting song
with an interesting message. So here now, fortified by the finest Saudi
Arabian Chablis that money can buy is Mr N! / There he goes, living
proof of the old saying that work is the curse of the drinking classes.

I CAN'T DO MY BALLY BOTTOM BUTTON UP   1916
(J. P. Long)
Ernie Mayne

(For portly man) When our next artiste first appeared in one of our
programmes he caused grave constip-consternation, but we've got
used to him now so let us brace ourselves for that gastronomical
geezer, Mr N. / Thank you, Mr N. A lunchtime in his own legend.
   (See also Boiled Beef and Carrots etc.)

I CAN'T REACH THAT TOP NOTE (AH! AH! AH!)   1909
(Worton David & George Arthurs)
Wilkie Bard, Herbert Rule

Now to an artiste whose vocal talents have made him wealthy
below the dreams of average. It has been said that he has the ideal
voice in the event of fire or shipwreck. Ear-plugs at the ready, then,
for a singer known and feared throughout the Thames Basin (or
local) Mr N. / We only put that in to make everyone else look good.

I CAN'T TAKE MY EYES OFF YOU   1904
(Rida J. Young: Paul Rubens)
Constance Windom
Interpolated into New York production of "Three Little Maids", Daly's

I Can't Take My Eyes Off You, sighs Miss N in No X. I wonder who the
lucky man is? And we shall find the same difficulty as we contemplate
an alluring mixture of the vulnerable and the brazen in the palpitating
person of Miss N.
   (For other "eye" songs see Algy etc.)

I CAN'T TELL WHY I LOVE YOU BUT I DO   1900
(Will D. Cobb: Gus Edwards)
Emma Carus, Lil Hawthorne, Julie Mackay, Harry MacDonough, Clarice Vance

Love is blind, so 'tis said, which is why Miss N declares in No X: I Can't Tell Why I Love You But I Do. Whatever the reason, he is the most fortunate of men. Just as we are fortunate enough to be spending the next few minutes in the company of the love-lorn Miss N.

I'D LIKE TO LIVE IN PARIS ALL THE TIME See COSTER GIRL IN PARIS, THE

I DO LIKE AN EGG FOR MY TEA   1919
(Frank Leo)
Bert Coote
Included in "Back Again", Ambassadors'

We all have our little fads and fancies, our little peculiarities, and Mr N's are more peculiar than most as we shall now discover. So let's take a leap into the unknown with that jocular and jovial josser Mr N! / So Mr N likes an egg for his tea. Ah well, *chacun à son gout*, which roughly translates as Jack's got the gout.
   (*See also* Boiled Beef and Carrots *etc.*)

I DO LIKE A S'NICE S'MINCE S'PIE   1914
(Worton David & Bert Lee)
Jay Laurier

Many Music Hall artistes have felt constrained to inform us of their favourite comestibles and to enthral us now with a lyrical tribute to his own preferred provender is the Galumphing Gourmet himself, Mr N. / Mince Pies, eh? I prefer kippers and custard myself...
   (*See also* Boiled Beef and Carrots *etc.*)

I DO LIKE TO BE BESIDE THE SEASIDE   1909
(John A. Glover Kind)
Mark Sheridan

Now to No X, the seaside. It's the only place for a holiday, isn't it? I always take the wife and kids to the seaside every year. Mind you, we always go in February. Well, we like to get in early while the sheets are still clean. So here now giving us a whiff of the briny and a tantalising glimpse of lower limb is Mr N! / There you saw Mr N, modelling next

Song Introductions

season's beachware exclusive to (*local store*). I'm sure you especially noticed the fashionable dropped crotch line...
(*See also* All the Girls are Lovely by the Seaside *etc.*)

I DO LIKE YOU SUSIE IN YOUR PRETTY LITTLE SUNDAY CLOTHES

(C. W. Murphy & Worton David)   1912
Daisy Dormer

Since giving us (*song title*) Miss N has effected a complete change of attire appropriate for No X. "I Do Like You Susie In Your Pretty Little Sunday Clothes", most prettily performed now by the young miss who can wreak havoc in manly bosoms any day of the week: Miss N! / Miss N, looking a picture.

I DON'T CARE WHAT BECOMES OF ME   1911
(A. J. Mills: Bennett Scott)
Fred Earle, Sam Mayo

Mr N is buoyant mood tonight and wishes to make a declaration of intent, to whit: I Don't Care What Becomes of Me. Don't care was made to care, that's what my old granny used to say and you know what a silly old bat she was. So here, throwing caution to the winds is the rackety, rip-roaring Mr N! / Mr N, getting married in the morning. We had a quiet family wedding, you know—just me, the wife and the kids.

I DON'T WANT TO PLAY IN YOUR YARD   1894
(Philip Wingate: H. W. Petrie)
Jenny Clare & Madeline Majilton

How often do we think of our childhood and of the playmates of those tender years. And though those friendships may sometimes come under strain, how proud and glad we are when they mature into a lifelong affection. Such as been the happy experience of our old acquaintance Miss N.

I DREAM OF JEANIE *See* JEANIE WITH THE LIGHT BROWN HAIR

I DREAMT THAT I DWELT IN MARBLE HALLS   1843
(Alfred Bunn: Michael W. Balfe)
Louisa Pyne, Elizabeth Rainforth (original singer)

Miss N's beautiful lyric soprano is now heard to advantage in an aria from Mr Michael Balfe's "The Bohemian Girl", first performed at Drury Lane in 1843. In this opera the heroine Arline has been abducted as a child by gypsies, but still she remembers the splendours of her father's mansion. I Dreamt that I Dwelt in Marble Halls, an aria whose demanding challenges are fully met by Miss N. / Marvellously sung by Miss N.

IF I COULD ONLY MAKE YOU CARE 1913
(J. E. Dempsey: Johann C. Schmid)
Zigeuner Quartet

Miss N now gives us that most soul-stirring of ballads If I Could Only Make You Care. "If", the saddest word in the English language, so here tugging at our heart-strings as only she can, is Miss N! / There she goes, in all her forlorn glory.

IF I HAD A GIRL AS NICE AS YOU 1904
(C. W. Murphy & Dan Lipton)
Alf Gordon, Herbert Payne, Ernest Pike

Mr N, the ranking lady-killer of our company has been the cause of many a flutter in feminine bosoms, especially with No X, If I Had A Girl As Nice As You. Let us all now luxuriate in the manly presence and the dulcet tones of Mr N. / Mr N, thanking his lucky star. Well, that's as may be but you know the old saying, boys: candy is dandy but liquor is quicker.

IF I ONLY KNEW THE WAY 1896
(Harry H. Greenbank: Howard Talbot)
Venie Belfry
From *"Monte Carlo", Avenue*

At no extra charge Miss N—she of the (*mention previous appearance*)— is about to essay the character of a young maiden who has lost her way... Frankly, I think Miss N knows the way rather better than she should. Be that as it may, let us all now delight in the elfin charms of Miss N.

IF I SHOULD PLANT A TINY SEED OF LOVE 1908
(Ballard MacDonald: James W. Tate)
Clarice Mayne, Maude Mortimer

Now for a melody by that master tunesmith Mr James W Tate, the man responsible for such memorable numbers as A Broken Doll, Every Little While, I Was A Good Little Girl, and the one we are about to hear now: No X on your song-sheets, dedicated to all romantically-inclined

Song Introductions   83

gardeners and entitled If I Should Plant A Tiny Seed of Love. To be propagated now by our very own little passion flower, Miss N! / Planting a tiny seed of love was that perennial favourite, Miss N.

(See also Biggest Aspidistra in the World, The *etc.)*

IF IT WASN'T FOR THE 'OUSES IN BETWEEN   1894
(Edgar Bateman: George Le Brunn)
Gus Elen

An Englishman's home, it is said, is his castle, and our Mr N gives us a tour of his humble abode in the East End of London—humble but one which nevertheless enjoys the most marvellous views. At least it would do, if—It Wasn't For The 'Ouses In—oh, you know it do you…? Despite this shortcoming Mr N has turned his home into a regular rural retreat, so to give us a conducted tour of his establishment is that prime performer Mr N.

(See also Patchwork Garden, The *for another gardening song and page 201 for further songs of London)*

IF THE MANAGERS ONLY THOUGHT THE SAME AS MOTHER
(Irving Berlin: Ted Snyder)   1910
Maidie Scott
From "The Jolly Bachelors", Broadway, New York

Now for a young hopeful whose swift ascent to stardom is but a foregone conclusion. At least that's her mother's opinion. Unfortunately it is not one shared by some rather important people. Nevertheless, here, with enthusiasm undimmed by experience, is Miss N. / I'm sure we all wish her well in her chosen career—if only it were deep-sea diving…

(See also Boers Have Got My Daddy, The *etc. for child songs. For stage songs see* Bedelia (2) *etc.)*

IF THE MISSUS WANTS TO GO LET HER DROWN   1902
(Phil Ray)
Phil Ray

Our next needs no introduction—he hasn't turned up. So as we like to encourage new talent here's a trial turn instead. May I ask for oodles of encouragement for the *(reading)* bubbly and buoyant Mr N! / Mr N. I said that turn would be a trial, didn't I…?

IF THOSE LIPS COULD ONLY SPEAK   1905
(Charles Ridgewell & Will J. Godwin)
Will Godwin

Though it can ease the pain of parting a portrait can never really compensate for the absence of a loved one. This is the point at issue in No X, If Those Lips Could Only Speak. But definitely singing for us now, in anguished loneliness, is Mr N. / Telling the sad story there—an epic in little—was Mr N.

IF YOU CAN'T DO ANY GOOD DON'T DO ANY HARM 1902
(Harry Bedford)
Kate Carney

Moses came down the mountain with ten commandments whereas Miss N offers you but one simple injunction: No X—If You Can't Do Any Good Don't Do Any Harm. And doing us a power of good is that most life-enhancing of artistes Miss N. / Miss N, helping us along life's sometimes thorny path.

IF YOU CAN'T GET A GIRL IN THE SUMMERTIME 1915
(Bert Kalmar: Harry Tierney)
Lou Lockett & Jack Waldron, Cissy Ramsden, Harry Tierney

"Summer is a-cummen' in, loudly sing cuckoo"—so runs the old mediaeval English glee song. We don't go back quite that far for our next number though its subject—romance in the summertime—is eternal. And eternally welcome in our midst as ever is the Lothario of Limehouse (*or local*) Mr N.

IF YOU WANT TO HAVE A ROW WAIT TILL THE SUN SHINES
(William Hargreaves) 1904
Victoria Monks

Miss N has long basked in our admiration, and maintains her excellent reputation now with No X, a tale of domestic discord in the Deep South: If You Want to Have a Row Wait till the Sun Shines. We wait no longer for that high-struttin', high-toned, Queen of the Cake Walk, Miss N. / What a performance there from Miss N! I think she should be on prescription.

IF YOU WERE THE ONLY GIRL IN THE WORLD 1916
(F. Clifford Grey: Nat D. Ayer)
George Robey & Violet Loraine

(*For solo male*) Time for us all to sing once again as Mr N brings us the hit song from the Alhambra revue *The Bing Boys Are Here*—that most celebrated of sentimental ditties: If You Were the Only Girl in the

Song Introductions 85

World. But serenading *all* the ladies here tonight is your own, your very own Mr N. / Mr N casting a potent spell as only he can.
(For other two-handers and/or possible concerted items see page 199)

I JUST CAN'T MAKE MY EYES BEHAVE 1906
(Will D. Cobb & Harry B. Smith: Gus Edwards)
Anna Held, Ada Jones
From "A Parisian Model", Broadway, New York

Our next song is entitled I Just Can't Make My Eyes Behave. It is not on your song-sheets—we thought you'd like a little rest—in any case who could tear their eyes away for a moment from the felicitously flirtatious Miss N. / Miss N, declaring that she just can't make her eyes behave—a song dedicated to the surgical registrar of Moorfields Hospital *or* The Royal College of Ophthalmology.
(For further "eye" songs see Algy etc.)

I LIFT UP MY FINGER AND I SAY "TWEET TWEET" 1929
(Leslie Sarony)
Stanley Lupino, Leslie Sarony

At which point in our programme I am contractually obliged to unleash upon you Mr N, a man with a simple but effective way of getting through life's petty vexations with the minimum of stress and aggravation. Here then as happy as a sandboy is Mr N. / Aren't you glad you came?

I LIKE YOUR APRON AND YOUR BONNET 1911
(J. P. Harrington: Alf J. Lawrence)
Mabel Green, Ella Retford

Miss N obliges with No X—I Like Your Apron And Your Bonnet. It has been said that Miss N's appearances here tend to excite the grosser passions, so if there are any grocers in, please try and keep yourselves under control as we exult in the sundry charms and dainty delights of Miss N.

I LIKE YOUR OLD FRENCH BONNET 1909
(Tom Mellor & Alf J. Lawrance & Harry Gifford)
Daisy Dormer

Miss N now warns you gentlemen of the follies of a holiday romance, especially a holiday taken in La Belle France! Mais oui! C'est le numéro

X sur le programme—(*in execrable French accent*)—I Like Your Old French Bonnet. Oh, la la! Mesdames et messieurs, bienvenue a Mademoiselle N! / Miss N and her old French bonnet. And she never even sent him a letter.

(*See also* Can-Can *etc.*)

I LIKE YOUR TOWN 1915
(Harry Bedford & R. P. Weston)
Harry Bedford

Mr N considers that he has had enough of Town—you may think the Town has had enough of Mr N ... whatever the truth of the matter he's packed his bag and sacked his valet. So, heading—as the poet Milton said—for fresh woods and pastures new, is the dashing and debonair Mr N. / Mr N, off to enjoy country pursuits. And good luck to him.

I LIVE IN TRAFALGAR SQUARE 1902
(C. W. Murphy)
Morny Cash

Mr N has, alas, seen better days. But he keeps smiling, despite all adversity and the buffetings of fate. What a privilege to meet, therefore, in all his shabby glory, Mr N! / Mr N, the defiant dosser of Trafalgar Square ... did you know Lord Nelson wrote a song once? Nelson, yes. It was called "Please Don't Talk About Me—One Eye's Gone..." I know how you feel.

(*See page 201 for further songs of London*)

I'LL BE YOUR SWEETHEART 1899
(Harry Dacre)
Lil Hawthorne, Marie Kendall

Things are looking up as I introduce that most ornamental of artistes Miss N, who in No X offers a tempting proposition: I'll Be Your Sweetheart—chance would be a fine thing. Ladies and Gentlemen, with a song of burgeoning romance, that sentimental and scintillating sprite, Miss N.

I'LL MAKE A MAN OF YOU 1914
(Arthur Wimperis: Herman Finck)
Clara Beck, Gwendoline Brogden
From "The Passing Show", Palace

We proceed apace with I'll Make A Man of You, a song respectfully

Song Introductions   87

dedicated to the surgical registrar of (*local*) hospital. This famous recruiting song will now be performed by a lady who has men flocking to the colours in their droves, and quite right, too. Yes, it's the Britannia of (*local*): Miss N! / (*For busty woman*) I'm asked to tell you that Miss N's figure was entirely supported by voluntary contributions. (*Or if in uniform*) The uniform's changed since my day. My sergeant wasn't a bit like that. Well, perhaps a little.
    (*See also* Army of Today's All Right *etc*.)

I LOVE A LASSIE   1905
(Harry Lauder & Gerald Grafton: Harry Lauder)
Harry Lauder

Anyone in from Scotland?... I remember a few years ago there was a great fuss—even questions asked in Parliament—about a road sign on the border. As you went north it said "Welcome To Scotland", but on the other side as you came south it said "Beware of the Sheep". Which brings us to No X, I Love A Lassie, that joyous evocation of dalliance in the glens, avidly pursued by Mr N.
    (*See also* Annie Laurie *etc*.)

I LOVE TO GO SWIMMIN' WITH WIMMIN   1921
(Ballard MacDonald: Sigmund Romberg)
Pat Rooney
From "Love Birds", Apollo, New York, though cut before opening night.

Our next artiste has enjoyed many successful seasons on Blackpool sands with Johnson's Jolly Joyboys, but it's the jolly girls at the seaside with which he is pre-occupied at the moment, for Mr N loves to Go Swimmin' With Wimmen, No X. So, let's dive straight into the deep end with that muscular man of the moment, Mr N! / I can tell you, ladies, in the water he's poetry in motion—they say his breast-stroke has to be experienced to be believed.
    (*See also* All the Girls are Lovely by the Seaside *etc*.)

I'M AFRAID TO COME HOME IN THE DARK   1906
(Harry H. Williams: Egbert Van Alystyne)
May A. Bell, Della Fox, May Irwin, Hetty King, Elizabeth Murray, Ella Retford, Maidie Scott, May Vokes
From "A Knight for a Day", Wallack's, New York

Our next song, No X, is entitled I'm Afraid To Come Home in the Dark. I can understand that, especially if you live in (*local*)—you never know what you might step in. But here now stepping boldly into the spotlight is the unafraid and unabashed Miss N! / Miss N with a song originally sung in this country by Miss Hetty King, no less.

I'M A LITTLE TOO YOUNG TO KNOW 1889
(Charles Reeves: F. W. Venton)
Ada Reeve

Now a tale of a young girl, retiring and shy, a maiden who while trembling on the very brink of womanhood is still A Little Too Young To Know. An expressive picture of innocence and modesty—we don't see too much of that here—brought to us by the divinely dimpling Miss N! / A little too young to know, eh...? If you believe that you'll believe anything.

I'M ALONE BECAUSE I LOVE YOU 1931
(Joe Young)
Bud & Joe Billings

The artistry of Miss N has long held our respect and admiration, not least for her version of that most plaintive of songs, I'm Alone Because I Love You, No X. Not that we could ever feel alone in the company of the ever-endearing, ever-enthralling Miss N.

I'M A MAN THAT'S DONE WRONG TO MY PARENTS
(trad: ed. Lucy Broadwood)
Published in English County Songs, 1889

We find Mr N in agonies of remorse having fractured the Fourth Commandment. While you're trying to work out whether that's one of the juicier ones let me remind you that it is Honour Thy Father and Thy Mother. Mr N has alas disobeyed this injunction and is now paying the price. Here he is, the distraught and distracted Mr N! / Let that be a terrible lesson to you all. Gawd 'elp 'im.

I'M GETTING READY FOR MY MOTHER-IN-LAW 1896
(Harry Wincott)
Harry Champion

Love and marriage: the two being by no means as mutually exclusive as folk-lore would have us believe. It's true there can be snags which have to be counter-balanced against wedded bliss, one being that when a man takes a wife he also takes on—her mother. So let us see how this sometimes fraught relationship fares in the domestic affairs of Mr N! / Thank you Mr N. Actually, he's very fond of his mother-in-law—he worships the ground that's coming to her.

I'M GLAD I TOOK MY MOTHER'S ADVICE c1895
(Percival Langley: Charles Osborne)
T. E. Dunville, Maidie Scott
This song seems not to have been published, but it was recorded by Miss Scott in 1915 on HMW 568.

In these modern days where women are claiming equality with men and even agitating for the vote you might think that young girls are totally lacking in modesty and propriety. It is nice to know therefore that some maidens are still prepared to take their Mother's Advice. One such an obedient virgin will now be impersonated for us ... by that innocuous and ingenuous incarnation of innocence Miss N. / What a lovely child. It's very late for her to be out, so even as we speak our producer is rushing her home to bed...
   (*See also* Boers Have Got My Daddy, The *etc.*)

I'M GOING BACK TO HIMAZAS 1927
(Fred Austin)
Harry Gordon

There are many music hall songs which deal with longing for one's roots, nostalgia for the old times and the old places. Mr N declares a profound desire to go back not to Old Virginny, or Michigan, but to a little place called Himazas. Let us bid him a safe journey and a speedy return, for where should we be without the irresistible, the inimitable, the indispensable Mr N! / Him-az-as the pub next door—it's difficult to believe that was written by a grown man, isn't it?

I'M GOING TO GET MARRIED TODAY—HOORAY! 1899
(Bennett Scott & C. G. Cotes)
Maggie Duggan

Miss N is so excited! And with good reason, for she is about to experience a profound change in her personal circumstances—indeed, the most profound change a young maiden can possibly undergo: marriage! Aaah! So let us wish every happiness to the Blushing Bride, Miss N. / What a splendid wife she'll make! My wife's very unsettled these days, I can tell something's wrong—she's taken to wrapping my sandwiches in a road map.

I'M HENRY THE EIGHTH I AM   1910
(Fred Murray & R. P. Weston)
Harry Champion

We present a man who likes to sing his little songs and tell his little witticisms ... he's a sort of half-singer, half-wit. So now, with an intriguing tale of marital multiplicity is your own, your very own Mr N! / Thank you Mr N, Henry the Eighth he is, he is. Have you ever heard that song before? ... well, you've just heard it again!

I MIGHT LEARN TO LOVE HIM LATER ON   1921
(R. P. Weston & Bert Lee)
Violet Loraine
From "London, Paris and New York", London Pavilion

It's very difficult finding reliable servants these days, isn't it? I mean, I must have been through six chambermaids in the last eighteen months alone. But we now meet a tweeny, a parlour maid who has designs on her aged employer. As you can see in No X I Might Learn To Love Him Later On is the title of the piece, and the piece about to sing it is the frisky and frolicsome Miss N. / Miss N—she's not really common—she comes from a good family ... very well-reared ... oh, you noticed, did you?
(*See also* I Ain't 'Arf a Lucky Kid *etc.*)

I'M LOOKING FOR MR WRIGHT   1909
(R. P. Weston & C. W. Murphy & Herman Darewski)
Madge Temple

In No X Miss N sighs for a Mr Wright to take her up on high. This I take to be a punning reference to those two foolhardy American brothers who are endeavouring to construct a flying machine. What folly! If they succeed I'll eat my gavel, and that's a promise. Another promise is that the next few minutes will be occupied most gladsomely by the lady with the finest fuselage in the business: Miss N! / Miss N, Looking For Mr Wright. I'm sure she won't have to wait long.
(*See also* Up in a Balloon)

I'M ONE OF THE BOYS *See* OH, I'M ONE OF THE BOYS

I'M 94 THIS MORNIN'   c1921
(Will Fyffe)
Will Fyffe

Now it is my privilege to welcome a true veteran of the Halls, a

Song Introductions   91

man who has been entertaining the great British public for so
many glorious years and can still cut the mustard, as they say. Yes,
it's that naughty nonegenarian, Mr N. / He joined an old folks
club—I don't know what he got up to but after one week he had
three notches on his walking-stick.

   (*See also* Annie Laurie *etc. for Scots songs and* Cowslip and the Cow *for country yokel songs*)

I'M SHY, MARY ELLEN, I'M SHY   1910
(Charles Ridgewell & George A. Stevens)
Jack Pleasants, Jack Smiles

Our next artiste is a touch nervous. Well, you see, he read in his stars
this morning that Taurus is rampant. And he's a Virgo ... or he used
to be. But rising above this baleful augury, with all the febrile and
feverish ferocity of a forceful—am I splashing you?—of a forceful and
frantic four-flusher, is Mr N! / Thank you, Mr N, the man of whom it
was once said "It's a boy!"

   (*See also* Billy Muggins *etc.*)

I'M TWENTY-ONE TODAY   1911
(Alec Kendal)
Jack Pleasants

It is my privilege to announce at this juncture that Mr N, a young man
much admired here for his talents and personableness, has today
attained his majority. So let us all offer our warmest congratulations
as he strides into the limelight, in the full flush of his ardent manhood,
Mr N. / Mr N—twenty-one today. Doesn't that take you back?
Twenty-one. To be so fit and full of *vim* and *vigour* ... I think I need a
lie down.

   (*See also* When a Fellow is Twenty-One)

I MUST GO HOME TONIGHT *See* OH, I MUST GO HOME TONIGHT

I'M WAITING HERE FOR KATE   1909
(Worton David & George Arthurs)
Wilkie Bard

Cupid's darts are aimed at all manner of persons, from those of high
society right down to the lewdest clodhopper, a character assumed
now with rather worrying conviction by our Mr N. According to No
X a country girl called Kate is the object of his amatory inclinations,

and now he awaits her at the garden gate. Let *us* wait no longer for the lubricious and licentious Mr N. / A sensitive soul, even if he is a little rough around the hedges.

(*See also* Cowslip and the Cow, The *etc.*)

IN JERSEY CITY   trad
(anon.)

We continue with Miss N who gives us a plaintive song from the United States of America entitled In Jersey City and based, I believe, on a European folk-song. But whatever its origin this song demonstrates the universal frailty of our emotions and the tragic consequences which may arise therefrom. With In Jersey City: Miss N.

IN OLDEN SPAIN   1888
(Clarence Lalo: Edward Lalo)
Julie de Savigny
From "Le Roi d'Ys", Opéra-Comique, Paris

(*For comedy version*) The great house curtains will shortly swing open to present us with a setting which evokes the torrid noonday heat of a small pueblo in central Espagne. A fit setting indeed for an artiste who has thrilled audiences all over Penge and the Home Counties (*or local*), and will now thrill us with In Olden Spain. Ladies and gentlemen, the Diva of Deptford (*or local*) Madame N. / I think her new singing teacher has been a great help, don't you?

(*See also* My Castle in Spain, Spaniard that Blighted My Life, She Does the Fandango All Over the Place, Tiddley-Om-Pom!)

IN OTHER WORDS   1916
(F. Clifford Grey: Nat D. Ayer)
George Robey
From "The Bing Boys Are Here", Alhambra

I'd like to introduce the next turn with a quotation from Henry IV Part II—but I've forgotten it. So here with his own brand of poetic licence is the Bard of Bermondsey (*or local*), Mr N! / Mr N—I can't tell you the trouble he had learning that.

IN THE DINGLE DONGLE DELL   1914
(Clare Kummer)
Margaret Cooper

(*For "Pixie" two-hander*) We waft you now to a fairy camp ... with a sylvan song about a misogynistic creature of the woods ... aren't you glad you came? Do you believe in fairies...? Just as well, because we are now about to meet the Peckham Pixies! (*or local*). / Pixie 1 was Miss N and the other understandably prefers to remain anonymous, so any resemblance between him and Mr N is entirely coincidental.

(*For other two-handers and/or possible concerted items see page 199*)

IN THE GLOAMIN' 1877
(Meta Orred: Lady Arthur Hill)
Signor Campobello, Will Oakland

In contrast we pass from a song expressing the joyous hope of future fulfilment to a wistful recollection of happier day: In the Gloamin', a tale of noble renunciation, and a ballad particularly suited to the clear lyric soprano (*alter to suit*) of Mr/Miss N.

IN THE GOOD OLD SUMMERTIME 1902
(R. E. N. Shields: "Honeyboy" George Evans)
Julie Mackay, Blanche Ring, Stewart & Gillen
From "The Defender", Herald Square, New York.

They say that only God can make a tree, but they reckoned without the limitless ingenuity of the (*local*) stage management! A sylvan setting, then, for No X, In The Good Old Summertime. Not that the artiste needs any assistance other than your kind attention, for she is that sunniest of soubrettes, Miss N.

IN THESE HARD TIMES 1915
(R. P. Weston & Fred J. Barnes)
Whit Cunliffe

One cannot help remembering even in this convivial atmosphere that we live in Hard Times. Such a sorry state of affairs has not escaped the attention of our next artiste, a young lady who has been called a baggy sausage... (*look at notes*)... I think that should be saucy baggage: ... yes, it's our very own Good-Time Gal, Miss N. / In These Hard Times, a political polemic from Miss N.

IN THE SHADE OF THE OLD APPLE TREE 1905
(Harry H. Williams: Egbert Van Alystyne)
Nora Bayes, Lillian Rosewood, Leona Thurber

Romance and nostalgia, two sentiments found at their lushest in No X, In The Shade Of The Old Apple Tree. So now let us welcome the apple of everybody's eye, the ever-lovely English delicious Miss N. / Miss N, and may her Pippins never fall.

IN THE TWI-TWI-TWILIGHT 1907
(Charles Wilmot: Herman Darewski)
George Lashwood

How many fond declarations have been made, I wonder, In The Twi-Twi-Twilight? With No X, treading a delicate path between the romantic and the risqué, is that roistering roué. Mr N. / There he goes, the Lothario of (*local*), Mr N.

IN THE VALLEY OF GOLDEN DREAMS 1913
(C. W. Murphy & Worton David)
Florrie Forde, Gertie Gitana

No X on your songsheets is steeped in regret for missed chances and lost opportunities: In The Valley of Golden Dreams. And few singers can bring such depth of feeling to a song as Miss N. / Miss N... isn't that a beautiful melody? That's what we miss today, isn't it? An honest-to-goodness tune.

I PARTED MY HAIR IN THE MIDDLE 1913
(Worton David & C. W. Murphy)
George Formby

Now a visit from a gentleman whose talent is matched only by his sheer animal magnetism. In fact the last time he appeared here many ladies took it upon themselves to hurl sundry nether garments over the footlights—a disgraceful exhibition. (*To woman in front row*) And you never got yours back, did you, Agnes? So take a grip on yourselves, girls, as we unleash upon you the Adonis of the Halls Mr N. / Thank you, Mr N. And I'm glad you ladies managed to keep yourselves under control this time.

I PUT ON MY COAT AND WENT HOME 1910
(Robert Hargreaves & William Hargreaves)
George Formby

I have to say the next artiste, Mr N, is an acquired taste—whenever I feel in need of some exercise I put on one of his records and let my flesh creep. Nevertheless he has lived a life of astounding variety and adventure, so here to recount some of his more startling exploits is Mr N. / What *will* he get up to next? Mr N, as intellectually-challenged as ever.

Song Introductions   95

IS ANYBODY LOOKING FOR A WIDOW?   1908
(Harry Gifford)
Vesta Victoria

Our Miss N has, I'm sorry to say, recently been bereaved. Her husband drank champagne from her slipper and succumbed shortly afterwards to a fatal attack of athlete's gullet. But now the sap's rising again and Miss N's eye has begun to rove. Is There Anybody Looking For A Widow? she cries. If so your search is over, gentlemen, because here she is with all mod cons and everything in full working order: Miss N! / (*Look off after her*) It's all right, she's gone...

I STOPPED I LOOKED AND I LISTENED   1916
(Joseph Tabrar)
George Robey
From *"The Bing Boys Are Here"*, Alhambra

So many of us saunter through life unaware, unobserving, but whenever Mr N comes across anything untoward he stops... he looks... and he listens. An autobiographical aria, so to speak, from the quintessence of quaintness: Mr N. / Mr N—little in life's rich pageant passes him by. But we pass on with...

IS YOUR MOTHER IN MOLLY MALONE?   1903
(A. J. Mills: George Everard)
Walter Munroe

We continue apace with our Irish troubadour, Mr N... who has been described as the original little bit of heaven that fell. He regales us now with a Celtic cantata, No X, Is Your Mother In Molly Malone?, so a warm welcome for that sparky spalpeen Mr N. / Mr N who leaves for Paris next week where he is appearing at the celebrated Irish cabaret on the Left Bank, the Follies Bejabers...

(*See also* Band Played On, The *etc.*)

I THINK I'LL BUY PICCADILLY   1927
(Ted Waite)
J. W. Rickaby

It has been said that our next artiste, Mr N, tends to sing flat. It's not surprising really as he's been spending some time recently in a place where he's not allowed anything sharp. So here now, on day release from B Wing, Mr N! / Harpic, eh? I must make a note of that... might make a change.

(*See page 201 for further songs of London*)

IT'S A BIT OF A RUIN THAT CROMWELL KNOCKED ABOUT A BIT
(Harry Bedford & Terry Sullivan: Harry Bedford)
1912
Marie Lloyd

Now for an hysterical—historical item concerning a certain Oliver Cromwell and an old ruin… (*To man or woman in audience*)… nothing personal, sir/madam… And to deliver tonight's lecture is Miss N, an artiste whose motto might be Virtue Won't Hurt You, But Vice is Nice. Stand well back for the lusty, gusty and bustling Miss N! / Thank you, Miss N, who next week will be going to Aldershot (*or local barracks*) to entertain the troops… one at a time.

IT'S A DIFFERENT GIRL AGAIN! 1906
(George Arthurs: Bennett Scott)
Whit Cunliffe

(*This intro was for a programme opener*) Hello! Hello! Hello! cries Mr N in No X, which seems to be an appropriate way to start our programme. After all, if he'd started with "Goodbye-ee" you might have all got up and walked out. It's not too late to make something of the evening. But now you've taken your coats off see what you make of the sprightly and engaging Mr N! / Mr N—light of heart and fleet of foot—he'd need to be with all those women in tow…

IT'S A GREAT BIG SHAME 1894
(Edgar Bateman: George Le Brunn)
Gus Elen

It says here "announce Mr N—it's a great big shame…" Oh, that's the title of the song!—I'm so sorry. It's a Great Big Shame, No X. And for why? Because Mr N has lost his pal, his best pal in all the world … not to the Grim Reaper but to a figure even more implacable— his best pal's wife! So let's all lend a sympathetic ear to the downcast and despondent Mr N. / Our thanks to Mr N, and I'm sure you know the old saying: a married man has just one wife but a navvy can take his pick.

IT'S ALL RIGHT IN THE SUMMER TIME 1902
(George Everard & Fred Murray)
Vesta Victoria

It's All Right in the Summertime, claims Miss N. I think it's not bad in the wintertime either, but that's a personal opinion. No X chronicles

Song Introductions 97

her experiences as an artist's model. So, direct from being hung at the Royal Academy, is the lithe and lissome Miss N. / A model performance from Miss N.

IT'S A LONG, LONG WAY TO TIPPERARY   1912
(Jack Judge & Harry J. Williams)
Florrie Forde, Jack Judge, Minnie Muir, Maude Mortimer

Our next number is one hallowed in the annals of popular music and is forever associated with Miss Florrie Forde and with the Army as a marching song. Its first singer however was its composer, Mr Jack Judge, who paid off a debt to a friend by assigning over part of the copyright. I don't know how big the debt was but even a small share of It's A Long Long Way to Tipperary must have gathered in a pretty penny. An imperishable song given a rousing performance now by Miss N.

(*See also* Army of Today's All Right *etc.*)

IT'S A PITY TO WASTE THE CAKE   1909
(J. P. Harrington: Orlando Powell)
George Lashwood

The bride left at the altar is so often regarded as a figure of fun but what of the groom in the same predicament? Our Mr N has just suffered this humiliating misfortune, so let us offer heartfelt commiserations to the betrayed, the benighted, the bereft Mr N! / Poor Mr N, looking for a bride. Any married couples in? ... that's nice. I'm married myself but my wife's not here tonight. She's down at the docks doing some overtime (*or local*).

(*See also* Boiled Beef and Carrots *etc.*)

IT'S LOVELY TO BE IN LOVE   1915
(F. Clifford Harris: James W. Tate)
Clarice Mayne

Some artistes do not always select songs entirely suitable for themselves. But No X, It's Lovely To Be In Love, could scarce find a more appropriate exponent than that most decorative adornment of the Halls, the lovely and the lovable Miss N. / There—told you it'd be good, didn't I...?

IT'S MY BATH NIGHT TONIGHT   1922
(R. P. Weston & Bert Lee)
Jack Pleasants

An ablutionary aria now from Mr N who in No X informs us that It's his Bath Night Tonight. On behalf of all of us in the dressing-room may I say I wish it had been last night. Still, let's all take the plunge now with the hopeless and soapless Mr N. / Mr N looking forward to his bath. May his loofah never droop.

IT'S ONLY A FALSE ALARM (GREAT EXPECTATIONS) 1889
(Wal Pink & Harry Randall)
Harry Randall

Our next song owes its origins to Mr Charles Dickens' famous novel Great Expectations. This is what is known in the trade as a point number, and few artistes can put across their points with more éclat and élan than your very own Mr N. / You see, Mother was right—always wear clean underwear... you never know, do you?

IT'S THE POOR THAT HELP THE POOR 1904
(A. J. Mills & Harry Castling)
Florrie Gallimore

A well-remarked characteristic of British working men and women is the sharing of what little they have with those even less fortunate, as reflected in No X, It's the Poor that Help the Poor. Helping us now is an artiste rich in talent and well worthy of your favour, Miss N. / A song of social comment from Miss N.

I'VE GOT MY EYE ON YOU 1913
(Fred W. Leigh & George Arthurs)
Clarice Mayne
(*Not Cole Porter's 1940 song* I've Got My Eyes On You)

I've Got My Eye On You declares our Miss N, which is very generous of her considering she's only got the two. But who, I wonder, is the lucky chap to be singled out by the languid and lyrical Miss N. / (*If she has picked out individual man in audience*) You got more than you bargained for, didn't you? No extra charge...
(*For further "eye" songs see* Algy *etc.*)

I'VE GOT RINGS ON MY FINGERS 1909
(R. P. Weston & Fred J. Barnes: Maurice Scott)
Ellaline Terriss
Included in "Captain Kidd", Wyndham's, 1910. In New York interpolated into "The Midnight Sons" (Broadway 1910) and "The Yankee Girl" (Herald Sq 1910) for Blanche Ring who also sang it in "When Claudia Smiles" (39th St, 1914) and "Right This Way" (46th St, 1938).

Song Introductions 99

Miss N now wafts us to exotic climes—to the South Seas, no less—where in No X she dilates upon the adventures of Jim O'Shea, a bold son of Erin who found himself upon an Indian isle wearing Rings on his Fingers. An unlikely tale indeed, verisimilitudinously performed by the twinkling and tinkling, Miss N! / Wasn't that fun! (*If she was in scanty costume*) Rather revealing costume, wasn't it? And she's got a nasty cough—I've promised to rub her chest with Vick and he's getting very impatient so let's move on with...

(*See also* I Wouldn't Leave My Little Wooden Hut for You)

I'VE GOT THE OOPERZOOTIC 1896
(Harry Hunter: Edmund Forman)
Johnny Danvers

Mr N is not well, ladies and gentlemen ... aaah! Yes, he's sickening for something. To those who know him socially he's been sickening for years ... but he's fallen victim to a very rare disease, so rare that he's the only person who's ever had it. And we've had it now for here direct from a bed of pain, comes that chronic tonic Mr N. / Mr N with the Ooperzootic, a most infections malady—melody. I've enjoyed a lot of bad health in my time. Do you know, I've had everything in the medical books except hypochondria...?

I'VE NEVER LOST MY LAST TRAIN YET c1906
(George Rollit: George Le Brunn)
Marie Lloyd

Living in the country Miss N has to endure the hazards of railway travel—if, that is, she wishes to sample the heady excitements of London, just as we now sample the seductive charms of everybody's favourite travelling companion, Miss N. / Tempting Providence there was the lady three times voted Miss Narrow/Broad Gauge, Miss N.

(*See also* Casey Jones *etc.*)

I WANT A GIRL JUST LIKE THE GIRL WHO MARRIED DEAR OLD DAD 1911
(Will Dillon: Harry Von Tilzer)
American Quartet, Al Jolson, Dorothy Ward

Next on the agenda is No X, a song called I Want A Girl Just Like the Girl Who Married Dear Old Dad, a title which when you come to think of it rather neatly encapsulates the entire plot of Oedipus Rex. It's an American song but it will be sung in English—we don't want to make things too difficult for you this early in the evening. So in sentimental vein and a striped blazer is your own Mr N! / My mother told me all about girls before I left home—that's why I left home.

I WANT TO BE A PRIMA DONNA *See* **ART IS CALLING FOR ME**

I WANT TO BE IN DIXIE (I WANT TO GO BACK TO DIXIE)
1911
(Ted Snyder: Irving Berlin)
American Ragtime Octette, Arthur Collins, Byron G. Harlan, May Irwin, Jen Latona, Ella Retford, Willie Solar, The Three Rascals
From "She Knows Better Now", Plymouth, Chicago, and interpolated into "The Whirl of Society", Winter Garden, New York

Our next artiste proclaims that she wants to be in Dixie, which is a great shame because we have always revelled—indeed wriggled with pleasure—in the company of the serenely sublime Miss N!

(*See also* Alabama Jubilee *etc.*)

I WANT TO GO BACK TO MICHIGAN (DOWN ON THE FARM)
(Irving Berlin) 1914
Daisy James, Murray Johnson, Beatrice Lillie, Frank Mullane, Bobbie Russell, Rae Samuels, Daisy Wood
Interpolated as Back at The Farm *with new lyrics by JP Long & Ernie Mayne into the 1914 revival of "The Earl and the Girl" at the Aldwych. The following year it was sung in its original form by Beatrice Lillie in the revue "Gerrard 5064" at the Alhambra.*

We discover Mr N in reflective mood, recalling in No X the manifold attractions of the great state of Michigan whither he wishes to return. He's staying in (*local*) at the moment and I can't understand why anyone should want to leave *there* ... but there's no accounting for taste so before he quits our shores let's give a rousing send-off to that song-and-dance man *par excellence* Mr N! / Mr N performing there with his customary poise and panache.

(*See also* Alabama Jubilee *etc.*)

I WANT TO GO TO IDAHO 1908
(Tom Mellor & Alf J. Lawrance & Harry Gifford)
G. H. Elliott

Mr N is positively aching to return to Idaho—funny, I thought he came from Willesden (*or local*)—but there it is. A certain Miss Lindy Lou is involved, which may have something to do with the matter.

Song Introductions   101

Let's find out from Mr N! / Mr N, wanting to go to Idaho. Which is a nice place to live, unless you happen to be a potato.

(*See also* Alabama Jubilee *etc*.)

I WANT TO PLAY WITH LITTLE DICK   1897
(Will J. Godwin)
Vesta Victoria

We like to give room in our programmes from time to time for the younger generation, the stars of tomorrow, and we see now a sweet little moppet making her debut. She's understandably very nervous, so as she tells us about her much-loved playmate let's give every possible encouragement to dinky little Miss N. / (*To pianist*) Was there a sub-text there that I was missing…? Miss N—they're lovely at that age, aren't they?

(*See also* Boers Have Got My Daddy, The *etc*.)

I WANT TO SING IN OPERA   1910
(Worton David & George Arthurs)
Wilkie Bard

Our next artiste, Mr N, has a voice that, er, well let me just say that when he sings deaf people won't even watch his lips moving. He has however long harboured operatic aspirations. Whether this is a realistic ambition you may judge for yourselves. Ladies and gentlemen, singing *molto gobbo* and entirely without the aid of a safety net, is Mr N. / Mr N will be appearing next week at the Royal Opera House—Sark.

(*See also* Bedelia (2) *etc*.)

I WANT TO TAKE A YOUNG MAN IN (AND DO FOR HIM)   1931
(Frank Wilcock)
Nora Blakemore

Despite her undeniable popularity with our audiences here Miss N has been unlucky in affairs of the heart, so let's hope that tonight she'll strike lucky. We certainly have since we are now to spend the next few minutes in the company of the ever-hopeful, ever-optimistic Miss N! / Miss N, looking for a nice young man… I think a dirty *old* man is the best she can expect this evening.

I WAS A GOOD LITTLE GIRL TILL I MET YOU   1914
(F. Clifford Harris: James W. Tate)
Clarice Mayne, Ella Retford
From "This And That", Comedy

Ladies and gentlemen, I Was a Good Little Girl Till I Met You. No, not an excerpt from my autobiography but the title of our next song, No X, to be brought to you by that captivating combination of comeliness and coquetry, Miss N. / What a sweetie! Miss N will be delighting us again with her ditties later on.

I WAS ONE OF THE RUINS THAT CROMWELL KNOCKED ABOUT A BIT *See* **IT'S A BIT OF A RUIN THAT CROMWELL KNOCKED ABOUT A BIT**

I WAS STANDING AT THE CORNER OF THE STREET 1910
(George Formby & J. Hunt: George Formby)
George Formby, Harry Randall

Mr N will shortly be dawdling down centre stage, to boast in No X of his prowess in that most soporific of activities: Standing at the Corner of the Street, a feat unparalleled since the discovery of chloroform. Loitering with intent, then, is the lethargic and languid Mr N! / He's a strange performer, isn't he? But I find he grows on you—like a goitre.

I WISH I'D BOUGHT DUCKS 1900
(Frank Leo)
Wilkie Bard

Mr N now essays a contemplative aria, a philosophical look at life. How often have we said "Oh, I wish I'd done this differently" or "I wish I could change that decision". Such thoughts are all part of life's rich tapestry as indeed are the confidential observations of Mr N.

I WONDER WHAT IT FEELS LIKE TO BE POOR? 1913
(C. W. Murphy & Dan Lipton & Magini)
Tom E. Hughes

We're all middle-class here, aren't we? I tell you why I ask—we've got No X now, a song entitled I Wonder What It Feels Like To Be Poor? I can't imagine—can you? Further discussion on this interesting proposition from that supercilious socialite Mr N. / Mr N, in ironical mood. We had nothing when I was a lad—nothing, I tell you! Yes, we may have been poor, but my God! we were miserable.

I WOULDN'T LEAVE MY LITTLE WOODEN HUT FOR YOU
(Charles Collins & Tom Mellor) 1896
Daisy Dormer

We now approach No X, I Wouldn't Leave My Little Wooden Hut For You, a song originated by the dainty and delectable Miss Daisy Dormer, who is not with us tonight on account of being dead ... so

Song Introductions   103

here instead, flaunting her wares, is the no less dainty and decidedly delectable Miss N! (*If in a grass skirt*) Miss N, not one to let the grass grow under her skirt.

(*See also* I've Got Rings on My Fingers)

JEANIE WITH THE LIGHT BROWN HAIR   1854
(Stephen Foster)
John McCormack

Admirers of Mr N—(*whom we saw earlier in X*)—know that he is the fortunate possessor of a most pleasing and melodious tenor voice, now heard to advantage in one of Mr Stephen Foster's most haunting ballads: Jeanie With The Light Brown Hair. And so it is my pleasure to welcome back Mr N.

JERE-JEREMIAH   1913
(C. W. Murphy & Worton David)
Florrie Forde, Clarice Mayne

Miss N now enumerates the charms of one Jerry Jeremiah, who as you can see in No X is apparently a whizz on the ragtime trombone. And what a lucky chap to have ensnared the affections of Miss Sadie Brown, as presented by that jewel in our crown Miss N! / A dazzling performance there from Miss N.

JERUSALEM'S DEAD, THE   1895
(Brian Daly: John Crook)
Albert Chevalier

In Cockney rhyming slang a donkey is known as a Jerusalem, from Jerusalem artichoke—moke. And for the costermonger selling his wares from a barrow his Jerusalem is his constant companion throughout every hour of the daily grind. What a grievous blow then, when that faithful and uncomplaining animal breathes his last. With The Jerusalem's Dead, a tender lament from Mr N. / Mr N bringing a lump to the throat and a tear to the eye.

JESSIE THE BELLE AT THE (RAILWAY) BAR   1867
(George Ware)
Annie Adams, Henri Clarke, Fred French, George Leybourne, Harry Liston, Mrs F. R. Phillips, Alfred Vance, Mrs G. Ware

So often, and quite unfairly, barmaids are regarded as being no better than they should be. But our Mr N was in no wise deterred when he found—or thought he'd found—the love of his life in Jessie, the Belle at the Bar. How this relationship fared we shall now discover as we welcome back the Moorgate (*or local*) Masher himself, Mr N. / Thank you Mr N—that was his first and doubtless last performance for the (*local*) company.

(*See also* Casey Jones *etc.*)

JINGO SONG, THE *See* MACDERMOTT'S WAR SONG

JOHNNIE   1923
(Sam Mayo)
Sam Mayo

N was going to sing a jolly song but he's feeling somewhat downcast due to a recent bereavement. He's just lost a close friend of many years, so a consolatory welcome if you please for Mr N. / Mr N, remembering his dear old pal—he sounded quite a character.

JOHNNY AT THE GAIETY   1895
(George Grossmith jnr)
George Grossmith jnr

At this point in the proceedings it is my honour to introduce that celebrated stage-door Johnny Mr N with a look at life among the nobs, the leisured classes, the future leaders of our country—God help us all... Tug your forelocks now if you please for the Honourable Mr N. / That was Mr N *en route* for yet another wild night of salacious carousing in the fleshpots of (*local*).

JOHNNY JONES *See* WHAT'S THAT FOR, EH?

JOHNNY MORGAN'S SISTER   1907
(Will Hyde)
Maidie Scott

(*This intro was for a performance given in a Morningside accent*)

Miss N takes us north of the border to present a little Scots schoolgirl—definitely teacher's pet. The reason for this favouritism as we see in No X is because she is Johnny Morgan's Sister. So let us enjoy now the canny Caledonian charms of Miss N. / That's a bonnie

wee lassie that. Her brother's a canny bairn too—he cannae sing, he
cannae dance, he cannae do anything...

> (*See also* Annie Laurie *etc. for Scots songs and* Boers Have Got My Daddy, The *for child songs*)

JOHN WILLIE, COME ON   1908
(George Formby)
George Formby

As a singer our next artiste has what might be called an interesting
voice ... it kept him out of the army. I refer to Mr N who now diverts
us with the adventures of John Willie. I have never met John Willie
myself—what about you, missus? ... what, never? ... this should be
a voyage of discovery for us all, then. Here then, with a smile on
his lips and a hand on his wallet, is Mr N! / Thank you, Mr N ...
there's a wife for you. What about you, sir? Are you married or
happy?

JOLLY GOOD LUCK TO THE GIRL WHO LOVES A SOLDIER
1906
(Fred W. Leigh: Kenneth Lyle)
Vesta Tilley

Jolly Good Luck, roundly declares Miss N, to the Girl Who Loves A
Soldier. I had the privilege of wearing Her Majesty's uniform for
several years ... mind you, it fitted her better. But in No X with a
costume which fits her very well indeed—a little too well for my peace
of mind—we salute our very own Daughter of the Regiment, Miss N!
/ That's the stuff to give the troops—Miss N on top form.

> (*See also* Army of Today's All Right *etc.*)

JOSHU-AH   1906
(Bert Lee & George Arthurs)
Clarice Mayne

In No X that charming chanteuse Miss N sings of a certain Miss May
who was enamoured of one Joshua, because it seems he was sweeter
than lemon squash ... which was why she had a *crush* on him ... God
make me funny! ... a *cordial* welcome, therefore ... for the delicious,
the delightful, the delectable Miss N! / Miss N's silvery soprano will
be heard to advantage again later on in the programme, never fear.

> (*See also* Now I Have to Call Him Father, Sophy, Turned Up, Why Am I Always the Bridesmaid, Waiting at the Church)

JUST A LITTLE BIT OF STRING *See* SIMPLE STRING, A

106   It Gives Me Further Pleasure

JUST A SONG AT TWILIGHT See LOVE'S OLD SWEET SONG

JUST LIKE THE IVY   1902
(Harry Castling & A. J. Mills)
Marie Kendall

Now to No X, Just Like The Ivy, a song whose chorus would seem to suggest the clinging embrace of a young woman and her sweetheart. But in fact the verses tell a very different tale, as we shall hear now from a loving and generous-hearted grand-daughter: Miss N. / There now. Wasn't that lovely? Miss N, Just Like The Ivy.

(*See also* Biggest Aspidistra in the World *etc.*)

JUST TOUCH THE HARP GENTLY   1870
(Samuel N. Mitchell: Charles Blamphin)
William Leslie

Shortly we shall find Miss N entertaining us with an elegiac and truly joyful little song called Touch the Harp Gently. And touching our affections as delightfully as ever is Miss N. / Miss N with her invisible harp. I'm not sure I understood all of that ... but it seems you did.

KASHMIRI SONG (PALE HANDS I LOVED)   1902
(Lawrence Hope: Amy Woodforde-Finden)
Clara Butt, Peter Dawson, Hamilton Earle, Ivor Foster, John McCormack
Extracted from Laurence Hope's "The Garden of Kama"

The English fascination with the mystery and romance of India is superbly caught in the Indian Love Lyrics, settings of Mr Laurence Hope's poetry by Mrs Amy Woodforde-Finden. The third of these in particular has stood the test of time: Kashmiri Song, or Pale Hands I Loved. A song of longing and regret, from Mr N. / Mr N, remembering an exotic entanglement.

KEEP THE HOME FIRES BURNING   1914
(Lena Guilbert Ford: Ivor Novello)
Stanley Kirkby, Sybil Vane
Note: This song was originally entitled Till the Boys Come Home

In time of war the prime topic of patriotic songs is, understandably, "Our country, right or wrong!" But No X offers a less strident and more domestic injunction: to Keep The Home Fires Burning, the beautiful melody written by that up and coming young Welsh composer Mr Ivor Novello, and exquisitely sung for us by Mr/Miss N.

(*See also* Army of Today's All Right, The *etc.*)

Song Introductions   107

KEYS OF HEAVEN, THE   trad
(anon.)
Clara Butt & Kennerley Rumford, Yvette Guilbert, Dora Labette & Hubert Eisdell

Miss M and Mr N now unite artistically in a duet derived, so I understand, from an old Cheshire folk ballad. It concerns two swains, one of whom—the young lady inevitably—coyly indulges herself in the age-old game of playing hard to get. The Keys of Heaven from Miss M and Mr N. / Miss M and Mr N, a match made in Heaven... (*strike a match*)... and there's one made in Sweden.

(*For other two-handers and/or possible concerted items see page 199*)

KISS THE GIRL IF YOU'RE GOING TO   1907
(Fred J. Barnes & R. P. Weston)
Marie Kendall

Now to a song I haven't heard for years, not since Big Ben was a watch and Hyde Park was flower-pot: No X, a song whose title says it all, Kiss the Girl If You're Going To, and the gentlemen to sing it all is the impish and impetuously impulsive Mr N. / What a jolly song that is. And given a jolly jolly performance by Mr N.

KITTY, THE TELEPHONE GIRL   1912
(Harry Gifford & Alf J. Lawrance & Tom Mellor & Huntley Trevor)
Jack Norworth
Interpolated into "Hullo, Tango!", Hippodrome 1913
Also "Gerrard 5064", Alhambra 1915

The new telephone system springing up all over the country is providing respectable employment for single women as operators, and in No X we meet one of these Hello Girls, as they're called, working in that most fashionable of London exchanges: Gerrard. So with Kitty the Telephone Girl, let us now connect with the larky and lyrical Miss N. / Miss N as Kitty the Telephone Girl. I proposed to my wife over the phone. I was so nervous! When she answered I blurted out "Darling! Will you marry me?" "Of course I will, you silly boy!" she said. "Who is it speaking, please?"

(*See also* Hello! Ma Baby *etc.*)

K-K-K-KATY   1918
(Geoffrey O'Hara)
Marie Brett & A. Frank Varney, Dan O'Neill, Walter Williams
From "Buzz-Buzz", Vaudeville

In the spring a young man's fancy lightly turns to what a young woman's been thinking about all winter. I even get a bit frisky myself and my wife starts her annual migraine season... But Mr N's fancy is none other than K-K-K-Katy, No X. In this item Mr N will not only sing but he'll also act, and if you watch very closely, you'll notice. With K-K-K-Katy its M-M-M-Mr N.

See also Cowslip and the Cow, The *etc.*)

KNOCKED 'EM IN THE OLD KENT ROAD *See* WOT CHER!

KNOCK THE TWO ROOMS INTO ONE 1900
(A. J. Mills & Bennett Scott)
Ethel Haydon

In No X on your song-sheets Mr N essays the character of Bertie, a telegraph clerk who wished to Knock Two Rooms Into One—a dashingly dotty idea, perhaps, but getting the message across in this cheery tale is the rhapsodically romantic Mr N.

LAMBETH WALK, THE 1899
(E. W. Rogers)
Alec Hurley
Note: This is not the song with the same title ("Any time you're Lambeth Way...") from Noel Gay's "Me and My Girl", Victoria Palace, 1937

America has given us the cake-walk and so Britain has responded with the Lambeth Walk, as strutted for us now by an artiste who will not only sing but also trip a tetrain of terpsichorean tours de jetés!... dancing... Your close attention please for the original Lambeth Walk, and for the original—indeed still the one and only—Mr N. / Mr N, of whom more anon.

(See page 201 for further songs of London)

LARK IN THE CLEAR AIR, THE c1850
(Sir Samuel Ferguson: air "An Tailliuir")

A few moments of genuine artistry now amongst the prevailing dross as admirers of Mr N's vocal excellence have their patience rewarded. This fine tenor has chosen for us a traditional Irish air with lyrics by Sir Samuel Ferguson: the Lark in the Clear Air. Ladies and gentlemen, Mr N.

(See also Band Played On, The *etc.)*

LAST ROSE OF SUMMER, THE *See* 'TIS THE LAST ROSE OF SUMMER

Song Introductions

LAUGHING SONG, THE 1876
(Eng w Hamilton Aïdé: Johann Strauss II)
Miss E. Chambers, Caroline Charles-Hirsch
From "Die Fledermaus", an der Wien, 1874. London: Alhambra

Now for an extract from the younger Strauss's light opera Die Fledermaus, a work which received its London premiere in 1876—perhaps some of you remember it? In this famous aria Adéle is a lady's maid masquerading at a high-society ball as a lady of quality; a Marquis thinks he recognises her, but she laughs him to scorn. Yes, it's The Laughing Song, consummately rendered by Miss N. / Miss N, giving it the full treatment.

LEAVE A LITTLE BIT FOR YOUR TUTOR 1901
(J. P. Harrington: George Le Brunn)
Harry Freeman

Our vicar as I expect most of you know is the slightly reverend Mr N, a cleric of great piety and energy. So large is his Sunday school that in order to teach the little mites adequately he has had to tutor no fewer than sixteen of their elder brothers and sisters to help him. He now tells us of the time he took the whole kit and caboodle on their annual summer outing. So may I ask for a warm liturgical welcome if you please for the Reverend Mr N! / Rev Mr N delivers wonderful sermons—I'm told that till he came here some of you didn't know what sin was...
  (*See also* at the Vicar's Fancy Ball *etc.*).

LET ME CALL YOU SWEETHEART 1910
(Beth Slater Whitson: Leo Friedman)
Mae Curtis, Beatrice Galbraith, Peerless Quartet

No X is that buoyant waltz in 3/4 time... you can't really have a waltz in any other time, can you? But I'm sure we all know this most tuneful of choruses, so let us assist to the best of our ability that blissful balladress: Miss N. / Let Me Call You Sweetheart from Miss N—ah! if only...

LET'S ALL GO DOWN THE STRAND 1908
(Harry Castling & C. W. Murphy)
Charles R. Whittle

The fact that Music Hall has its origins in London is reflected in the large number of songs which feature the Metropolis. And in the heart of dear old London Town, joining the City to the West End, lies the

Strand. In No X you are invited to perambulate down this famous thoroughfare in company with the very glass of fashion, the mould of form, Mr N. / Mr N down the Strand. He's a genuine cockney, you know. Oh yes—born within the sight of bow legs.

(See page 201 for further songs of London)

LET'S HAVE FREE TRADE AMONGST THE GIRLS 1911
(Harry Castling: John A. Glover Kind)
Whit Cunliffe

A political item now. Let's Have Free Trade, asserts Mr N in No X, Amongst the Girls, a title positively dripping with innuendo. But he comes from the House of Commons and so naturally adopts the high moral stance that we have come to expect from our legislators. Ladies and gentlemen, it's the stately and the statesmanlike Mr N! / " ... anything up to forty...!" That's a bit offensive. Hands up all those girls over forty ... hands up all those under forty ... hands up all those on the turn...

LET'S WAIT AND SEE THE PICTURES 1910
(Frank W. Carter & John A. Glover Kind)
Tom Clarke, Arthur Lennard

Other lesser Halls at the end of their programmes are demonstrating that new French invention known as the cinematograph. It'll never catch on. Why look at flickering shadows when you can see the likes of me in the flesh...? And in fact many Halls use this contraption merely as a chaser to get people out quickly. But in our next item one young lady asks her beau if they can Wait and See the Pictures. So let us wait no longer to see N!

(For other two-handers and/or possible concerted items see page 199)

LET THE GREAT BIG WORLD KEEP TURNING 1917
(F. Clifford Grey: Nat D. Ayer)
Laddie Cliff & Violet Loraine
From "The Bing Girls Are There", Alhambra

Let The Great Big World Keep Turning—No X—so let Mr/Miss N now join us to celebrate the universality of love with a song whose lyrics and melody so beautifully complement each other, as do they highlight the talents of that universal favourite, Mr/Miss N.

LILY OF LAGUNA, THE 1898
(Leslie Stuart)
Eugene Stratton, G. H. Elliott

Song Introductions   111

And now a favourite artiste: Mr N, with that most lilting of Music
Hall songs, No X, Lily of Laguna. The composer, Mr Leslie Stuart,
always maintained that the Laguna he had in mind was a little
town in California though he never actually went there himself.
Whatever the truth of the matter let us enjoy not only the choruses
but also the no less tuneful verses from Mr N.

LINGER LONGER LOO   1893
(Willie Young: Sidney Jones)
Yvette Guilbert, Millie Hylton, Cissie Loftus, Ellaline Terriss, May Yohe
From "Don Juan", the last of the Gaiety burlesques

Note: Harry Champion sang a parody with the same title by George Maurice

In No X Mr N requests Lucy to Linger Longer. And surely no lady,
whatever her name, could possibly resist the charms of the pressing
and persuasive Mr N. / Mr N, pitching a little woo.

LITTLE ANNIE ROONEY   1889
(Michael Nolan)
Lottie Gilson, Michael Nolan

A trip over the Irish Sea now where we meet that broth of a bhoy,
Mr N, who, so No X informs us, has a sweetheart, Little Annie Rooney,
and he's stuck on her like nobody's business. So your kind attention
please for the Sligo Spalpeen himself Mr N! / What a lucky girl that
Annie Rooney is, to be sure to be sure to be sure.
    (*See also* Band Played On, The *etc.*)

LITTLE BIT OF CUCUMBER, A   1915
(T. W. Connor)
Harry Champion

A comestible cantata now, for Mr N has an all-consuming passion for
a certain vegetable—whether a large bit or a little bit he can't get
enough of it. So here direct from the Tango Tea Rooms in Acton High
Street (*or local*) is Mr N! / Mr N with the Cucumber Song, which will
doubtless be repeated several times throughout the evening.
    (*See also* Boiled Beef and Carrots *etc.*)

LITTLE BIT OFF THE TOP, A   1898
(Fred Murray & Fred W. Leigh)
Harry Bedford

Mr N now hurtles onto the podium. (*Reading from notes*) He comes, I
understand from (*local*), his hobbies are reading, country walks, and

doing charity work which includes raising money for the Music Hall Chairmen's Benevolent Fund. And if he thinks he can get round me like that—he's quite right. With A Little Bit off the Top, here he is, a great deal over the top, Mr N. / Mr N, a man with more talent in his little finger than the rest of his little body.

(*See also* Get Your Hair Cut)

LITTLE DAMOZEL, THE   1912
(F. E. Weatherly: Ivor Novello)
Lucrezia Bori, Evangeline Florence

As I am sure you're all well aware our Miss N is a superb soprano whose vocal agility and sweetness of tone are matched only by her personal charms. With the young Mr Ivor Novello's very charming ballad, The Little Damozel, it's my delight to introduce Miss N. / Ahhh—ain't love grand?

LITTLE OF WHAT YOU FANCY DOES YOU GOOD, A   1915
(Fred W. Leigh & George Arthurs)
Marie Lloyd

Now for a great threat... (*look at notes*)... treat—as we welcome a lady who while never overstepping the bounds of propriety declares roundly that A Little of What You Fancy Does You Good—and she's prepared to prove it! So let us wait no longer to meet that boisterous and bouncy (little) bundle Miss N! / Frankly, I don't believe Miss N ever fancied a *little* of anything...

LITTLE YELLOW-BIRD   1903
(C. W. Murphy: William Hargreaves)
Ellaline Terriss, Flo De Vere
From "The Cherry Girl", Vaudeville

Every true-born Briton values freedom above all, regarding liberty as a birthright to be cherished and defended. This is the theme of our next item, No X, Little Yellow Bird, exquisitely performed by the superbly gowned and infinitely attractive Miss N. / Miss N, in all her numinous beauty.

LIZA JOHNSON   1901
(Edgar Bateman: George Le Brunn)
Kate Carney

In her next song entitled Liza Johnson—No X—Miss N demonstrates the influence of ragtime on our British Music Hall songs, because its sub-title is "The Ragtime Coster". My delight now to welcome a lady whose plangent tones have thrilled us so often: Miss N. / Miss N—taking no prisoners tonight.

LORD MAYOR'S COACHMAN, THE   1881
(Harry Hunter: David G. Day)
H. P. Matthews

The Lord Mayor's golden coach is one of the great sights of London, but of the driver? To be the Lord Mayor's Coachman requires not only the utmost skill in handling the reins, but also an encyclopaedic knowledge of our capital's highways and byways. As we shall discover from the redoubtable Mr N! / A tour de force there from Mr N.

(See page 201 for further songs of London)

LOST CHORD, THE   1877
(Adelaide A. Procter: Arthur Sullivan)
Clara Butt, Enrico Caruso, Alma Gluck (w. Efrem Zimbalist), Louise Kirkby Lunn, Antoinette Sterling

Now to one of the most renowned and revered ballads ever written—Sir Arthur Sullivan's setting of the poem by Miss Adelaide A Procter and composed while his much-loved brother lay dying. It is of course The Lost Chord, to be sung now by Mr/Miss N.

LOST, STOLEN OR STRAYED   1897
(A. J. Mills: Bennett Scott)
Millie Lindon, Sisters Lloyd

(For woman in Salvation Army costume) Music Halls are often castigated as being places of sin and impropriety—such criticisms are totally without foundation ... more's the pity ... and to prove it we have now a sermon calculated to strike terror into the heart of any maiden here tonight tempted to sacrifice her most sacred possession—her honour! Quake now to the awful events unfolded by a lady willing and eager to save us all: Sister N!

(See also Happy Eliza *and* Converted Jane *etc.)*

LOVE, GOODBYE   1911
(Adrian Ross: Franz Lehár)
Lily Elsie
From *"The Count of Luxembourg"*, an der Wien, Vienna 1909. London: Daly's

Miss N now thrills us with her silvery soprano in an aria from Herr

Franz Lehár's light opera The Count of Luxembourg. In this excerpt Sonia has been promised in marriage to a man she has never met, an arrangement which fills her with disdain. With Love, Goodbye let us bid welcome to Miss N.

LOVE'S OLD SWEET SONG 1884
(C. Clifton Bingham: J. L. Molloy)
Clara Butt, Antoinette Sterling, Edna Thornton

Next a song that you might call the parlour ballad's parlour ballad. Yes, No X, Love's Old Sweet Song, that unsurpassed and unsurpassable mingling of twilight, nostalgia, and true love. A potent combination indeed, most potently sung by Miss N. / That's made us all misty-eyed, hasn't it? Love's Old Sweet Song from Miss N.

LOWTHER ARCADE, THE *See* TIN GEE-GEE, THE

LUCKY JIM (HOW I ENVY HIM) 1896
(Charles Horwitz: F. V. Bowers)
Harry Davenport
Interpolated into first UK production of "The Belle of New York", Shaftesbury, 1898

Of the seven deadly sins Mr N is guilty of the most heinous—envy, for jealousy of his erstwhile friend Jim has turned a once fine upstanding figure of a man into a husk! This is a truly pitiable turn, ladies and gentlemen, the only consolation being it doesn't last long. It gives me far-flung pleasure to introduce the glum and gloomy Mr N. / You're easily pleased.

MACDERMOTT'S WAR SONG 1877
(G. W. Hunt)
G. H. Macdermott

"We don't want to fight," declares Mr N in No X, "but By Jingo! if we do!" Mr N himself served for many years in the Post Office Rifles, until he was unfortunately cashiered after some untoward dealings with the mails. Nevertheless, here he is, positively foaming with patriotic fervour: Mr N! / The embodiment of Jingoism, Mr N. We're all a little shell-shocked after that show of belligerence, so in contrast I'm happy to announce…

(*See also* Army of Today's All Right, The *etc.*)

Song Introductions 115

McNAMARA'S BAND 1914
(Terrence O'Shaughnessy / John J. Stamford?: Shamus O'Connor)

The Irish as a nation have a fine tradition of music making, a tradition energetically maintained by our next artiste. A credit to Ould Ireland indeed, is not only MacNamara's Band but also Mr N!

(*See also* Band Played On, The *etc.*)

MA BLUSHIN' ROSIE 1900
(Edgar Smith: John Stromberg)
Fay Templeton
From "Fiddle-Dee-Dee", Weber & Fields' Music Hall, New York

All the world loves a lover, so they say, and in No X Mr N serenades the light of his life, a sweetly blushing maiden called Rosie. Let us all now share in the happiness of the blissful and besotted Mr N. / Mr N and his coy maiden.

MACUSHLA 1910
(Josephine V. Rowe: Dermott MacMurrough)
John McCormack

Our next item finds the song and the singer perfectly blended. The song from Ireland is that distillation of tenderness and regard: Macushla, and the singer? I know you're going to enjoy the next few minutes in the company of Mr N.

(*See also* Band Played On, The *etc.*)

MAJOR-GENERAL WORTHINGTON 1916
(Ted Waite)
J. W. Rickaby

Ladies, you now have the thrill of seeing on our stage a proud member... (*looks at notes*)... of Her Majesty's Armed Forces, resplendent in his dress uniform—and how you ladies love a uniform, eh? So, gentlemen, how can we mere civilians compete with the magnificent Major-General Worthington, as embodied in the fine upstanding specimen of Mr N! / It's soldiers like him that made Britain what she is today ... yes...

(*See also* Army of Today's All Right, The *etc.*)

MAN ON THE FLYING TRAPEZE, THE *See* **FLYING TRAPEZE, THE**

MANSION OF ACHING HEARTS, THE   1902
(Arthur Lamb: Harry Von Tilzer)
Florrie Forde

There are (as I've mentioned before) so many Music Hall songs which treat of love eternal and of love betrayed. Now a lament for love denied, stamped with all the emotional power and truth that so mark our next artiste's performances. Ladies and gentlemen, with No X, the Mansion of Aching Hearts, may I ask you to welcome back Miss N.

MAN THAT BROKE THE BANK AT MONTE CARLO, THE 1891
(Fred Gilbert)
Charles Coborn, Maggie Duggan, William Hooey
Note: this song was inspired by the celebrated feat of Charles De Ville Wells

Our Mr N has recently been in foreign parts—always very enjoyable—where he had an astounding stroke of good fortune. He's positively bursting to tell us all about it, so without further ado let us welcome to our stage the incandescent, the incomparable, the incontestable Mr N. / Thank you, Mr N, the man that broke the bank at Monte Carlo. I broke the bank once—my sister's piggy-bank—she was furious. She'd been saving up for the operation.

MARRIED TO A MERMAID   1866
("AJC": M. Watson)
Arthur Lloyd
"AJC" was alleged to have been William Makepeace Thackeray

Britain is a sea-girt island and thus owes her pre-eminence in the world to her brave mariners, whose ancestors sailed the seven seas in search of fame, fortune, crumpet—er—glory. But sometimes tragedy intervenes as when Mr N tells us of a refugee from Davy Jones' Locker. Here then, veering hard a-starboard, is that very extraordinary seaman Mr N. / Must be wonderful to be a sailor ... all those rowlocks and bollards and things...

(*See also* All Hands on Deck *etc.*)

MARROW SONG, THE   1952
(Edrich Siebert)
Billy Cotton

We last saw Mr N in a double act, but now we see him singly-lili-lily in a vegetarian vignette, a culinary cantata which has been described as a millstone... (*look at notes*) ... milestone in Music Hall history, so I will say no more other than to utter the name of the assassin of

Song Introductions   117

gloom himself, Mr N! / Mr N—I'm sure that performance will be remembered long after it's forgotten.

(*See also* Boiled Beef and Carrots *etc.*)

MARTHA SPANKS THE GRAND PIANNA   1899
(George Dance: Howard Talbot)
Louie Freear, Alma Jones, Hilda Trevelyan
From *"A Chinese Honeymoon"*, *Theatre Royal, Hanley, (Strand 1901)*

Miss N has long harboured the desire to be a conductress, not of an omnibus but of an orchestra, as you might expect from someone who comes from a musical family. For as No X informs us Martha Spanks the Grand Pianna. A spanking good number given a spanking good performance now by Miss N. / Miss N, still banging 'em across like a good 'un.

MARY ANN SHE'S AFTER ME   1911
(Fred W. Leigh)
George Bastow

We present now a lad from Lancashire (*or local*) who has had a very sheltered upbringing leaving him extremely naive and unsophisticated, especially where the fair sex is concerned—his mother wouldn't even let him see the ladies side of the laundry list. Nevertheless a certain Mary Ann has set her cap at him, and the poor boy seems quite unable to cope. Let's see what we can do therefore to raise the spirits of the mournful, the melancholy Mr N! / Keeping everything crossed there was Mr N, a man of many parts, some of which are no longer manufactured.

MARY'S TICKET   1909
(J. P. Long: Gilbert Wells)
Florrie Forde

A lady travelling unescorted upon our railways, alas, risks untoward advances; but now we learn of a young lady in a very different but nonetheless awkward predicament. Here then, the prettiest piece of rolling stock I've seen in many a day, steaming silkily out of the sidings, is Miss N. / There's not much I can say about that without getting us closed down.

(*See also* Casey Jones *etc.*)

MATTINATA   1904
(Edward Teschemacher: Ruggiero Leoncavallo)
Enrico Caruso, John Coates, Ben Davies, Beniamino Gigli, John Harrison

Now to one of Signor Leoncavallo's most popular songs, Mattinata—'Tis the Day, which is a great deal easier to say than to sing. As we shall discover from the jubilant performance of Mr N. / Splendidly sung—and a very difficult accompaniment brilliantly played by Maestro N. (*To pianist after applause*) That kept you busy, didn't it?

MEET ME IN ST LOUIS, LOUIS 1904
(Andrew B. Sterling: Kerry Mills)
Nora Bayes, Lew Dockstader, Lottie Gilson, Ethel Levey, Billy Murray, Bonnie Thornton, Gus Williams

The Louisiana Purchase was the celebrated transaction in which Napoleon Bonaparte sold off a large part of the Deep South for little more than a song. The centenary of this event is shortly to be marked by a World's Trade Fair in St Louis, where in No X we are invited to meet the petite and prodigiously personable Miss M. / Miss N with Meet Me In St Louis. What a cheery performance. The Home Counties equivalent doesn't have quite the same ring, does it? (*Sing*) "Meet me in St Alban's, St Alban's..."—no, not really.

MERRY WIDOW WALTZ 1907
(Basil Hood: Franz Lehár)
Lily Elsie & Joe Coyne, Constance Drever & Joe Coyne, Mizzie Gunther & Louis Treumann
From "The Merry Widow", an der Wien, Vienna 1905. A greatly altered version was first seen in London at Daly's

(*For solo performance*) Miss N shows us her mettle once again, this time leading us into the heady realms of romantic light opera with Herr Franz Lehár's Merry Widow Waltz. This surely most seductive of songs is brought to us now by the glittering and glamorous Miss N. / Miss N with the Merry Widow Waltz, touching us all with a little of that Viennese magic.

(*For two-handers and/or possible concerted items see page 199*)

MIDNIGHT SON, THE 1897
(E. W. Rogers)
Vesta Tilley

To find the Midnight Son "you needn't go trotting to Norway—you'll find him in every doorway". Indeed we now find one of these rakish rascals here upon our very own stage. So a guarded welcome for that ultra-refined and insufferably fashionable midnight son himself: Mr N! / Such depravity from Mr N! Next thing you know he'll be reading the Daily Mirror. *(If a girl)* In a vain attempt to hide her womanly figure beneath a suit of male attire there was Miss N.

MILLER'S DAUGHTER, THE   1894
(Peter Carroll: Carl Zeller)
Alexander Girardi
From "The Miner" ("Der Obersteiger", an der Wien, Vienna)

Interpolated briefly into "An Artist's Model" (Gaiety) to lyrics by Adrian Ross and sung in a duet version by Marie Tempest and Hayden Coffin. Originally written for tenor voice.

Carl Zeller's operetta Der Obersteiger is remembered today principally for one song—The Miller's Daughter, better known perhaps as Don't Be Cross which tells the tale of a spirited lass who plays hard to get once too often. Now to be given a most spirited performance by our favourite soprano, Miss N.

MINER'S DREAM OF HOME   1891
(Leo Dryden & Will J. Godwin)
Leo Dryden

Once again Mr N leaps into the breach, this time bringing us a elegiac ditty concerning the homesickness suffered by a poor miner who for a decade or more has been far from home. I refer you to No X, The Miner's Dream of Home. The warmest of welcomes is due therefore to Mr N. / Mr N, longing for home. *(If played for comedy see back announcement for* Our Lodger's Such A Nice Young Man)

MOLLY O'MORGAN   1909
(Fred Godfrey & Will Letters)
Nora Emerald, Ella Retford, Charles R. Whittle

Now a treat for admirers of Miss N—as who is not?—as she informs us in No X of one Patsy Burke, who came from Dublin to London looking for work, and of Molly O'Morgan who came looking for him, the spalpeen! So now let us follow the fortunes of that captivating colleen Miss N! / Miss N told me she was at one time engaged to an Irishman. I said, "Oh, really?" She said, "No, O'Reilly"... I paid for these jokes—I'm going to use them.

   (*See also* Band Played On, The *etc.*)

MOON HAS RAISED HER LAMP ABOVE, THE   1862
(John Oxenford: Jules Benedict)
Ivor Foster & Hubert Cave, Charles Santley & William Harrison

From "Lily of Killarney", Covent Garden. Based on Dion Boucicault's play "The Colleen Bawn", itself an adaptation of Gerald Griffin's 1829 three-volume novel "The Collegians"

It's a long time since we had a really good duet in our shows, and tonight ... is no exception, as we endure—enjoy—The Moon Has Raised Her Lamp Above, to be sung by two of our leading luminaries, Messrs M & N. / Thank you indeed, gentlemen. Mr M was the corduroy baritone and the tenor of no fixed pitch was Mr N.

(For other two-handers and/or possible concerted items see page 199)

MOONLIGHT BAY (ON) 1912
(Edward Madden: Percy Wenrich)
Dolly Connolly, Herbert Payne, Esta Stella

A four-hander now, consisting of two artistes with two hands each—now there's a novelty—essential equipment for cuddling and caressing. According to No X, the location for all this unsavoury activity is Moonlight Bay, so let's get over there now to watch the action and eavesdrop upon the infatuated Miss N and the besotted Mr M! / Don't they make a lovely couple?

(For other two-handers and/or possible concerted items see page 199)

MOONLIGHT BLOSSOMS 1899
(E. W. Rogers)
Vesta Tilley

(*For two boys and a girl*) We ask you now to journey in imagination to the heart of London's West End where we find cavorting three artistes with a song whose intriguing lyrics equate London's Gilded Youth with garden flowers. So now with No X it's my privilege to introduce that toney trio: the Piccadilly Peonies! / There you saw Messrs M and N, and the rose between two thorns was Miss N.

(See also Biggest Aspidistra in the World, The *etc.)*

MOONSTRUCK 1909
(Lionel Monckton)
Gertie Millar
From "Our Miss Gibbs", Gaiety

In his musical comedy Our Miss Gibbs the composer, Mr Lionel Monckton, wrote a number which perhaps more than any other epitomises the frothy, frivolous charm of the old Gaiety Theatre. Moonstruck is the song, and who could endow this evanescent piece

Song Introductions   121

of nonsense with more rapturous vitality than Miss N. / Wasn't that absolutely delightful?

MORE WORK FOR THE UNDERTAKER   1895
(Fred W. Leigh)
Charles Bignell

(*For two-handed version*) We continue with those two fine artistes the Zola Brothers, Emile and Gorgon. We all try and make a few extra pennies these days (I myself do the occasional morning shift at the (*local*) abattoir) so here are these two gentlemen in their daytime attire direct from their latest undertaking. A cheery little number from those two rascally rapscallions: the Zola Brothers. / There were your very own Messrs M and N, who ask me to advise you they also do embalming while you wait.

(*For other two-handers and/or possible concerted items see page 199*)

MOTHER MACHREE   1910
(Rida J. Young: Ernest R. Ball & Chauncey Olcott)
Ernest R. Ball, Beniamino Gigli, Charles W. Harrison, John McCormack, Will Oakland, Chauncey Olcott
From "Barry of Ballymore", New York. Also interpolated into "Isle o' Dreams", Grand Opera House, New York, 1913

The eminent composer Mr Ernest R Ball seems to have cornered the market in sentimental Irish songs, what with When Irish Eyes are Smiling, A Little Bit of Heaven Fell, Kathleen Aroon, and his latest offering in this vein Mother Machree. Many fine singers have been attracted to this heartening melody but few finer than Mr N.

(*See also* Band Played on, The *etc.*)

MOTHER'S ADVICE *See* I'M GLAD I TOOK MY MOTHER'S ADVICE

MOTHER WAS A LADY (IF JACK WERE ONLY HERE)   1896
(Edward B. Marks: Joe Stern)
Meyer Cohen, Lottie Gilson

Our status in society is usually irrevocably determined by the circumstances of birth and family, but Miss N now suggests that true class is more a matter of self-respect, consideration for others and a kind heart. My Mother Was A Lady, proudly declares Miss N. / Miss N, showing that breeding is not necessarily important—though it can be fun ... or so they tell me.

MRS CARTER 1900
(C. W. Murphy & Edgar Bateman: C. W. Murphy)
Gus Elen

(*If the performer has appeared in a previous "disaster" song this can be referred to*)

Mr N's experience of life has alas tended to make him a touch cynical, if not downright misanthropic. In No X, Mrs Carter, he displays a deeply jaundiced view of marriage, at least as experienced by *Mr Carter*, a very gloomy groom indeed as we shall discover from Mr N! / Well done, sir. A Gus Elen song marvellously delineated by Mr N. (*If appropriate*) I thought it was wonderful how he kept his moustache on right through!

MUFFIN MAN, THE 1889
(Harry King)
Dan Leno

We strike a more sombre note now, for our Mr N has been most cruelly used by the lady to whom he had lost his heart. He was working as a baker, only to learn one of life's bitterest lessons: never trust a woman who likes a roll. All sympathy therefore for the deceived, the deluded, the disconsolate, Mr N. / Don't tell him but the other man was me! I loved her muffins but I wasn't so fond of her—and we continue with...

MURDERS c1914
(Dick Henty & Louis Rihill)
George Grossmith jnr, Leslie Henson
Interpolated into "Tonight's The Night", Gaiety

We all have to suffer the slings and arrows of outrageous fortune, do we not? but Mr N has devised his own particular way of coping with life's petty niggles and frustrations, and especially with the anti-social behaviour of those we meet in our daily round. An instructional and inspirational item from Mr N! / (*Looking after him off-stage*) Yes, well done, Mr N ... excellent ... very good indeed! (*To audience*) I'm always very careful what I say about Mr N...

MY ACTOR MAN 1913
(F. Clifford Harris: James W. Tate)
Marie Lloyd

The peer who falls madly in love with an actress is a commonplace in today's liberal society. Not so frequently seen, however, is the lady of

Song Introductions

breeding whose amorous proclivities are aroused by an actor. Here then in No X, with passion's fires damped down—but only just—is the sultry and susceptible Lady N! / That was our Miss N— I wish it was the interval ... pffoa! (*If she wears a revealing dress*) I think it's that final bow that really makes the act, don't you, chaps?

MY AIN FOLK 1904
(Wilfrid Mills: Laura G. Lemon)
Clara Butt, Maggie Teyte, Edna Thornton

What is it, I wonder, about Scottish ballads that so grips the imagination and plays upon the heart-strings? My Ain Folk is certainly one that has this effect on me, especially when so tellingly sung by Mr N. / Miss N with that timeless tale of longing and regret.

(*See also* Annie Laurie *etc.*)

MY BEAUTIFUL LADY 1911
(Hugh Morton: Ivan Caryll)
Hazel Dawn
From "The Pink Lady", Globe

No X now wafts us into a never-never land of romance and high society—the world of operetta. From Mr Ivan Caryll's The Pink Lady we shall now be regaled with a waltz song redolent of glittering ballrooms and silken dalliance. My Beautiful Lady, appropriately sung by the exquisite and exultant Miss N!

MY BLUSHING ROSIE *See* MA BLUSHING ROSIE

MY BOY'S A SAILOR MAN 1909
(A. J. Mills & Bennett Scott)
Daisy Dormer

In No X we discover that My Boy's A Sailor Man, and what a very jolly jack tar he must be to have captured the heart of our Miss N. But sailors are known to have a roving eye which somewhat clouds her effulgent happiness. So it's helm alee for the captivatingly coy Miss N. / That song reminds me of my youth ... *he* joined the navy...

(*See also* All Hands on Deck *etc.*)

MY CASTLE IN SPAIN 1906
(Tom Mellor: Alf J. Lawrance & Harry Gifford)
Lil Hawthorne

We were to have had two artistes from Spain at this point: the exciting knife-throwing act Los Calamitos and Doris. But Doris isn't out of bandages yet, so instead of a Spanish artiste we have an artiste just back *from* Spain. She is an acknowledged virtuoso of the art of Flamenco, and with My Castle in Spain she gives us the authentic flavour of Andaluthia. Tho it'th—so it's Olé! Olé! for Senorita N! / (*If showing prominent bust*) Miss N proudly displaying a bal*con* known and feared throughout the Iberian peninsular.

(*See also* In Olden Spain *etc.*)

MY GIRL'S A YORKSHIRE GIRL 1908
(Dan Lipton & Fred Murray)
Florrie Gallimore, Charles R. Whittle

Anyone here from Yorkshire...? Well, we have this Lancashire song ... no, it's No X, in which Mr N offers a proud declaration concerning the lady in his life. Yes, it seems that his girl's a Yorkshire girl—well, it's better than being a Yorkshire pudding. To tell us more is the Bradford Balladeer himself Mr N! / You can't trust those fact'ry lasses, can you?

MY HERO 1910
(Stanislaus Stange: Oscar Straus)
Constance Drever, Olga Petrova
From "Der Tapfere Soldat", an der Wien, Vienna 1908. London: Lyric

Bernard Shaw was once appalled to discover that he had inadvertently given permission for one of his plays, "Arms and the Man", to be adapted as a musical comedy. But under the title "The Chocolate Soldier" the results were nowhere near so dire as he had feared, and we hear now the most celebrated of Oscar Straus's arias from this show, My Hero. Ladies and gentlemen, the magical voice and presence of Miss N.

MY MOTHER WAS A LADY (IF JACK WERE ONLY HERE) *See* MOTHER WAS A LADY

MY MOTTER 1909
(Arthur Wimperis: Lionel Monckton)
Alfred Lester
From "The Arcadians", Shaftesbury

A gentlemen renowned for the energy and vitality of his performances now explodes upon our stage. A whirlwind of activity in both his professional and his private life, here he comes, hurtling across the theatrical firmament like a meteor: Mr N! / And as Mr N meanders off-stage for a quick rub-down with a damp songsheet we pick up the pieces with...

(*See also* Billy Muggins *etc.*)

MY OLD DUTCH 1892
(Albert Chevalier: Charles Ingle)
Albert Chevalier

The comic hazards of married life are so often iterated in Music Hall song that it's a welcome change to meet one man at least whose relationship with his wife is as close today as it was on their wedding-day forty years ago. No X, My Old Dutch. Sing your hearts out please—(*aside*) 'cos he's getting a bit Mutt and Jeff—for that venerable veteran of the Halls: Mr N! / That was Mr N making his fourteenth farewell appearance. Make-up by Plaster of Paris.

MY OLD MAN'S A DUSTMAN *See* WHAT D'YER THINK OF THAT?

MY OLD PAL JOE 1906
(Edgar Bateman: Maurice Scott)
Tom Costello

(*For weedy character*) Friendship, true friendship is something to be cherished as we go through this vale of tears. That is the theme of our next item, penetratively performed by that prodigal powerhouse of personality and passion, Mr N. / Mr N has asked me to let you know he can now accept a few selected pupils for his weight-lifting and body-building classes.

MY OWN LITTLE GIRL 1902
(Percy Greenbank: Lionel Monckton)
Hayden Coffin
From "The Country Girl", Daly's

Mr Lionel Monckton is rightly famed as the composer of any number of successful musical comedies, many of which have the exciting word "girl" in the title—The Gaiety Girl, The Shop Girl, The Circus Girl, and so on. No Mr N sings for us a jubilant and impassioned number from Mr Monckton's latest show The Country Girl. With My Own Little Girl—your own, your very own Mr N!

MY SON (MY SON, MY ONLY SON)
(E. W. Rogers: George Le Brunn)
Charles Godfrey

For our next item Mr N re-enacts the tragic story of trust betrayed in one of our noble families. Mr N comes from an excellent family himself—he's the son of a belted earl (*indicate belt round waist*) and a high-slung countess (*"lift" sizable bosom*). So stand by for a cataclysmic display of emotion from Mr N! / I'm sorry you couldn't accept that in the spirit in which it was offered.

MYSTERY OF A HANSOM CAB, THE   1889
(E. W. Rogers: A. E. Durandeau)
Walter Munroe

As the lights lower (*cue electrics*) a sense of unease, of foreboding permeates the orgytorium... no, I'm not going to sing... but to set the scene for Mr N to recount The Mystery of the Hansom Cab. I would advise those of a nervous disposition to keep everything crossed for with this strange and sinister tale comes creeping the strange and sinister Mr N! / What a zwizz...! Mr N getting us all in a tizwoz for nothing.

(*See page 201 for further songs of London*)

MY SWEETHEART'S THE MAN IN THE MOON   1892
(James Thornton)
Marie Kendall, Bonnie Thornton

My Sweetheart's the Man in the Moon, chirrups little Miss N in No X. Her Sweetheart's the Man in the Moon, eh? That's a long way to go for a cheesy embrace, but she seems happy enough and so shall we be in the company of the ardent and amorous Miss N. / Miss N, in love with the Man in the Moon. Which brings us reluctantly down to earth with...

MY WIFE'S FIRST HUSBAND   1898
(Nat Clifford)
Ernie Mayne

Our Mr N has recently undergone a change of status—he's got himself married! But he didn't just marry a wife—he married a widow-woman! Yes, she's been round the course a few times... Since when he has become the unwitting target for a barrage of complaints. Nevertheless, he has managed to maintain his usual cheerful and carefree disposition, so we can expect the customary lively performance from Mr N! / So much for marriage. (*To man in audience*) Are you married, sir? Or have you always been round-shouldered...?

MY WIFE'S GONE TO THE COUNTRY 1909
(George Whiting: Ted Snyder & Irving Berlin)
Arthur Collins, Byron G. Harlan, Mabel Hite, Phil Parsons

Our Mr N is in playful mood because His Wife's Gone to the Country. Well, you know the old saying: while the cat's away the mice will play, and so all a-twitter and a-twitch comes scampering Mr N. / Mr N, whose wife's gone to the country. Nothing she likes better than a vigorous tramp in the woods.

NATURE'S MADE A BIG MISTAKE 1910
(Alf Ellerton & Worton David: Alf Ellerton)
Gus Elen

Mr N tells me he's got a new act off the back of a fag packet so anything can happen. What more can I say other than to demand a thunderous round of indifference for the oldest infant prodigy in the business, Mr N. / Don't worry—he's in rude health. Well, rude, anyway. I'm told he likes his vice versa ... whatever that may mean.

NELLIE DEAN 1916
(Billy Clarke: Harry Armstrong)
Gertie Gitana

The American composer Mr Harry Armstrong is not exactly a household name but he did come up with two imperishable tunes: Sweet Adeline, which he wrote at the age of seventeen, and the other—written twenty years later and perhaps even more widely sung—is the immortal Nellie Dean, first sung on the Halls in Britain by Miss Gertie Gitana, and now re-created for us by our very own Mr/Miss N. / Mr/Miss N with Nellie Dean, a song long recognised as landmark in American popular song which is why the original manuscript is preserved in the Library of Congress. You didn't know that, did you? ... and you don't care either, do you?...

NEVER INTRODUCE YER DONAH TO A PAL 1891
(A. E. Durandeau & Albert E. Ellis: A. E. Durandeau)
Gus Elen

Some advice when embarking upon courtship is now offered by a man who looks to me frankly a bit... (*aside*) ... common. I must say I hadn't realised the lower classes went in for love and courtship and marriage just like you and me ... well, me, anyway. So a word to the wise then from the Sage of Stepney (*or local*) Mr N. / Mr N—the working class can be so pathetic, don't you find?

NEVER MIND 1913
(Harry Dent & Tom Goldburn)
Gertie Gitana, Eric Marshall

"All's for the best in the best of all possible worlds"—that's the encouraging and positive philosophy with which our next song is imbued—whatever blows Fate cares to visit upon us—Never Mind. So sings the ever-optimistic and ever-welcome Mr/Miss N. / Never Mind, Mr/Miss N. My old granny used to say "Keep smiling—things could get worse. And she was right. I kept smiling—and they did..."

NEXT HORSE I RIDE ON, THE 1905
(George Everard & Fred Murray)
Vesta Victoria

We turn to the Sport of Kings. I'm very fond of riding myself... it's all that leather... (*breathing hard*)... and the whips... and the motion... (*recovering*) Sorry about that. But our Miss N loves the gee-gees and anything to do with racing. So here, weighing in at ninety-eight pounds, six and fourpence, is that fascinating filly, Miss N! / Miss N, a lady also fond of literature. There's nothing she likes better than curling up with a good bookie.

NICE QUIET DAY, A 1901
(Edgar Bateman & Eustace Baynes: Maurice Scott)
Gus Elen

Mr N occasionally earns an extra bob or two as a postman. This can be an extremely tiring job, especially if you have to deliver my fanmail, and Mr N obliges with a reminiscence of how he spent a precious day off, a Bank Holiday, with his family. So here is the very essence of relaxed contentment: Mr N. / A postman's day off, remembered for us by Mr N, who asks particularly to be remembered at Christmas.

(*See page 201 for further songs of London*)

NIGHT I APPEARED AS MACBETH, THE 1919
(William Hargreaves)
Billy Merson

I have the distinction now of introducing the eminent Shakespearean

Song Introductions   129

actor Mr N. I remember him years ago at the Old Vic in "Midsummer Night's Dream", and those of us who saw his Bottom on that occasion have yet to recover from the experience. He will now relate the first time he attempted to scale one of the great peaks of British drama, so here from a record-breaking run at the Harringay Dog Track (*or local sports ground*) is the eminent Thespian, Mr N. / Thank you Mr N. We'll let you know...

NO, 'ARRY, DON'T ASK ME TO MARRY   1893
(Harry Castling: George Le Brunn)
Marie Lloyd

That great Music Hall artiste Miss Marie Lloyd is generally associated with songs of a saucy and boisterous nature, but No X, No, 'Arry, Don't Ask Me to Marry demonstrates a gentler and less strident aspect of her art. A touching tale, then, to be unfolded for us now by Miss N.

NOBODY LOVES A FAIRY WHEN SHE'S FORTY   1934
(Arthur Le Clerq)
Tessie O'Shea

As a lad my favourite pantomime character was not the principal girl or the dame or any of the comics but the Fairy Queen, who with a wave of her wand could bring triumph out of tragedy, happiness out of disaster. And I've had an abiding interest in fairies and queens ever since... But I wonder, do we ever consider what happens to a Fairy Queen who is a little past her best? A little over the hill? For as we know, Nobody Loves A Fairy—When She's Forty. But I know I can rely on you all for a considerate and kindly welcome for Fairy Snowdrop! / (*If a man in drag*) That was Mr N, who will be available for clinical examination after the performance. (*If a woman*) I'm sure we all found that deeply moving... I was so moved I nearly went.

NOBODY KNOWS YOU WHEN YOU'RE DOWN AND OUT
(Jimmie Cox)   1923
Bobby Baker, Jimmie Cox

Now to a lady with alas a cynical, bitter attitude to life, for as she sings in No X, Nobody Wants You When You're Down And Our. But we certainly want her whatever the state of her fortunes, for she is none other than our very own Miss N.

NOBODY NOTICED ME   1918
(Nat D. Ayer & Bert Lee)
Jack Pleasants

Our next artiste is one of those men of whom it is said that he can light up a room just by leaving it. Yes, there's no beginning to the talents of that paragon of personality, poise and panache: Mr N! / We certainly noticed him, didn't we?

NONSENSE! YES! BY JOVE! 1881
(Harry Nicholls: Oscar Barrett)
George Barrett & J. L. Shine, Robert Brough & Harry Nicholls, Herbert Campbell & Charles Grosse, Fred Stimson & Fawcett Lomax
From "Whittington and His Cat", Gaiety.

We British are renowned, are we not?, for our imperturbability in the face of adversity, for keeping a stiff upper lip when all seems lost. And maintaining this fine tradition of sang froid... *French!* ... are those two legendary Stage-Door Johnnies: Messrs Gus and Algy! / Algy and Gus, better know as our very own Messrs M and N, proving the truth of the old saying that you can always tell Old Etonians—but you can't tell 'em much.

(*For other two-handers and/or possible concerted items see page 199*)

NORA MALONE (CALL ME BY PHONE) 1909
(Junie McCree: Albert Von Tilzer)
Hedges Brothers & Jacobson, Herbert Payne, Blanche Ring
Interpolated into "The Yankee Girl", Herald Square, New York, 1910

Nora Malone, commands the masterful Mr N, Call me by Phone—No X upon yer songsheets, begorrah. And to be sure no young woman, whatever her name, could possibly resist his blarney-ish blandishments. So here, with a smile, a song and a stretch of the imagination, is Mr N. / Mr N, as incorrigible as ever.

(*See also* Kitty the Telephone Girl *etc. For Irish songs see* Band Played On, The *etc.*)

'NORRIBLE TALE, A 1865
(E. L. Blanchard: arr. M. Hobson)
Sam Cowell, J. L. Toole, Alfred Vance

Prepare now for your withers to be wrung. How long is it since your withers were wrung, madam?... I see. Prepare to shudder at a catalogue of gruesome and grisly horrors, a 'norrible tale of a most mournful family brought to us by Charnel House Charlie himself, Mr N. / Thank you Mr N, the only man I know to be made a Freeman of (*local*) Cemetery.

Song Introductions 131

NOW I HAVE TO CALL HIM FATHER 1908
(Charles Collins & Fred Godfrey)
Vesta Victoria

Love and marriage have ever been popular themes for Music Hall songs, and while our Miss N did have an admirer her romance was sadly punctured, as we shall hear. A consolatory welcome therefore for the depressed, the disheartened, the despondent, Miss N! / If she hasn't clicked by the end of the week she's going back to the convent... The Little Sisters of Perpetual Outrage.

(*See also* Joshu-ah *etc.*)

NOW YOU'VE GOT YER KHAKI ON 1915
(Charles Collins & Fred W. Leigh)
Marie Lloyd

In these troubled times it is imperative that we keep the Army up to strength and in this regard we find our Miss N doing her bit with a little song entitled "She Was Only A Colonel's Daughter—But She Knew What Regiment". Yes, with No X, it's Britain's one-woman recruiting drive, Miss N! / Miss N, promising an extra cuddle to Cocky. (*To man in audience*) You're looking all smiles—you're not Cocky, are you? No...? I wish I was.

(*See also* Army of Today's All Right, The *etc.*)

NURSIE-NURSIE 1910
(Worton David & Bert Lee)
Clarice Mayne

Did you know that our Miss N is a nurse? The definition of a good nurse is one who can make the patient without disturbing the bed. Be that as it may No X tells us that she has a very special private patient. So let us all take a turn for the nurse—it's the enticing and inviting Miss N. / I understand Miss N used to shave the patients before their operations. Which is why her favourite song is Nobody Knows the Stubble I've Seen.

OH, FLO! (WHY DO YOU GO?) 1901
(Harry Dacre)
Harry Dacre, Harry Taylor

In No X we learn of Flo who was wont to go riding alone on her motor-car—the fast hussy! So here at full throttle... (*for solo woman*) ... is the Boadicea of Balham (*or local*) Miss N. (*For two women*) ... are no fewer than two young ladies! Yes, it's that toothsome twosome The Misses M & N! / Thank you Miss N, elegantly modelling the very latest motoring attire from (*local down-market clothes shop, charity shop or flea-market*). OR Miss M was on one side and Miss N was—on the other.

(*See also* Get Out and Get Under *for another car song and page 199 for further two-handed and/or concerted items*)

OH, FRED! TELL THEM TO STOP   1880
(George Meen)
George Leybourne, Tony Pastor

Oh, Fred Tell Them To Stop! cries our next artiste in No X. Tell them to stop? Why? What were they a-doing of? All will be revealed, in a manner of speaking, by that innocuous and ingenuous incarnation of innocence Miss N! / Miss N, who's always been unlucky with men. She used to be married to a trapeze artiste, but she caught him in the act.

(*See also* Swing Me Higher Obadiah)

OH, HOW RUDE!   1899
(Bennett Scott: C. G. Cotes. From E. W. Rogers' original)

Now a treat for the ladies as sauntering into view comes one of the handsomest men on the Halls—though good looks can be such a curse as I know from experience. It's extraordinary how aggressive and rude some people can be when confronted with male beauty, as outlined in the first verse and chorus of the next song from the Greenwich Ganymede (*or local*): Mr N. / Mr N. A bit saucy that last bit, wasn't it? A bit cheeky. Yes, I was relieved when he finished.

OI I, I'M ONE OF THE BOYS   1907
(R. P. Weston & Fred J. Barnes: Maurice Scott)
George Formby

Mr N is feeling very pleased with himself—I'm One of the Boys, he insists, which must be a great relief to Mr N senior. Nevertheless, here he is, the unabashed, the unashamed, the unavoidable Mr N! / Thank you, Mr N, who considers himself one of the boys. Personally, I think he should go for a second opinion.

OH, I MUST GO HOME TONIGHT   1909
(William Hargreaves)
Billy Williams

Mr N has contracted to favour us with No X, entitled I Must Go Home Tonight. Why the rush? you are asking ... go on then, ask! (*Audience: "WHY THE RUSH?"*)... I don't know, I'm just the chairman. But here to explain the reasons for this domestic imperative is the Rotter of Rotten Row: Mr N! / Mr N there in a *perpetuum mobile* performance. I've known him for years—in fact we're related through drink.

OH! JACK, YOU ARE A HANDY MAN   1901
(Nat Clifford)
Katie Lawrence

Traditionally your British sailor can turn his hand to anything, whether it's splicing the crow's nest or weighing the bilge. Batten down the hatches, then, ye lubbers, for here luffing round the headland is Pretty Petty Officer N! / Miss N, steering a true course as ever.

   (*See also* All Hands on Deck *etc.*)

OH! MR PORTER   1893
(Thomas Le Brunn: George Le Brunn)
Norah Blaney, Marie Lloyd

Miss N recently underwent, I'm sorry to say, an unfortunate experience on a railway train—no, it wasn't standing in the station at the time. No, this is the sorry tale of a girl who wanted to go to Birmingham but was taken on to Cr- oh, you know her, do you? Here she is then, that lost little baggage with a first-class carriage, Miss N. / Wasn't that fun?

   (*See also* Casey Jones *etc.*)

OH! OH! ANTONIO   1908
(C. W. Murphy & Dan Lipton)
Edith Fink, Florrie Forde

The achingly attractive Miss N outlines in No X the adventures of an unfortunate young maid from Italia, searching the streets of London for a certain ice-cream vendor called Anton- oh, you know him, do you?... Here she is then, little Miss Tutti Frutti herself, Miss N. / She loves her ice-cream, does Miss N. I wouldn't mind joining her in a tub...

OH, WHAT A BEAUTY! *See* MARROW SONG, THE

OH, YOU BEAUTIFUL DOLL   1910
(A. Seymour Brown & Nat D. Ayer)

American Ragtime Octette, Ida Barr, Gene Green, Clarice Mayne, Billy Murray

Oh, You Beautiful Doll, No X, was first sung in this country by that magnificent star of the Halls, Miss Ida Barr, a generously-proportioned lady of whom it was once said "Ida Barr? She could 'ide a pub!" Of more svelte proportions but no less capable of commanding our attention is that succulent songstress Miss N. / A great big beautiful doll indeed, Miss N.

OH! YOU LITTLE DARLING 1882
(Joseph Tabrar)
Nellie L'Estrange, Kate Vaughan
Interpolated into "Whittington & His Cat", Gaiety

Mr Joseph Tabrar claims to have written more Music Hall songs than anyone else and we continue with one his latest effusions No X, Oh! You Little Darling. And to sing it we welcome just about the darlingest little darling imaginable: Miss N!

OLD BRIGADE, THE 1881
(F. E. Weatherly: Odoardo Barri)
Norman Allin, Ian Colquhoun

Men who have heeded their country's call to arms are rightly honoured and revered, even when Old Father Time has touched their hair with grey. With No X we salute one of the Old Brigade; still sprightly, still smart and soldier-like: Private N! / I was in the Army myself, you know. I reached the rank of Private, Third Class, Smoking.

(*See also* Army of Today's All Right, The *etc.*)

OLD DICKY BIRD 1901
(T. W. Connor: arr. Fred Eplett)
George Lashwood

Mr N now annoys us with something called Poor Old Cock, a pathetic tale of blighted hopes and fowl frustration. Here then, hatching the plot... with egg-ceptional virtuosity... is the man with the pigeon toes and the crow's feet, Mr N. / And as Mr N flaps back to his roosting box, we flutter on with...

OLD MAN'S DARLING, AN 903
(Fred Murray: George Everard)
Vesta Victoria

Song Introductions   135

What does a woman look for in a prospective husband? Such is the interesting question posed by our next song, No X, and indeed by our next singer. Food for thought then, from the scrumptious and altogether edible Miss N. / If a young woman marries an old man she'll soon know what it is to have old age creeping up on her...

OLGA PULLOFFSKI THE BEAUTIFUL SPY   1935
(R. P. Weston & Bert Lee: R. Harris Weston)
Jack Hylton and his Band

The life of the spy, the double-agent, is one of constant danger, intrigue and duplicity. And in these times of international tension even a female can become a double-agent, so here, stirred but not shaken, is that tricky little traitress, Miss Olga Pulloffski! / Miss Olga Pulloffski, a lady who has slept—swept—her way across Europe, heavily disguised as our own Miss N.

ONE OF THE BOYS *See* OH, I'M ONE OF THE BOYS

ONE OF THE SHABBY GENTEEL   1902
(Harry Castling)
Harry Bedford

With No X Mr N presents a pathetic but all-too-familiar figure in our present day society, the man of substance reduced to penury. What more greater humiliation for a man once well-to-do than to be considered as One of the Shabby Genteel. A figure of fun, maybe, but not as portrayed by the resolute and undaunted Mr N. / Mr N, a man with true grit.

ONLY A GLASS OF CHAMPAGNE   1939
(Arthur Wimperis: Noel Gay)
Evelyn Laye
Included in "Lights Up", Savoy 1940

The innocent abroad is a character much favoured by song-writers, and we hear now a graphic account of what can befall a young gel after Only A Glass of Champagne, given by a lady who has herself perhaps drunk a little too deep from the Cup of Experience: Miss N.

   (*See also* Gipsy's Warning, The *etc.*)

ONLY A PANSY BLOSSOM   1883
(Eben E. Rexford: Frank Howard)
Mohawk Minstrels, Will Oakland (Moore & Burgess Minstrels)

(*For "badly-sung" comedy version*) Only a Pansy Blossom sighs Miss N in a song which compares the withering of a flower to an aching heart. And as the artiste pines for a summer long ago, we look forward with the keenest of anticipation to the bell-like tones of Miss N. / Miss N. (*To pianist*) Are you sure that piano's in tune?

(*See also* Biggest Aspidistra in the World, The *etc.*)

ONLY A WORKING MAN 1923
(Herbert Rule & Fred Holt)
Lily Morris

Behind every good man there's an even better woman, so 'tis said, and as you can see in No X Miss N's old man is the apple of her eye, just as the apple of our collective eye is the unconquerable, the unmatchable, Miss N! / What a wonderful song, don't you think, ladies? ... we enjoyed it, didn't we, chaps?

ON MOTHER KELLY'S DOORSTEP 1925
(George A. Stevens)
Fred Barnes, Randolph Sutton

One of the best known and in my far from humble opinion best-written of all Music Hall songs is to be found at No X, On Mother Kelly's Doorstep. Bringing us this truly delightful song in his own highly individual style is that positive Prince of balladeers, Mr N. / And chorus singing doesn't come much better than that—On Mother Kelly's Doorstep from Mr N.

ON THE GOOD SHIP "YACKI HICKI DOO LA" 1917
(Billy Merson)
Billy Merson

No X brings us a touch of mal-de-mer and the dastardly doings of a brigand of the high seas—a man steeped in thuggery, skulduggery and bu-ccaneering. Yes, it's the piractically plaguy and pixilated Cap'n N! / Shivering our timbers there was Mr N.

(*See also* All Hands on Deck *etc.*)

ON THE ROAD TO MANDALAY 1907
(Rudyard Kipling: Oley Speaks)
Peter Dawson, Lawrence Tibbett
From Kipling's "Barrack-Room Ballads"

When I say that the words of our next number are from Mr Rudyard Kipling's Barrack-Room Ballads and the music is by Mr Oley Speaks, many of you I'm sure will have guessed the title—yes, we travel now On the Road to Mandalay, in which a cockney soldier recalls his time in that mysterious and strangely compelling corner of Empire. Let us now enjoy this immortal ballad in a grand performance from Mr N. / Mr N, thrilling us with On the Road to Mandalay.

OOH! 'ERI (THE SLAVEY) 1927
(Wish Wynne)
Wish Wynne

When not delighting us on the boards Miss N does a little light skivvying to make ends meet, an occupation not without its hazards as we shall discover from the boisterous, breezy and bumptious Miss N! / Miss N, not a girl, it seems, to remain in any position for long...

(*See also* I Ain't 'Arf a Lucky Kid *etc.*)

OUR HANDS HAVE MET BUT NOT OUR HEARTS (THE FALSE FRIEND) 1889
(Thomas Hood: W. Vincent Wallace)
Lucy Clarke

The poems of Thomas Hood have fired the inspiration of many musicians, including Mr Vincent Wallace, a fellow Irishman, whose setting of Our Hands Have Met But Not Our Hearts we hear now. The sub-title of this ballad is The False Friend, and as it happens it's a great personal favourite of mine, especially when sung with such truth and such artistry by Miss N.

OUR LODGER'S SUCH A NICE YOUNG MAN 1897
(Lawrence Barclay & Fred Murray)
Vesta Victoria

We continue with Miss Vesta Victoria's celebrated—one might even say notorious—song Our Lodger's Such A Nice Young Man, No X. And having given you the title of the song let me tell you that the singer is none other than that adolescent acne—acme—of excellence Miss N. / Next week little Miss N will be giving us that doleful ditty: Don't Go Down in the Mine, Dad—There's Plenty of Slack in your Trousers...

(*See also* Boers Have Got My Daddy, The *etc.*)

OUR THREEPENNY HOP 1901
(Harry Castling)
Kate Carney

Once again we descend into the murky underworld of the working classes with an artiste who will not only sing but also oscillate her nether limbs in a series of spasms loosely connected with the terpsichorean arts—dancing. Here then to describe the sheer fun to be experienced at her local Threepenny Hop is Miss N! / A most energetic and incisive performance from Mr N, the man who put the turps into terpischore.

OURS IS A NICE 'OUSE OURS IS   1921
(Herbert Rule: Fred Holt)
Alfred Lester

Miss N trips daintily into view with an elegant and refined performance as is her wont ... and if Miss N won't nobody will. I gather the point of her display this evening is to delineate the delights of her domestic demesne—in other words, to tell us about 'er 'ouse. If there's no place like home, there's no performer to compare with Miss N.

PACK UP YOUR TROUBLES IN YOUR OLD KITBAG   1915
(George Asaf: Felix Powell)
Florrie Forde, Adele Rowland
Note: To avoid unnecessary complication this intro ignores George Powell's use of the pen-name George Asaf

At the start of the Kaiser's War there was a competition for a new marching song. Two brothers, Felix and George Powell, submitted an entry which won hands down. The melody is fiendishly singable, the rhythm is perfect for marching, and as for the lyrics—well, few songs can have caught the spirit of their time more vividly than Pack Up Your Troubles, now splendidly recalled by our very own Forces' Favourite, Miss N. / Miss N with a classic not just for its age, but for all time.

   (*See also* Army of Today's All Right, The *etc.*)

PADDY McGINTY'S GOAT   1917
(R. P. Weston & Bert Lee & The Two Bobs)
The Two Bobs

Here now heavily encumbered in a check suit and an Irish accent is Mr N, a man who if rumour be true has not just kissed the blarney stone but carnally embraced it. So then, with Paddy McGinty's Goat and coming to us direct from Sodom and Begorrah, is Mr N. / Mr N. You'd never guess to look at him now that when he was a boy he used to dig for peat. Pete was his brother, he was always falling in the bog...

   (*See also* Band Played On, The *etc.*)

Song Introductions   139

PALE HANDS I LOVED See KASHMIRI SONG

PANSY FACES
(Harry B. Smith: William H. Penn)
Irene Bentley, Leila McIntyre, Ellaline Terriss
From "Mother Goose", Drury Lane, and in New York interpolated into "The Girl From Dixie", Madison Square, New York

There is great debate nowadays as to whether trees and plants understand English. Have you ever tried to parley with the barley? Would talking to a dahlia be a failure? I think there can be no doubt that flowers do respond to nobility of soul and integrity of character, both of which are possessed in abundance by our next artiste. With Pansy Faces, No X on your songsheets, is that most fragrant and flagrant of floribundas, Mr/Miss N. / Thinking beautiful thoughts there, Mr/Miss N. Needs a good mulch if you ask me.

(See also Biggest Aspidistra in the World, The etc.)

PARADISE FOR TWO, A   1916
(F. Clifford Harris & Valentine: James W. Tate)
Thorpe Bates & José Collins
From "The Maid of the Mountains", Daly's

A romantic duet by definition needs not just vocal excellence but two artistes who can convince us that the spark of attraction has ignited between them, and that is what we offer you now. From "The Maid of the Mountains": A Paradise for Two, brought to us in a blaze of passion by Miss M and Mr N. / Spontaneous combustion there from Miss M and Mr N.

(For other two-handers and/or possible concerted items see page 199)

PARTED   1901
(F. E. Weatherly: F. Paolo Tosti)
Hubert Eisdell

A very popular item always in our programme is the parlour ballad, and you are about to hear one of the very finest. With lyrics by FE Weatherly and composed by Tosti, it is Parted. But joining us now I am most happy to welcome Mr N. / Mr N with Parted—singer and song in perfect accord.

PATCHWORK GARDEN, THE   1902
(Edgar Bateman & Paul Mill: J. Arlie Dix)
Paul Mill, Walter Passmore & Florence Lloyd

Interpolated into "The Earl and the Girl", Adelphi

When the curtains part I should like you to imagine a little piece of garden in a humble artisan's dwelling in the Borough (an area of London just below Southwark Bridge). Here Mr N has gathered bits and pieces from hither and yon to create a perfectly paradisiacal Patchwork Garden. Let us luxuriate now in a wholly engaging performance from Mr N. / Mr N in a characteristic performance of strength and unforced charm.

>(*See also* If It Wasn't for the 'Ouses in Between *and page 201 for further songs of London*)

P.C. 49   1913
(William Hargreaves)
J. W. Rickaby

The boys in blue have long been familiar and welcome figures on our streets—pounding their beats in all weather, upholding the Queen's peace and the rule of law which we Britons hold so dear. But what is required of the British police officer? Courage, honesty, dedication, intelligence—everything in fact that our local bobby lacks... Not surprisingly, for who should he be but Police Constable N. / And they say our police are the envy of the civilised world ... doesn't say much for civilisation.

>(*See also* Ask a P'liceman *and* Gendarmes' Duet)

PERCY FROM PIMLICO   1898
(Tom Leamore)
Tom Leamore

We proudly present—at e-*nor*... (*let audience finish*"... *mous expense*)—oh, you know what's coming, do you?—a man whose fame has spread to the four corners of Christendom, a man who needs no panegryics from me such is his renown. Ladies and gentlemen, that magisterial magnifico: Percy from Pimlico! / Percy from Pimlico, better known as our own Mr N, putting on the style in no uncertain terms.

>(*See page 201 for further songs of London*)

PER TUPPENCE PER PERSON PER TRIP *See* RUNCORN FERRY, THE

PHILOSOPHY (A BEE ONCE LIGHTED ON A FLOWER)   1904
(anon.: David Emmell)
Margaret Cooper, Maurice Farkoa

Song Introductions   141

A brief but meaningful item now in which Miss X discourses in philosophical vein as she explores one of life's eternal verities. Yeah, a parable for our time, offered by the bounteously bewitching Miss X. / That's the way the world is, alas.

PHIL THE FLUTER'S BALL   1889
(Percy French)
Peter Dawson, Percy French, Denis O'Neil, Albert Whelan

Now to a number performed almost entirely from memory as Mr N animadverts upon a gentleman called Phil who apparently played the flute at a ball. This is of course an Irish song, so let's roll up the carpet for a touch of the ceilidhs from the Pride of Erin Mr N. / Thank you Mr N, who I think needs a whiff of oxygen after that—I could do with a lie-down myself. I've been up all day, it is a shame.

(*See also* Band Played On, The *etc.*)

PIANO TUNER, THE   c1906
(C. G. Cotes)
George Robey

(*For Welsh performance*) An ethnic item now from wild and woolly Wales. I'm English myself but I can say that famous place name, you know, the sign on the railway station. Are you ready?—Cardiff. But now we present an honest boyo going about his lawful occasions to earn enough to put the leeks and lava bread on the family table. So here, all the way from glittering and glamorous Glamorgan, is Mr N! / He does have problems with his wife. She's Presbyterian and he's Sunday opening.

(*See also* Tuner's Oppor-tuner-ty, The)

PICCADILLY   1921
(Walter Williams & Bruce Sievier: Paul Morande)
Hetty King

Now to that great Metropolitan thoroughfare Piccadilly, leading from Hyde Park Corner to the very heart of Empire, Piccadilly Circus. Strolling nonchalantly along Piccadilly is very much the smart thing to do, so let us now join the fastidiously fashionable Mr N! / Mr N comes as you would expect from a very genteel family. He tells me that in his house they have ashtrays with no adverts on!

(*See page 201 for further songs of London*)

PIGTAIL OF LI FANG FU, THE   1919
(Sax Rohmer: arr. T. W. Thurban)
Bransby Williams

We take you on a trip to the mystic East, to the mysterious Orient—not to mention the Arsenal and West Ham. A recitation featuring sin, squalor, violence, lust, depravity ... should make you feel at home. As the great house curtains jerk aside, imagine yourselves in an opium den somewhere in China where smokers of the black chandu dream their lives away. A grim tale, majestically recited for us by (*local's*) own remittance man: Mr N. / There must be a moral there somewhere. Confucius he say: man who make love to girl on side of hill—not on level.

(*See also* Billy's Rose *etc.*)

PIPES OF PAN, THE   1909
(Arthur Wimperis: Lionel Monckton)
Florence Smithson
From "The Arcadians", Shaftesbury

Mr Lionel Monckton's "The Arcadians" contains more good tunes per square foot than any other musical comedy of its time. From this delightful show Miss N, our resident coloratura soprano, has chosen the joyous and florid "Pipes of Pan". Ladies and gentlemen, Miss N. / Miss N with the Pipes of Pan—and you certainly need a good set of pipes to sing that little aria.

PLAY A SIMPLE MELODY   1914
(Irving Berlin)
Elsie Baker & Billy Murray, Sallie Fisher & Charles King, Ethel Levey & Blanche Tomlin
From "Watch Your Step", New Amsterdam, New York. London: Empire, 1915

A melody which is both simple and catchy is not so easy to write as you might think, but that young lion of Broadway Mr Irving Berlin has come up with two simple melodies that intertwine in perfect harmony. Two for the price of one, therefore, presented by Miss M and Mr N! (*If two girls*) ... presented by a brace of beauties: the Misses M & N! / Did you enjoy that? Of course you did ... a simple melody for simple people...

(*For other two-handers and/or possible concerted items see page 199*)

PLAYING THE GAME IN THE WEST   1910
(George Formby & Alec Kendal)
George Formby

Mr N has arrived in the heart of London. We find him up West, where despite his provincial origins he holds his own effortlessly amongst the smart set, taking his place as of right in the most fashionable

Song Introductions

circles. Here then, redefining the phrase "La Dolce Vita", is the vigorous and vibrant Mr N! / Mr N, proving if proof were needed that the country's goin' to the demnition bow-wows.

(*See also* Billy Muggins *etc.*)

PLEASE SELL NO MORE DRINK TO MY FATHER   1884
(Mrs F. B. Pratt: C. A. White)
From "The Temperance Vocalist", published by Charles Sheard.

Not all is well, I regret to say, in our beloved Britain. But what is the major problem threatening to undermine the very foundations of our society? I will tell you in one word—and it's a four-letter word: drink!... Yes, alcohol! We illustrate this grave contemporary problem with No X, Please Sell no more Drink to my Father. And the desperate, distraught daughter is Miss N! / Miss N, the poor drunkard's child. (*Emotionally*) I tell you ladies and gentlemen, if my daughter ever feels constrained to sing of me in those terms... I'll give her a good clip round the ear-'ole.

(*See* 'Arf A Pint of Ale *etc. for Drink songs and* Boers Have Got My Daddy, The *etc. for Child songs*)

PLEASE WILL YOU HOLD THE BABY, SIR?   1898
(R. E. Bays)
Percy Beaufoi

In the latest addition to his extensive repertoire Mr N utters an anguished cri de coeur—*French!*—Please Will You Hold The Baby, Sir? A casual enough request, you might think. But you would be wrong. Blench now at the piteous spectacle of the bereft and the beleaguered Mr N. / There you witnessed another defective—effective—performance from Mr N.

POLKA AND THE CHOIRBOY, THE   1889
(Corney Grain)
Corney Grain

On the Halls we hear so many songs of differing kinds, but have we ever considered how these songs come to be written? Or the manner of person who composes them? Some light will now be shed on this little-regarded aspect of the world of popular music by a man of whom it was once said "If music be the food of love, pass the bicarb." So here, snatched from the jaws of the Royal Albert Hall, is Mr N. / The Polka and the Choirboy perpetrated thereby Mr N.

POLLY PERKINS OF PADDINGTON GREEN 1863
(Harry Clifton)
Harry Clifton
Trad air, Nightingales Sing (?) Also used by George Ridley for Cushie Butterfield *qv*

Did you know that our Mr N, when not upon the Halls, works as a milkman? But I'm sorry to say that his love-life, like his cream, has not run smooth... And the name of the minx who led him such a dance? Pretty Little Polly Perkins of—oh, you know her, do you? Yes, she gets about, the hussy. Lend your attention, therefore, to the curdled and clotted career of Mr N! / Poor Mr N, looking very woebegone, poor chap.

> (*See also* Young Man Who Worked at the Milk Shop *and page 201 for further songs of London*)

POOR BUTTERFLY 1916
(John L. Golden: Raymond Hubbell)
Regine Flory
From "The Big Show", Hippodrome, New York

Here as promised is Miss N to sing for us again, this time that haunting melody Poor Butterfly. Now, although this song is not from Puccini's Madame Butterfly, the lyrics do tell a very similar story and there is indeed a cheeky musical quotation from the opera in each stanza. So now with Poor Butterfly, it's that treat for the eye and the ear, Miss N. / What a tonic! Miss N with Poor Butterfly.

POOR JOHN 1906
(Fred W. Leigh: Henry E. Pether)
Ada Jones, Vesta Victoria

We soldier on with an epic story of thwarted romance—I like saying that—*thwarted*—d'you want to try? *Thwarted*... very good. In No X Miss N relates the dire events which befell when John took her round to see his mother. Let us offer our commiserations now to the predictably peevish Miss N! / Did you like Miss N's dress, ladies? I've been interested in women's clothes for the past thirty years... on and off.

POOR OLD COCK *See* OLD DICKY BIRD

POPSY WOPSY 1913
(A. J. Mills: Bennett Scott)
Daisy Dormer, Molly McCarthy Ella Retford, Lilian Shelley

Song Introductions   145

Our programme tonight advances with a taste of the very latest form of entertainment known as Revue. We are delighted to welcome a young lady who is considered a leading light of this new style of diversion and is something of a protégé of mine... I've been giving her some very private coaching... So a very special welcome if you please for that tantalising tease, Miss Popsy Wopsy! / That was our very own Miss N, from the world of Revue. And now back to good old Music Hall with... (*Or if performed "badly"*) Needs a little more work perhaps...

POSTMAN'S HOLIDAY, THE *See* NICE QUIET DAY, A

PREACHER AND THE BEAR, THE   1903
(Joe Arzonia)
Albert Whelan

Miss N's voice has been heard so often from this stage in arias, songs and ballads of all kinds. But now the singer demonstrates her versatility with something quite different: that superb spiritual from the American Deep South, The Preacher and the Bear. Miss N. / The Preacher and the Bear. A performance of vibrant energy from Miss N.

PRETTY LIPS   1872
(Arthur Lloyd)
Arthur Lloyd

A major star on the Halls in the 1870s and 80s was Mr Arthur Lloyd. Most of his songs he wrote himself, including the one we are to hear now—a love song, a tribute to his sweetheart's Pretty Lips. Saucy stuff indeed, but let's throw caution to the winds and welcome Mr N / There! Pretty Lips, from the truly irresistible Mr N.

PRETTY LITTLE GIRL FROM NOWHERE, THE   1909
(E. W. Rogers: arr. John Neat)
Edith Fink, Florrie Forde, Ella Retford

A very popular song of its day is No X, the Pretty Little Girl from Nowhere, to be sung by a pretty little girl from stage left. To whom do I refer? To none other than the beguiling and the bewitching Miss N. / Miss N, the pretty little girl from nowhere but certainly going somewhere, even if it's only back to my place... I should be so lucky.

PULLING HARD AGAINST THE STREAM   1867
(Harry Clifton)
Harry Clifton

In the 1860s there was a great vogue for what were called motto songs—songs with lyrics of high moral tone and salutary intent. Ever mindful of our obligation not only to entertain but also to edify we now offer one of these improving items, No X. Pulling Hard against the Stream. And to lead us in this hymn is a man of unimpeachable rectitude Mr N. / Mr N, Pulling Pulling Hard against the Stream. Nobly done, sir.

(*See also* Row, Row, Row 1)

PUSHING YOUNG MAN, THE   1906
(Sam Mayo)
Sam Mayo

We continue apace with a gentleman whose marked individuality and strength of personality put one in mind of a manic-depressive gerbil. His declared ambition—one which we can all share—is to get the next few minutes over as soon as possible, so here he is: the unimaginable, the unassailable, the unavoidable Mr N! / Pushing his luck there, Mr N!

PUT A BIT OF TREACLE ON MY PUDDEN, MARY ANN   1922
(Fred W. Leigh & Harry Champion)
Harry Champion

The way to a man's heart, so 'tis said, is through his stomach. An interesting anatomical proposition, to be further propounded in No X by the vigorous and vehement Mr N! / Thank you Mr N, for a lively if somewhat coarse-grained performance.

(*See also* Boiled Beef and Carrots *etc.*)

PUT ME AMONGST THE GIRLS   1907
(C. W. Murphy & Dan Lipton)
Charles R. Whittle

In No X Mr N makes a fervent request: to put him amongst the grils— (*looks at notes*)—girls... an ambition which will find an echo amongst all red-blooded males, and perhaps even some of the men here tonight. So stand by for the carefree and cocksure Mr N. / Thank you, Mr N who wishes to be amongst the girls.... It's tragic - he's never got over the shock of being told he was a mixed infant.

Song Introductions 147

PUT ON YOUR SLIPPERS 1911
(J. P. Harrington: Orlando Powell)
Marie Lloyd

Put On Your Slippers, instructs Miss N in No X, You're In For the Night! After which, it's every man for himself. So let us wait not a moment longer for that torrid temptress, Miss N. / Put On Your Slippers, You're In For the Night, Miss N. And I can tell you from personal experience, boys, if you do, Miss N will give you the finest ... cup of cocoa you've ever tasted.

PUT ON YOUR TAT-TA, LITTLE GIRLIE 1910
(Fred W. Leigh)
Clarice Mayne

No X offers assistance to any young man here tonight wondering how best to approach the object of his heart's desire. Put on your Tat-Ta, declares Johnny, and come out a tat-ta with me—in other words: don your titfer and let's go walkies. Further instruction on this interesting topic will now be offered at no extra charge by that Master Masher, Mr N. / Mr N, putting us all in a good mood.

RATCATCHER'S DAUGHTER, THE c1852
(Rev. Edward Bradley: anon. (Sam Cowell?))
Sam Cowell

Now a song that became immensely popular in the 1850s, the very early years of the Halls. All the more surprising therefore to learn that the lyrics were written by a clergyman, the Reverend Edward Bradley. The title is The Ratcatcher's Daughter, and the executant is the mordant and melancholy Mr N. / Mr N with the sad tale of the Ratcatcher's Daughter. He's not common really, you know. He's just like you and me ... well, me, anyway.

(*See page 201 for further songs of London*)

REST OF THE DAY'S YOUR OWN, THE 1915
(Worton David & J. P. Long)
Jack Lane

Now we come to a local yokel, from a little village just outside (*local*) called Effingham Blindings. He regularly performs in the village hall so he has often been tried, tested and found wanting. So, telling us about life on the farm, it's that horny—(*look at* notes)—handed son of the soil, Mr N! / I said to him "Would I do any good on the farm?" He said "No, we got special stuff for that".

(*See also* Cowslip and the Cow, The *etc*.)

RIDING DOWN FROM BANGOR   trad
(anon.)

An artiste with a prominent place in our affections is Miss N. Riding Down From Bangor is the title of her next rendition, a gently rhythmic ballad, so here most definitely on the right lines, sliding sinuously into view, is Miss N! / Miss N, a young lady with a permanent way in all our hearts.

(*See also* Casey Jones *etc*.)

RIDING ON A LOAD OF HAY   1877
(Hope Arden: Harry Birch)
Harry Birch

A change of location as Miss N takes us to the countryside, where in tranquil mood she informs us "someone stole my heart away, riding on a load of hay". Stealing our hearts away is the enchanting and endearing Miss N. / A capital song, capitally sung.

RIDING ON TOP OF THE CAR   1905
(Fred W. Leigh: Harry Von Tilzer)
Alf Gordon, George Lashwood
The melody is Harry Von Tilzer's Down Where the Wurzburger Flows *with the American lyrics completely re-written by Fred W Leigh, literary editor to the publishers Francis, Day & Hunter. The original version was sung by Nora Bayes and by Arthur Collins.*

The next song, No X, is entitled Riding On Top Of The Car. The top deck of an omnibus certainly provides opportunities for amorous dalliance, and who better to dally with, ladies, than the doughty and definitely desirable Mr N. / I tried riding on top of a bus once but I couldn't get the horse up the stairs.

(*See also* Chalk Farm to Camberwell Green)

RILEY'S COWSHED   1924
(Stanley J. Damerell & Robert Hargreaves)
George Bass

This is where the show takes a bit of a dip ... as we present a gentleman from a little village a few miles away from here called Wedlock. Well, he comes from just outside it, actually. He's had a hard day muck-

Song Introductions 149

spreading so here he is now to spread a little more: Mr Mangel Wurzel! / Thank you, Mr N. (*To audience*) You try and get your money back...

(*See also* Cowslip and the Cow, The *etc.*)

RING DOWN THE CURTAIN 1902
(Robert H. Brennan: Pauline B. Story)
J. K. Emmett, Herbert Payne

The show, we are told, must go on, a tradition honoured and respected by generations of performers. But just occasionally an artiste is so laden with grief and care that when his cue comes, he fails his public. "Ring down the curtain," he cries. "I can't sing tonight". A dramatic situation indeed, given full measure by a man who will nevertheless sing here and now, Mr N. / Mr N, ringing down the curtain.

(*See also* Bedelia (2) *etc.*)

RING THE BELL, WATCHMAN 1872
(G. F. Root)
Christy Minstrels

Now for Mr N, who used to work as a grave-digger—did you know that? Mind you, he only did it to fill in... And he fills in the next few minutes with an assault upon the words and music of that maudlin masterpiece, Ring the Bell, Watchman. Let us all assume appropriately mournful attitudes now for Mr N. / That was his best number!

ROAMIN' IN THE GLOAMIN' 1911
(Harry Lauder)
Harry Lauder

We now pay tribute to a true giant of the Halls, Mr Harry Lauder. One of the reasons for his success was his immense skill not only as a performer but as a song-writer. He wrote, for instance, both the words and music of No X, Roamin' in the Gloamin', and what a marvellously infectious lilt the tune has. To sing this happiest of songs we naturally chose a fellow Scot, so from north of the border we welcome Mr N! / I'm Scotch myself—not so much by birth as by absorption.

(*See also* Annie Laurie *etc.*)

ROSE OF TRALEE c1850
(William P. Mulchinock (?))
John McCormack

Some publishers ascribe the lyrics to E Mordaunt Spencer and the music to Charles W Glover. The Irish publishers Soodlum's however give the writer and the story of the song as follows.

Our next song is from Ireland, written in the 1850s by one William Mulchinock who fell in love with a young servant girl in his Tralee family home. He was packed off to London, returning to discover that, tragically, she had passed away. But she lives on in song, for she was Mary, the Rose of Tralee, tenderly and yet vividly recalled for us now by Mr N. / Mr N with Rose of Tralee, and what a sweet nature as well as beauty Mary must have possessed to have inspired so lovely a memorial.

(*See also* Band Played On, The *etc.*)

ROSES OF PICARDY 1916
(F. E. Weatherly: Haydn Wood)
Joseph Cheetham, Peter Dawson, Hubert Eisdell, Ernest Pike, Philip Ritte, Florence Smithson

A treat indeed for lovers of the vocal art as, with your kind permission, we bring you Mr Henry Wood's ever-green melody Roses of Picardy. A favourite song needs a favourite singer, and as we aim to please we can surely do no better than invite onto the platform Mr N.

ROSIE'S YOUNG MAN 1909
(Fred W. Leigh & Henry E. Pether)
Eileen Douglas

A poignant narrative is brought to us by Miss N, in which Rosie is all of a palpitating pit-a-pat over her young man. Hope springs eternal in the human breast, so to discover the latest news let us waste no more time in welcoming to the boards Miss N! / Miss N, and if that young man doesn't come up to scratch I'll horsewhip the fellah till he begs for mercy! ... ooh, I got all fierce then—did you notice?

ROW, ROW, ROW 1912
(William Jerome: Jimmie V. Monaco)
Daisy Jerome, Lillian Lorraine
From "Ziegfeld Follies" Moulin Rouge, New York. In London interpolated into "Hullo, Ragtime!", Alhambra

1) Getting us off to a flying start—or should I say a boating start—with No X, Row Row Row, is a gentleman who spends a lot of time with his back between his knees... I didn't like to ask what for but anyway here direct from the Shadwell Basin (*or local*) is that riverboat rambler Mr N!

2) When the curtain rises I want you to imagine an idyllic summer afternoon in the countryside in the heart of England; I want you to

Song Introductions   151

imagine a cloudless sky, a shady river bank with little rowing-boats drifting idly past in the gentle current—you'll have to imagine it because we couldn't afford any scenery... But I'm sure you get the general background to No X, Row Row Row. So it's applause, applause, applause for (those lithe and lissome lovelies) N!

(*See also* Floating With My Boating Girl)

RUM-TIDDLEY-UM-TUM-TAY   1908
(Fred W. Leigh: Orlando Powell)
Marie Lloyd

(*For two-hander*) The next item concerns a group of ladies who decided to hire a couple of brakes and pay their very first visit to the countryside, to discover whether there really is life beyond Lewisham (*or local*). Here then are two members of this intrepid band to give us the low-down on their hoe-down in a song entitled: Rum-Tiddley-Um-Tum-Tay! / What a wonderful day that turned out to be! There you saw Miss N and Miss O—Miss N was the one with the hat on... (*when both are wearing hats*)

(*For other two-handers and/or possible concerted items see page 199*)

RUNCORN FERRY, THE   1933
(Marriott Edgar)
Marriott Edgar, Stanley Holloway

To the north of England now, to those hard-working and industrious folk whose thrift is one of the cardinal virtues. Take care of the pennies and the pounds will look after themselves—this is the lesson to be learned from our very own Lancashire Lad/Lass N! / I thought that was absolutely *pehr*fect.

(*See also* Billy's Rose *etc.*)

SAFTEST O' THE FAMILY, THE   1904
(Harry Lauder & Bob Beaton: Harry Lauder)
Harry Lauder

A visitor now from north of the border—from Neasden (*or local*). I won't say he's a bit slow on the uptake but when an old lady said to him "can you see me across the road?" he said "I dunno—I'll go and have a look...!" Make of that what you will, but he's definitely the Saftest o' the Family, and his name is Mr N. / I hope he gets home all right—he's got a back basement in Fingal's Cave.

(*See also* Annie Laurie *etc.*)

SAILOR'S FAREWELL, THE 1879
(J. Goddard: A. E. Armstrong)
Frederick Federici

Our Empire was founded on the exploits of those seafaring men whose skill, bravery and spirit of adventure made this right little, tight little island the centre of the greatest Empire the world has ever known! (*Encourage cheers*) A tribute now to the British sailor in the form of a dramatic monologue, given by that fine actor Mr N! / Last boat I went on was a luxury cruise liner. Marvellous vessel—even the toilet rolls were two inches wider than usual to allow for bad weather.

(*See also* All Hands on Deck *etc. for sailor songs and* Billy's Rose *etc. for monologues*)

SALUTE MY BICYCLE 1895
(J. P. Harrington: George Le Brunn)
Marie Lloyd

The influence of Mrs Amelia Bloomer from the United States can be seen in this country's Campaign for Rational Dress and indeed our Miss N now models the very latest in ladies' cycling attire. In No X she salutes her bicycle so let us now salute the sporty and rorty Miss N! / After which Miss N now cycles back to Penge (*or local*). Safe journey, and good luck with the talcum powder...

(*See also* Daisy Bell)

SARAH (SITTING IN THE SHOE SHINE SHOP) 1919
(Jimmy McHugh & J. E. Gilbert & Steve Conley & Joe Macey)
Jack Hylton's Band

Now Mr N will be giving a turn—giving us all a turn, I shouldn't wonder. But seriously, folks, in an endeavour to raise the tone of the proceedings let us meet the incontrovertible, the incoherent, the incontinent Mr N! / Mr N, never knowingly overpaid...

SEASIDE GIRLS, THE 1899
(Harry B. Norris)
Vesta Tilley
(*This intro is for a three-hander. Alter to suit for a solo version*)

Our next item takes us to the briny, to the seaside—very appropriate for the time of year—where we find three johnnies, blades, toffs, men about beach positively oozing bonhomie and heartiness from every pore. Yes, those three heavy swells, the Margate

Mashers! / With such young men in our midst the Empire's future is assured.

    (*See also* All the Girls are Lovely by the Seaside *etc*.)

SEAWEED 1905
(Fred Earle)
Fred Earle, "Alf Gordon" (Will Terry)

Music Hall songs cover every imaginable subject, but only one to my knowledge has ever been based upon that species of marine flora known as seaweed. The words and the music will now be attempted by Mr N, which is only appropriate since he's a bit of a weed himself. But let's be extra kind and give an encouraging round of applause for that soggy songster, Mr N! / Thank you, Mr N—a man born to have sand kicked in his eyes.

    (*See also* All the Girls are Lovely by the Seaside *etc*.)

SHE COST ME SEVEN AND SIXPENCE 1904
(James Hargreaves & Sam Mayo. Air: Early In The Morning)
Sam Mayo, Wilkie Bard

Now for what can only be described as a vulgar musical hall song ... to be sung by a vulgar musical hall artiste. So stand well back—this could get nasty—yes, you've guessed it: it's Mr N! / Mr N, showing us that gallantry is not yet dead.

SHE'D A BROTHER IN THE NAVY 1877
(Geoffrey Thorn: Walter Redmond)
James Francis, Howard Paul

Mr N now tells us of his intended. Or rather of his intended's family, because as we know when a man marries he acquires a whole new set of relations. That, then, is the lyrical argument of our next song, She'd A Brother in the Navy, to be developed by that Apollo of the 'Alls: brace yourselves, ladies, for Mr N! / There he goes, a fine strapping figure of a man. Pity the straps broke.

SHE'D NEVER HAD A LESSON IN HER LIFE 1903
(Fred Murray: Orlando Powell)
Marie Lloyd

We now learn of a young lady entirely untutored in the ways of the world, yet somehow managing to surmount the obstacles and dangers which she so guilelessly encounters. Her story will be recounted by a lady who is herself a graduate of the University of Life, so if you're sitting comfortably I will announce Miss N! / Miss N, and if you believe that you'll believe anything.

SHE DOES THE FANDANGO ALL OVER THE PLACE   1883
(G. W. Hunt)
Henri Clarke, George Leybourne

Mr N recently returned from abroad. He loves being abroad, only tonight's he's a chap. But on his last trip overseas he became enamoured of a foreign party—what's wrong with a British girl, eh? Foolish fellow—caused him no end of grief, as we shall see. Here then, wandering lonely as a cloud, is Mr N. / Thank you Mr N, for that triumph of nerve over talent.

(*See also* In Olden Spain *etc.*)

SHE PUSHED ME INTO THE PARLOUR   1912
(Alf Ellerton: Will Mayne)
Ernie Mayne

Mr N tells me he's been entertaining royalty—well, he was muttering something about being detained for HM's pleasure—how honoured we are therefore to have him with us tonight and to be treated to the intimate details of his private life. So, fingers in ears please, for Mr N. / Mr N, a man of whom it has often been said ... yes ...

SHE'S A LASSIE FROM LANCASHIRE   1907
(Dan Lipton & C. W. Murphy & John Neat)
Florrie Forde, Ella Retford

For No X, She's A Lassie From Lancashire, we find our Miss N authentically clad in clogs and shawl as the lyrics demand. A joyous idyll, joyously performed by the Bolton Belle herself Miss N!

SHE SELLS SEA-SHELLS   1908
(Terry Sullivan: Harry Gifford)
Wilkie Bard, Sam Mayo
First sung by Wilkie Bard in "Dick Whittington", Drury Lane

The next artiste to expose his art to your gaze is Mr N, and he has asked me not to give him the usual jocularly insulting introduction. He wants to be treated with respect. Personally I think he should be treated with creosote ... be that as it may, a nicer chap you couldn't meet. And here to prove it is: Mr N! / Mr N—once seen, soon forgotten.

SHE'S ONLY A WORKING GIRL 1898
(J. T. Kelly)
Florrie Forde, Charles Foster

I sometimes worry that with all these agitators and Bolsheviks at large common people may start imagining themselves as good as you and me ... well, me, anyway. But one who certainly doesn't have ideas above her station is Miss N who in No X sings She's Only a Working Girl. So a condescending welcome if you please for Miss N. / Miss N, who's welcome to scrub my area any time.

(*See also* I Ain't 'Arf a Lucky Kid *etc.*)

SHE'S PROUD AND SHE'S BEAUTIFUL 1906
(Fred W. Leigh & George Bastow)
George Bastow

When the great house-curtains rise/part, rather against their better judgement, you will see a gentleman who has come from far afield. In fact he comes from—a field. But he's fond of everything to do with the countryside—he loves the Call of Nature. And answering it for us now is Mr N. / Don't applaud too much—he might do it again.

(*See also* Cowslip and the Cow, The *etc.*)

SHE TOLD ME TO MEET HER AT THE GATE 1923
(Harry Castling & Charles Collins)
S. W. Wyndham

Mr N is not a happy chap, ladies and gentlemen, for as you can see in No X his new-found lady love arranged to meet him at the gate. The trouble is she didn't specify *which* gate. Here then to take us on a topographical tour of London and environs thereof is the frantic and footsore Mr N! / Mr N last gave that performance for the unfortunate inmates of Wormwood Scrubs prison (*or local*), so we apologise to any gentlemen in the audience who may have seen it before.

(*See page 201 for further songs of London*)

SHE WAS ONE OF THE EARLY BIRDS 1895
(T. W. Connor)
George Beauchamp

Poor Mr N has not been feeling himself lately ... having been crossed in love by a ballet girl in the pantomime at Drury Lane. Yes, he thought her as cute as a fairy, but she tinkered with his bell. In No X and giving us further observations on this unedifying subject is that stark, staring, stagnant stage-door johnny: Mr N. / Mr N will be appearing again tonight—I mention that for his fans just in case either of them is in tonight.

SHE WAS POOR BUT SHE WAS HONEST Early 20th cent?
(anon.)
Note: Claims that Weston & Lee originated this song are spurious, though they were responsible for a version performed by Billy Bennett. George R Sims is sometimes suggested as the poet-lyricist but with no evidence. A very rude version is published by Music Sales in "Bawdy Ballads"—not for the parish hall. A milder version is in Robbins Music Corp's "Twenty Four Folk Songs" (1965).

(*For "tarty" performance*) A tragic tale dedicated to all young maidens here tonight in the audience... No?... I see... Well, anyway, our next song depicts in grim and grisly detail the ghastly fate which befell a country girl alone and at large in the streets of London Town. And brought to us by a lady who has been described as a legend—(*look at notes*)—*legend*—of the Halls, the tart with a heart, Miss N. / Wasn't that nice of the vicar's wife to oblige?

(*See also* Gypsy's Warning, The *etc.*)

SHINE ON HARVEST MOON 1908
(Jack Norworth: Nora Bayes & Jack Norworth)
Nora Bayes & Jack Norworth, Olive Lenton
Included in "Ziegfeld Follies of 1908", Jardin de Paris, New York. In London interpolated into "Hullo, London!", Empire, 1910

We proceed with a romantic song in which a country boy looks to those warm, moonlit nights of summer in order to—shall we say?—further a relationship. No X, Shine on Harvest Moon, irresistibly sung by the moony and spooney, Mr N. / There's an old flirty boots, eh?

(*See also* Cowslip and the Cow, The *etc. for rural songs*)

SHIP AHOY! *See* ALL THE NICE GIRLS LOVE A SAILOR

SHIP I LOVE, THE 1898
(Felix McGlennon)
Tom Costello

It is a matter of honour amongst sea-faring men the world over that in the event of disaster at sea the Captain goes down with his ship. In No X, The Ship I Love, we celebrate this harsh but proud tradition, as dramatically re-enacted by Mr N. / Mr N, with The Ship I Love. (*If*

Song Introductions 157

comic) There he goes, back to the bridge on the Isle of Wight Ferry (*or local*).

(*See also* All Hands on Deck *etc.*)

SHOOTING OF DAN McGREW, THE   1917
(Robert Service: Cuthbert Clarke)
Bransby Williams
From "Songs of a Sourdough"

For our next item we transport you in the twinkling of an eye to Alaska—a fitting location for Mr Robert Service's apocalyptic poem The Shooting of Dan McGrew. Accordingly we find ourselves in the Malamute saloon, somewhere in those grim trackless wastes where life can be harsh and brutal—Penge (*or local*) rather springs to mind... Our guide is none other than that eminent recita-tationalist, Mr N. / Thank you, Mr N, one of the finest electro-elocutionists in the business (*or local*). What a performance!

(*See also* Billy's Rose *etc.*)

SIDEWALKS OF NEW YORK, THE   1894
(James W. Blake & Charles B. Lawlor)
Lottie Gilson, Charles B. Lawlor
See Dancing on the Streets

SIGNALMAN ON THE LINE, THE   1893
(Brian Daly: C. Bond Andrews)
Frank Celli

(*If appropriate:* And now—can you hear it? Yes, it's smoke machine time!) Every technical resource at our command is pressed into service in order to do justice to Mr N's dramatic portrayal of a man torn between family and duty. A deeply significant moral tract for our times, brought to us by Mr N. / Mr N there on the horns of a dilemma, and judging by his singing, his trousers were a bit tight as well.

(*See also* Casey Jones *etc.*)

SILVER THREADS AMONG THE GOLD   1873
(Eben E. Rexford: H. P. Danks)
Christy Minstrels, Moore & Burgess Minstrels, Will Oakland, Emily Soldene

What greater contrast can there be between (*mention previous item*) and our next song? Amidst the general hilarity and hurly-burly of our programme so far we take a welcome break for one of those honest-to-goodness sentimental ballads so popular in Victorian drawing-rooms. No X, Silver Threads Among the Gold, and to lead us in the choruses that Master (or Mistress) of Melody: N. / N, leaving us all aglow with tenderness.

SIMPLE LITTLE MAID IN THE CORNER, THE 1896
(H. A. Duffy & J. M. Harrison)
Kitty Dee

As you may know our Miss N lives in the heart of (*local posh area*). She recently gave a select little dinner party, just for the county set, you understand—I wasn't invited for a start. But one of her guests was a shy, simple little thing who sat demurely in the corner. To hear more of this genteel soiree we now meet the hostess. Graciousness personified: Miss N. / Living dangerously there, Miss N.

SIMPLE LITTLE STRING, A 1896
(Lionel Monckton)
Ellaline Terriss
From *"The Circus Girl"*, Gaiety. Interpolated into *"Bluebell in Fairyland"*, Vaudeville

For her next appearance our Miss N has selected a song by the prolific Mr Lionel Monckton with the curious title of A Simple Little String. If, as the Bard declares, there are Seven Ages of Man, we now learn of the Three Ages of a Young Woman, as delineated by a young lady of ineluctable and inexhaustible charms Miss N! / Isn't she absolutely delicious?... Don't you just adore those dimples? (*alter to suit*)

SINCE I BECAME A MARRIED MAN 1907
(Walter P. Keen)
G. W. Hunter

Marriage, they say, is a wonderful institution, but then—who wants to live in an insti... you're ahead of me, aren't you? Our Mr N recently entered holy deadlock—wedlock. Whether this was a wise decision or not we shall soon discover as we welcome the bedraggled bridegroom, Mr N! / I'll never forget the hotel where I spent my honeymoon. On the wall over the bed were two embroidered texts. On the wife's side it said "I Need Thee Every Hour" and on my side it said "Lord, Give Me Strength".

SINCE I CAME TO LONDON TOWN 1900
(P. Mario Costa: Richard Morton)
Armand 'Ary

Song Introductions   159

Melody adapted from P Mario Costa's "A Frangesa"

A visitor from the United States now treads the boards. Boys, she's got pots of money and she's looking for an English husband. I offered her myself ... well, I'm a husband ... but she said she wants one with a title. I told her my grandfather was a peer ... and grandmother had kidney trouble as well ... but enough of this persiflage—do you know Percy?—and let's welcome the radiant and randy Miss N.

(*See page 201 for further songs of London*)

SINCE I WALKED OUT WITH A SOLDIER   1909
(Arthur Davenport: H. G. Pelissier)
H. G. Pelissier

Miss N has recently had a close encounter, you might say, with a member of the rude and licentious soldiery, leaving her only a little bit older but ever so much wiser. Here then, direct from hut number fifteen on Salisbury Plain, is the bruised and bemused Miss N! / Miss N—tender to the core (corps)...

(*See also* Army of Today's All Right, The *etc.*)

SING! SING! SING!   1910
(Stanley J. Damerell & John Rutland)
Damerell & Rutland

To keep the ball rolling Miss N now invites us all to Sing Sing Sing— well, that's what we're all here for, isn't it?—details given at No X. So let us give the heartiest of welcomes to that vision in lilac pink (*alter to suit*) and 3/4 time—Miss N! / A spirited and sparkling start to our show, and may I thank you on behalf of Miss N for your excellent vocal response.

SING US ONE OF THE OLD SONGS   1900
(W. B. Kelly & J. H. Woodhouse)
Millie Lindon

We performers who strut our hour upon the stage are supposedly immune from the cares and worries of everyday living. But a lifetime of striving to please and entertain the public can take its toll, as we see in No X, Sing Us One of the Old Songs. A dash of good old-fashioned sentiment now most potently expressed by Miss N.

(*See also* Bedelia (2) *etc.*)

SISTER 'RIA   1895
(A. J. Mills & Arthur Lennard)
Lizzie Fletcher

Note: I have only seen this number played as a three-hander, giving it much the same intro as for Happy Eliza and Converted Jane *qv.* / There you saw Miss M and Mr N, with Miss O on the tambourine and on the bottle, I shouldn't wonder...

(*See also* Lost, Stolen or Strayed)

SISTER SUSIE'S SEWING SHIRTS FOR SOLDIERS 1913
(R. P. Weston: Herman Darewski)
Harry Cove, Al Jolson, Jack Norworth
From "Hullo, Tango!", Hippodrome

In No X we discover—and I quote—that: "Sister Shusie's Shewing Shir... (*to front row after slurping incoherently a few times*)... oh, dear, it's going to be a damp evening for you, isn't it?... Never mind, for here now is none other than Sister Susie's big brother himself, our very own: Mr N! / How did you get on, madam?... took your teeth out?... very wise.

(*See also* Army of Today's All Right, The *etc.*)

SKYLARK! 1901
(E. W. Rogers)
Arthur Lennard

Now I ask you to surrender yourselves to a song which is almost cruel in its effect upon our sensibilities. It's a real old tear-jerker: No X, Skylark, a song which needs only a good voice and oceans of sincerity, both of which we shall find in requisite measure in Mr N. / Lashings of honest sentiment there from Mr N with Skylark. My congratulations to you sir.

SMILES 1917
(J. Will Callahan: Lees Roberts)
Nell Carrington, Elsie Janis, Millie Lindon, Blossom Seeley
Included in "The Passing Show of 1918", Winter Garden, New York (Not Felix McGlennon's 1890 song of the same title sung by Little Tich)

Now our stage is given over to Miss N with a gentle sentimental number, and none the worse for that. As we see in No X "there are smiles that make us happy, there are smiles that make us blue". But I'm sure the next few minutes will be most happily spent in the company of Miss N!

SMILIN' THRU 1918
(Arthur A. Penn)
Jane Cowl, Walter Glynne, John McCormack

Song Introductions 161

Some songs drift in and out of fashion but here's one that's as popular and affecting as the day it was composed, and that was many years ago now. Smilin' Thru—I thought that would bring a smile to your faces. Even greater cause for delight is the singer, Mr N.

SOLDIERS OF THE QUEEN 1891
(Leslie Stuart)
Albert Christian, Hayden Coffin
Interpolated into "An Artist's Model", Daly's 1895

Ladies and gentlemen, what a wonderful thing it is to be British! Let us rejoice in our country, our Armed Forces, and our Queen—for our next song invites us to do just that. No X, Soldiers of the Queen, sung by that grand British baritone, Mr N. / Mr N lashing us into a patriotic frenzy with Soldiers of the Queen—words and music by Mr Leslie Stuart.

(*See also* Army of Today's All Right, The *etc.*)

SOMEBODY'S COMING TO TEA 1917
(Clay Smith & R. P. Weston & Bert Lee)
Kirkby & Hudson, Lee White

A significant moment for any family is the occasion when their daughter first brings home a very special young gentleman. Such doings! Such upheavals! A light-hearted look, then, at a family in turmoil: Somebody's Coming To Tea. And the somebody about to come on stage now is that tremulous little cup-cake Miss N. / Miss N— and I think he's a very lucky chap...

SOMEBODY WOULD SHOUT OUT "SHOP"! 1915
(R. P. Weston & Bert Lee)
Stanley Kirkby & Harry Hudson

Now for an item rarely seen at this price range: none other than Mr N, who comes to the fore with the tale of a shop-keeper called Ebenezer Johnson and the conflicts which arose between his social life and his professional obligations. Stand well back for the grossest grocer of them all Mr N! / It must be terrible to have to work for a living, don't you think?

(*See also* Girl that I M.A.R.R.Y, The)

SOME OF THESE DAYS 1910
(Shelton Brooks)
Shirley Kellogg, Carl McCullough, Ella Retford, Sophie Tucker

Now to what I believe is known in the United States as a torch song, Some of These Days. And which red-blooded man would not carry a torch for the Red-Hot Momma of Reigate (*or local*) herself, the magnificent, the majestic, Miss N. / Phew...! If only I were ten years younger... I'd be nineteen... (*alter to suit*).

SONG OF THE THRUSH, THE 1897
(Walter Hasting: George Le Brunn)
Peggy Pryde

A change of pace now as we bring you a song of longing and heartache inspired by those enterprising men who have journeyed to Australia to seek their fortunes in the goldmines and whose thoughts so often return to home. No X, the Song of the Thrush, reflectively and effectively sung by Mr N.

SONS OF THE SEA 1897
(Felix McGlennon)
Arthur Reece

For centuries Britain has ruled the waves, acquiring an empire and becoming the most powerful—and just—nation on earth. And we owe much of this greatness to those Boys of the Bulldog breed: the Royal Navy. No X, Sons of the Sea, for which, coming up alongside, is Mr N. / Sons of the Sea from Mr N—I liked the cut of his jib, didn't you?

(*See also* All Hands on Deck *etc.*)

SOPHY 1913
(Bert Lee: T. C. Sterndale Bennett)
T. C. Sterndale Bennett

Hope springs eternal, we are told, in the human breast. And it is surely the hope of any sensible girl to find a man, a husband—someone like me, for instance... Miss N now tells of one Sophy who went on hoping and hoping and then finally—but let us hear the story in full from the quaintly coy Miss N. / Aaah... isn't there one red-blooded man here who would take her on? (*If "Yes!" look off and shout "You've clicked! Well done, sir. You won't regret it." If no response: "No? Chicken, eh...? Alter to suit, perhaps making fun of a party booking.*)

(*See also* Joshu-ah *etc.*)

SPANIARD THAT BLIGHTED MY LIFE, THE 1909
(Billy Merson)
Al Jolson, Billy Merson

Song Introductions 163

Note: Before using this intro check that the artiste is adopting a Spanish characterisation! Our next artiste comes from overseas—from sunny Spain, but he is not a sunny señor, for he has been cut out of his señorita's affections by a fellow countryman, one Alfonso Spagoni who according to No X is the Spaniard that Blighted his Life. List now to El Cocones himself, Senor N! / I don't speak much Spanish myself. Just two words—manana which means tomorrow and pyjama which means tonight!

(*See also* In Olden Spain *etc.*)

SPIDER AND THE FLY, THE   c1830
(Thomas Hudson: anon.)
Kate Castleton, Thomas Hudson, Henry Russell

The battle of the sexes is now enjoined between two artistes old enough to know better but not too old to undertake a spot of musical cut and thrust. With The Spider and the Fly: Miss M and Mr N. / And the mere male is vanquished as usual—we don't stand a chance, do we, fellows?

STOP YER TICKLIN', JOCK   1904
(Harry Lauder & Frank Folloy: Harry Lauder)
Harry Lauder

Our next turn quite frankly is not one I would wish my maiden aunt to witness. Nor my maiden uncle, for that matter. Stop Yer Ticklin', Jock is the song about to be visited upon us, and I can only hope that the artiste's Scottish accent obscures the more questionable undertones. This artiste being none other than the Laird of Mucklecrankie (*or local*) himself, Mr N. / Mr N—lang may his lum reek.

(*See also* Annie Laurie *etc.*)

SUNSHINE OF YOUR SMILE   1913
(Leonard Cooke: Lilian Ray)
Norman Blair, John Coates, Olga & Elga & Eli Hudson, John McCormack

Time for us all to sing once again, this time with Miss N who brings a ray of sunshine to our stage with No X, that evergreen ballad The Sunshine of your Smile. Let us bask now in the effulgent charms of Miss N. / The Sunshine of your Smile. And what a lovely smile indeed there from Miss N.

SWANEE   1919
(Irving Caesar: George Gershwin)
Laddie Cliff, Al Jolson

Interpolated into "Sinbad", Winter Garden, New York. London: included in "Jig-Saw!", Hippodrome

A song of the Deep South—no, not Croydon (*or local*)—but the Southern States of the good old US of A. Mr N now takes us right down the Swanee—that could have been better phrased, never mind. He takes to the Swanee River down in Dixie, to his old home which he misses so much. As indeed we have been missing the cheery and chirpy disposition of Mr N!

(*See also* Alabama Jubilee *etc.*)

SWEET ADELINE *See* YOU'RE THE FLOWER OF MY HEART

SWEET GENEVIEVE 1869
(George Cooper: Henry Tucker)
Miss E. Blanchard, John McCormack, Will Oakland
George Cooper's poem was written as a tribute to his beloved wife who died young; Henry Tucker's melody was added some fifteen years later

"The blissful dreams of long ago"—the last line of the chorus of our next song, that melodious sigh for past joys, now gone but leaving the sweetest of memories. Sweet Genevieve is the title, with which we welcome to our stage Mr/Miss N.

SWEETHEART MAY 1894
(Leslie Stuart)
Vesta Tilley

Mr N now solicits our approbation with No X, a song from the prolific Mr Leslie Stuart and written for his daughter May. So here with Sweetheart May, a touching tale of what might have been, is Mr N.

SWEETHEARTS STILL 1902
(E. W. Rogers)
Vesta Tilley

We maintain the high standard of our programme with a heart-warming story of abiding affection: No X, Sweethearts Still. I need say no more other than to pronounce the name of the bearer of these excellent tidings: Miss N. / Miss N, still everybody's sweetheart.

SWEET LITTLE ROSE OF PERSIA 1900
(Fred J. Barnes & Charles Collins: Charles Collins)
Tom Leamore

Our next song is almost impossible to categorise so I shall simply tell

Song Introductions 165

you that the chorus is No X, the title being Sweet Little Rose of Persia, from which you might surmise correctly that the lyrics are full of floral references. Here now then, surefootedly treading that delicate line between pathos and bathos, is the Waif of Waterloo, Miss N.

(*See also* Biggest Aspidistra in the World, The *etc*.)

SWEET ROSIE O'GRADY 1890
(Maude Nugent)
Annie Hart, Lil Hawthorne, Marie Kendall, Walter Munroe, Maude Nugent, Pat Rafferty

Now to a lilting waltz of an irrepressibly romantic nature, as indeed is the singer of No X, Sweet Rosie O'Grady. So let us delay no longer in meeting the smitten and starry-eyed Mr N. / Aaah, brings tears to your eyes, ladies, does it not...?

SWIMMING MASTER, THE c1904
(Herbert Darnley)
Dan Leno, Max Miller

Let us consider the happy subject of holidays, which I suppose more often than not take us to the seaside, giving us the opportunity to indulge in that most healthful exercise: swimming. And if you can't swim, ladies and gentlemen, have no fear for we have engaged—at minimal expense—our very own Swimming Master. Here he comes in all his glory, the louche and lubricious Mr N. / Polluting our beaches there was Mr N.

(*See also* All the Girls are Lovely by the Seaside *etc*.)

SWIM! SAM! SWIM! 1916
(R. P. Weston & Bert Lee)
Jay Laurier

I'm sure we would all agree there is nothing more delightful on a hot summer's day than a dip in the briny, a pastime which with a bit of luck and a following wind will now be discussed by that one-man lunatic fringe Mr N! / Mr N, you may recall was this year's Best in Show at Cruft's.

(*See* All the Girls are Lovely by the Seaside *etc*.)

SWING ME HIGHER, OBADIAH 1907
(Alfred E. Rick: Maurice Scott)
Florrie Forde, Lily Lena, Mabel Thorne

What unimaginable thrills are in store for Miss N we can only surmise as in No X she begs Obadiah to Swing Her Higher! And as you can see she also wishes to be tied on ... these are deep waters, Watson. Let us hear further without delay from the joyous, the jubilant Miss N! / Love in a swing, how delightful. Mind you, love in a hammock needs perseverance as well... Hello, Percy...

(*See also* Oh Fred! Tell Them to Stop)

TAKE A LOOK AT ME NOW 1911
(Andrew B. Sterling: Harry Von Tilzer)
Ella Retford, Beth Tate

Miss N now demonstrates the remarkable changes in manner, style and dress which may be observed in a young lady after only the briefest of sojourns in London. Take A Look At Me Now, she commands, and who amongst us would not leap to obey so welcome an injunction from the fascinatingly feminine Miss N! / And we'll be taking another look at Miss N later on in the programme, never fear.

(*See page 201 for further songs of London*)

TAKE ME BACK TO DEAR OLD BLIGHTY 1916
(A. J. Mills & Fred Godfrey & Bennett Scott)
Ella Retford, Dorothy Ward

Serving one's country in the Army gives a chap an honourable purpose in life, and looking forward now in No X to a spot of home leave is that "unaffected undetected well-connected warrior"*Private N! / I took the Queen's shilling once, but she asked for it back.

* *From Gilbert & Sullivan's "The Gondoliers"*

(*See also* Army of Today's All Right, The *etc.*)

TAKE ME IN A TAXI, JOE 1913
(A. J. Mills: Bennett Scott)
May Moore-Duprez, Vesta Victoria

"Take me in a taxi, Joe" insists Miss N in No X. I can only hope for the sake of the vehicle's suspension she does not wish to be taken in the Biblical sense. No, I'm sure it's all quite proper since nothing unladylike could ever sully the lips of the angelic, the adorable, the altogether alluring Miss N. / Wasn't that a nice dress? Very becoming ... looked as though it'll soon be coming off.

(*See page 201 for further songs of London*)

Song Introductions   167

TALE OF ACKMED KURD, THE   1925
(Cedric Forbes: Minnie G. Crispen)
Kit Keen

It is said that a man should try everything in life except incest and folk-dancing. I don't know why those two should be singled out for prohibition. I've always rather enj—anyway, our Mr N is gradually working his way through the card, having tonight reached M for Monologue: The Tale of Ackmed Kurd. Batten down the hatches then for a full-blooded and full-throated recitation from Mr N. / Mr N. You know what they say: the Lord giveth and the Chinese take-away...

TA-RA-RA-BOOM-DE-AY   1891
(Richard Morton: Alfred Moor-King arr. Angelo A. Asher)
Lottie Collins, Alice Leamar
An adaptation of Henry J Sayers' Ta-Ra-Ra Boom-Der-É, said to have been first heard in a St Louis brothel/cabaret called Babe Connor's.

(*For French Can-Can style performance*) A Parisian flavour now and from where I sit more than a whiff of garlic as we bring you a French lady... ah, Paris! The Eiffel Tower, the Arc de Triomphe, the Taj Mahal ... but cementing the Entente Cordiale as only she can is that scintillating soubrette: Mademoiselle N! / (*If she finishes with flying splits—wincing:*) I wish she wouldn't *do* that...

    (*See also* Can-Can *etc.*)

TELL ME, DEAR FLOWER   1922
(Adrian Ross: Franz Schubert)
Courtice Pounds
From "Blossom Time", Ambassador, New York, 1921. London: re-titled "Lilac Time", Lyric.

At this time of year (*alter to suit*) our gardens are coming into bloom, reminding us that flowers have long provided inspiration to painters and poets and indeed composers such as Franz Schubert whose immortal melody Tell Me, Dear Flower with its bitter-sweet lyrics we hear now. To sing it for us I'm delighted to introduce Mr N.

    (*See also* Biggest Aspidistra in the World, The *etc.*)

TELL ME, PRETTY MAIDEN   1899
(E. Boyd Jones & Paul Rubens: Leslie Stuart)
Sextet
From "Florodora", Lyric

Now for a sextet ... a sextet with no fewer than two artistes! We all have to economise in these difficult times, don't we? From "Florodora" we give you Mr Leslie Stuart's delicious melody Tell Me, Pretty Maiden, deliciously sung by that handsomest of couples: Miss N and Mr N. / *(If the woman is large and overbearing)* Miss N and Mr N ... rather him than me...

(For other two-handers and/or possible concerted items see page 199)

TENOR AND BARITONE 1896
(H. Broughton Black: H. Lane Wilson)
Ernest Pike & Stanley Kirkby

Two gentlemen appear forthwith on this very stage to give a musical demonstration of the differences between the tenor and the baritone. Wittily entitled Tenor and Baritone, the lecture will be delivered by Messrs M and N. / Showing us their sterling qualities—Messrs M and N.

(For other two-handed and/or possible concerted items see page 199)

THAT GORGONZOLA CHEESE 1894
(Fred W. Leigh: Harry Champion)
Harry Champion

We press on with Mr N, whom God preserve—and I understand they have an arrangement—who is about to unburden himself at our expense with the tale of a cheese. But not any old cheese, no—That Gorgonzola Cheese, No X! An olfactory aria, then, richly and ripely delivered by Mr N! / Thank you Mr N, who is about to tour in that fine old musical comedy, The Desert Pong.

(See also Boiled Beef and Carrots *etc.)*

THAT IS LOVE! 1891
(Felix McGlennon)
Marie Loftus

A deeply emotional performance now by a man of exquisitely sensitive temperament, in which the poet addresses the ethical implications of that age-old question What Is Love? So here now, direct from the more select salons of *(local)* and *(local)*, let us meet the "Grosvenor Gallery, Greenery-Yallery"* Mr N! / What an artiste! Such delicacy of taste. And having often shared an dressing-room with him I can personally vouch for the sensitivity of his scruples.

* *From Gilbert & Sullivan's "Patience"*

Song Introductions

THEN YOU'LL REMEMBER ME 1843
(Alfred Bunn: Michael W. Balfe)
Beniamino Gigli, William Harrison, Edward Lloyd
From "The Bohemian Girl", Drury Lane

Mr Michael Balfe's opera The Bohemian Girl is rarely performed today, though it does contain two much-loved arias—I Dreamt That I Dwelt in Marble Halls and the one we are about to hear now Then You'll Remember Me, sometimes known by its opening words When Other Lips. To be recalled by that fine tenor, Mr N. / Well, she did remember him and all ended happily.

THERE ARE FAIRIES AT THE BOTTOM OF OUR GARDEN 1907
(Rose Fyleman: Liza Lehmann)
Dora Labette, Beatrice Lillie

One of the most profound philosophical dilemmas facing society today: are there indeed fairies at the bottom of our gardens? Our next artiste certainly believes so and who would dare to contradict the preternaturally paranormal Miss N. / A transcendental performance by Miss N. (*For longer back announcement, see* Gypsy Warned Me, The)

THERE ARE NICE GIRLS EVERYWHERE 1909
(R. P. Weston)
Whit Cunliffe

"Bliss was it in that dawn to be alive", declared the poet Wordsworth, "but to be young was very heaven". How blissful indeed to be a young blade, a young man-about-town who has just come upon the realisation that There are Nice Girls Everywhere—No X. Here he comes, swaggering into sight, the philandering and flamboyantly fashionable Mr N. / He's full of himself, isn't he? And why not…

THERE'S A LONG LONG TRAIL A-WINDING 1913
(Stoddard King & Zo Elliott)
Ernest Pike, Ada Reeve

The parting of lovers has prompted song-writers to indulge themselves in any number of doleful dirges, but No X has a truly inspired melody. There's a Long Long Trail A-Winding, hauntingly sung by Mr N. / N, and what a shame we have to break the mood…

THERE'S DANGER ON THE LINE c1885
(George P. Norman)
G. H. Macdermott

Two ladies now teamed together with a song inspired by that most exciting mode of transport: the railway. The interesting lyrics form an extended metaphor in which our journey through life is likened to a journey on a train. So here now, chugging coyly into view, are the Piston Sisters. / The Misses M & N. If you don't know which is which Miss M was in green and pink and Miss N was in pink and green (*alter to suit*). We steam ahead full throttle with...

(*See page 199 for two-handers and concerted items and* Casey Jones *etc. for train numbers*)

THERE THEY ARE—THE TWO OF THEM ON THEIR OWN 1898
(Fred Murray & Fred W. Leigh: adap. by George Le Brunn from Elthelbert Nevin's Narcissus)
Marie Lloyd

As Shakespeare might well have said: we now move on to our next item. This is No X, with the provocative title There They Are, the Two of Them On Their Own. The singer is no less provoking, being as nasty a child as ever disgraced herself on the parlour carpet—and in front of the vicar, too... Yes, it's dinky little Miss N! / There she goes, a little girl who always makes her mark. I only hope we can clean it off.

(*See also* Boers Have Got My Daddy, The *etc.*)

THEY ALL WALK THE WIBBLY WOBBLY WALK 1912
(J. P. Long: Paul Pelham)
Jack Sharman, Mark Sheridan

Now to three artistes (of assorted genders) who remind us of our summer holidays at the seaside—my favourite part of the coast is Dorset. I love going there and looking at all those pretty little coves... but there is something about the seaside air which makes holiday-makers walk in a strange wibbly wobbly kind of way, as demonstrated for us now by three artistes known collectively and imaginatively as the Three Artistes! / Last time I was at the seaside I saw two young women in the water. One was breasting the waves and the other was doing exactly the opposite...

(*See also* All the Girls are Lovely by the Seaside *etc.*)

THEY ALWAYS PICK ON ME 1911
(C. W. Murphy: Harry Von Tilzer)
Ada Jones

We come now to the youngest member of our company—not a happy little girl. The trouble is she's a youngest child, and as you can see in No X she's always being picked on—aaah! So let us see whether we can't bring a smile to the wan cheek of that pathetic little parcel Miss N! / And all ended happily and most satisfactorily there for Miss N.

(*Also see* Boers Have Got My Daddy, The *etc.*)

THEY BUILT PICCADILLY FOR ME 1913
(William Hargreaves)
J. W. Rickaby

London's Piccadilly has long been a thoroughfare notorious for high-living, debauchery and depravity—rather like (*local street*). Mr N claims that Piccadilly was built for him, and here to prove it is the ineffable, the insouciant, the irrepressible, Mr N. / They Built Piccadilly for Mr N—and quite right too!

(*See page 201 for further songs of London*)

THEY DIDN'T BELIEVE ME 1914
(M. E. Rourke: Jerome Kern)
George Grossmith jnr & Adrienne Brunne, George Grossmith jnr & Haidee de Rance, George Grossmith jnr & Madge Sanders, Julia Sanderson
From *"The Girl From Utah" (New York version, "Knickerbocker")*.
London: interpolated into *"Tonight's The Night"*, Gaiety

We are beginning to experience new flavours in popular song from our cousins across the herring-pond, and especially the work of a talented young man called Jerome Kern. One of his latest offerings, a sophisticated duet called They Didn't Believe Me, we hear now from that dreamy duo Miss M and Mr N.

(*For other two-handers and/or possible concerted items see page 199*)

THEY'RE ALL SINGLE BY THE SEASIDE 1911
(Worton David & C. W. Murphy)
Florrie Forde, Ella Retford

The season of summertime and holidays have prompted Miss N to make an interesting observation in her next song, which is that apparently They're All Single by the Seaside, No X. Further revelations from our very own Brighton (*or Blackpool or Bournemouth or local*) Belle, Miss N.

(*See also* All the Girls are Lovely by the Seaside *etc.*)

THOSE WEDDING BELLS SHALL NOT RING OUT 1893
(Monroe H. Rosenfeld: Edward Jonghman)
Leonard Barrie, Gus Edwards, Helene Mora, Arthur Reece, W. H. Windom
Based on The Fatal Wedding *by Gussie L Davis*

(*For concerted version in church setting*) Even as we speak our highly-trained staff are springing into action like an extremely well-oiled machine ... in order to erect an exact facsimile of the sanctuary of Brompton Oratory (*or local*). I'm told that after seeing it the Prior had himself barmitzvahed ... as well. Be that as it may we now find the company assembled for a wedding. Yes, a wedding has been arranged, all is in readiness, but Those Bells Shall Not Ring Out! / I'm not sure whether that was a happy ending or not.

(*For other possible concerted items see page 199*)

THOUGH ALL YOUR FRIENDS MAY LEAVE YOU 1903
(Harry Castling)
Kate Carney

Miss N now offers a poignant little vignette on a theme rarely dealt with in Music Halls songs and entitled Though All Your Friends May Leave You. And how bereft we here at (*local*) should be if ever we were to be deserted by the matchless Miss N.

THREE POTS A SHILLING *See* WHEN THE SUMMER COMES AGAIN

TIDDLY-OM-POM 1907
(Fred W. Leigh: Orlando Powell)
Marie Lloyd

Though British to the core Miss N does have a penchant for Spain—its music, its culture, its literature—its men. Treating us now to what I trust will be a heavily-expurgated version of her adventures in the Iberian peninsular is that tasty little enchilada, Miss N. / Gra*th*ias to Miss N, enthusing there about Spain, the Land of the Midnight Paella.

(*See also* In Olden Spain *etc.*)

TIN GEE-GEE, THE 1891
(Fred Cape)
Mel B. Spurr, Fanny Wentworth

In 1845 Charles Dickens wrote that we should "bless the squire and his relations ... and always know our proper stations". But irony can be a dangerous weapon and our next song, written nearly half a century later, shows that class divisions in our society remain as deep as ever. The Tin Gee-Gee, sung by the incomparable Mr N. / The Tin Gee-Gee by Mr N—definitely a two and three in my book.

Song Introductions 173

'TIS THE LAST ROSE OF SUMMER 1807
(Thomas Moore: Richard A. Milliken: arr. Thomas Moore)
Catherine Hayes, Christine Nilsson, Adelina Patti, Emma Thursby

Many of the works of the Irish poet Thomas Moore cried out to be set to music—Believe Me If All Those Endearing Young Charms, The Harp That Once Through Tara's Halls, Oft In The Stilly Night and also our next ballad, whose limpid beauty requires very special qualities. And I am sure you will agree that for 'Tis the Last Rose of Summer we have an ideal interpreter in Miss N. / A luminous performance by Miss N.

TO CHEER HIM UP AND SEND HIM ON HIS WAY 1912
(Alec Kendal)
Jack Pleasants

In these increasingly fraught and materialistic times it behoves us all to remember the Christian duty of charity that we all owe to one another. Help our neighbour as we would ourselves, that is the lesson offered by our next artiste, an exemplary specimen of muscular Christianity: Mr N. / Lashing us into paroxysms of apathy there was Mr N, who has been described as being not so much in the forefront as the U-Bend of British comedy.

TOMMY MAKE ROOM FOR YOUR UNCLE 1876
(T. S. Lonsdale)
W. B. Fair, Tony Pastor

Courting a widow lady is not without its special difficulties and hazards, especially if the object of one's affections has a child in tow. Not easy, trying to whisper sweet nothings with a bumptious brat in attendance, but the problem is triumphantly surmounted by Mr Fred Jones, better known to us as Mr N. / I'm sure they'll live happily ever after.

TOUCH THE HARP GENTLY See JUST TOUCH THE HARP GENTLY

TRICKY LITTLE TRILBY 1895
(J. P. Harrington: George Le Brunn)
Marie Lloyd

In recent years few fictional characters have captured the imagination so sensationally than Trilby, the vulnerable young woman hypnotised by the wicked Svengali. There have been Trilby hats and Trilby dresses and—Trilby songs. Putting the fluence on us now as Tricky Little Trilby is the memorable and mesmerising Miss N.

TRAMP TRAMP TRAMP THE BOYS ARE MARCHING See WORK BOYS WORK AND BE CONTENTED

TRIXIE OF UPPER TOOTING 1896
(Ada Reeve: Paul Rubens)
George Grossmith jnr, Lionel Mackinder, Ada Reeve

The lyrics of our next song were written by the lady who first sang it, the great Music Hall artiste Miss Ada Reeve, and the music is by that prolific composer of popular songs and musical comedies, Mr Paul Rubens. The title? Trixie Of Upper Tooting, a topical song given a topping performance by the lively and lovely Miss N.

(*See page 201 for further songs of London*)

TRULY RURAL See I CAN SAY "TRULY RURAL"

TUNER'S OPPOR-TUNER-TY 1879
(Harry Adams & Fred Coyne: Fred Coyne)
Fred Coyne

Every self-respecting parlour contains a pianoforte nowadays, and when you have a piano you must have recourse from time to time to the services of a piano-tuner. Mr N now expatiates upon his unhappy encounter with one of these peripatetic functionaries, so let us offer a sympathetic welcome to the betrayed and benighted Mr N. / Thank you, Mr N. He leaves nothing to the imagination, does he?

(*See also* Piano-Tuner, The)

TURNED UP 1924
(Harry Castling & Herbert Rule)
Florrie Forde, Lily Morris

Miss N returns with a song about Big Amy... (*look at notes*) ... bigamy... No X, Mary Ellen at the Church Turned Up. Has Miss N turned up? Yes? Oh well, we'll have to get on with it then. Here she is, plucking at our heart-strings, the lugubrious yet larky Miss N! / Wasn't that a lovely dress? I wonder who shot the couch...

(*See also* Joshu-ah *etc.*)

Song Introductions 175

TWIDDLEY BITS, THE 1901
(George Dance & J. Adams: Ernie Woodville)
Louie Freear, Alma Jones, Hilda Trevelyan
Interpolated into "A Chinese Honeymoon", Theatre Royal, Hanley (Strand)

Miss N has so often delighted us in the past as a singer, dancer and actress. But she is ambitious to extend her versatility by taking piano lessons, and we all look forward to her first recital. In the meantime, singing for us *dolce e molto espressivo* is the divinely delectable Miss N. / I'd like to be her tuner, wouldn't you, maestro?

(*See also* Piano-Tuner, The)

TWO LITTLE GIRLS IN BLUE 1892
(Charles Graham)
Lily Burnand, Marie Kendall, Horace Wheatley

In Music Hall songs, as in life, love sometimes leads to lasting happiness and sometimes not. Unrequited affection is the gist of No X, Two Little Girls in Blue, a bitter-sweet song of tender regret and given a most trenchant performance by Mr N.

TWO LITTLE SAUSAGES 1907
(Adrian Ross: Lionel Monckton)
Gertie Millar & Edmund Payne

Two artistes now grace the stage with a duet from Mr Lionel Monckton's latest Gaiety success "The Girls of Gottenburg", a song all about two little sausages who fall in love ... kosher, of course. Ladies and gentlemen, Miss N and Mr N. / What a ridiculous song!

TWO LOVELY BLACK EYES 1886
(adap. Charles Coborn)
Charles Coborn
Adapted by Coborn from My Nellie's Blue Eyes, *a Christy Minstrel song (lyrics: Edmund Forman) derived from the Venetian ballad* Vieni Sul Mar

There now follows a party political piece from Mr N, who comes to us fresh—or fairly fresh—from the hustings. As we see in No X, political debate can land you in very hot water, as was the lot of that very cross cross-bencher indeed: Mr N. / (*To accompanist*) You don't get involved in political arguments, do you?... No... He's been sitting on the fence so long his bottom looks like a hot-cross bun ... or so they tell me...

(*For further "eye" songs see* Algy *etc*)

UNDER THE BED 1929?
(Harry Castling)
Nellie Wallace
Unpublished but available in manuscript from EMI

What with young men discarding their spats all over the Home Counties (*or local*) and young ladies' skirts rising to a full three inches below the knee it's good to know that one of Britain's daughters at least is prepared to follow her mother's advice. I won't mention her name as she is from a good family and wishes to remain synonymous. So I will simply introduce her as A Debutante! / Who could fail to respond to such unspoiled innocence?

UNDER THE DEODAR 1902
(Adrian Ross: Lionel Monckton)
Aileen D'Orme, Evie Green, Maggie May

That great impresario Mr George Edwardes has kindly given us permission to include a song from his latest Gaiety success "A Country Girl", composed by Mr Lionel Monckton. And I know you will agree with me that the lovely melody Under the Deodar is eminently suited to the vocal talents of Miss N.

UP IN A BALLOON 1868
(G. W. Hunt)
George Leybourne
Ladies' version lyrics written for Nellie Power by her mother were also sung by Annie Adams, Alice Dunning and Louie Sherrington

I understand that attempts are being made in America to construct a heavier-than-air flying machine. Our Astronomer Royal has declared this to be a scientific impossibility. And he must be right, 'cos he's British! However, there is one proven way of defeating gravity and that is by hot-air balloon, and who would not wish to ascend into the blue with that radiant aviatrix Miss N! / Taken for a ride there was Miss N... (*If accompanied*) with her inspid ... intrepid companions Messrs (*give names*). And now down to earth with a bump with...

(*See also* I'm Looking for Mr Wright)

VARMER GILES 1902
(T. F. Robson & Gilbert Wells)
George Bastow
Air, Villikins and His Dinah *qv*

We continue with a yeoman of Old England, a denizen of Cranborne Chase in the heart of the lovely Dorset countryside—I love being in the country, don't you?, watching all those young couples on the verge. But here to give us the countryman's view of the great Metrollops of London is a name celebrated in the fields and operating theatres of Britain: Varmer Giles! / Thank you Mr N, appearing as Varmer Giles. That really was piles of fun.

(*See also* Cowslip and the Cow, The *etc.*)

VICAR AND I WILL BE THERE, THE   1919
(F. Clifford Grey: Nat D. Ayer)

Here's a surprise—guess who's paying us a flying visit? Our old curate, Mr Meek! You remember him, don't you...? We haven't seen much of him since he moved away from us here at St Cuthbert's-on-the-Verge and I thought it might be nice to find out how he's getting on with his new parish. So let's give a respectful welcome back to the Reverend Mr Meek. / Thank you, Mr N, who used to be our chaplain. We called him chaplain 'cos he was a bit of a charlie.

(*See also* At The Vicar's Fancy Ball *etc.*)

VILIA   1907
(Adrian Ross: Franz Lehár)
Constance Drever, Lily Elsie, Mizzie Gunther
From *"The Merry Widow"* (*"Die Lustige Witwe"*, an der Wien, Vienna 1905). An adapted version was first seen in London at Daly's.

No musical comedy has caused a greater sensation than Herr Franz Lehár's The Merry Widow. All Europe went Merry Widow mad, and one of its songs swiftly became a standard in the soprano repertoire. It tells of a young hunter who falls in love with a beautiful and mysterious maiden, unaware that she is in fact Vilia, a witch of the woods. And the lady about to work her magic on us is Miss N. / Miss N. Took me years to get her to sing like that...

VILLIKINS AND HIS DINAH   1836
(anon.)
Sam Cowell, Frederick Robson, J. L. Toole

Now for an epic disaster on a scale unparalleled since Mr Gladstone dropped his bags, and brought to you by Mr N ... who relates a grim but gripping tale of tragedy amongst the hoi polloi: Villikins and his Dinah. And in the character of a coarse, cockney costermonger sort of person is, believe it or not, Mr N. / Well done, Mr N. And I must say, ladies and gentlemen, I did admire the way you picked up the chorus—it's not even on the songsheet...

WAIT FOR THE TURN OF THE TIDE 1868
(Harry Clifton: Charles Coote)
Harry Clifton

A song now of a type which has rather fallen out of fashion and so we are indebted to Mr N for demonstrating for us now what used to be known as a "motto" song. This kind of number was popularised back in the 1860s by Mr Harry Clifton with such titles as Paddle Your Own Canoe, Pulling Hard Against The Stream, Work Boys Work and be Contented, and the one we are about to hear now, No X, Wait For The Turn of The Tide. Let us wait no longer for Mr N. / What a load of old...

WAITING AT THE CHURCH 1906
(Fred W. Leigh: Henry E. Pether)
Vesta Victoria

The young lady who has been jilted, left at the altar, is so often a figure of odium, obloquy and opprobium ... don't you think? Nevertheless I am sure we here are made of more compassionate clay so may I ask for the optimum courtesy, kindness and consideration for Miss N! / (*If she plays it pregnant look off stage and say "Get the water boiling! ... nothing to do with me..."*)

(*See also* Joshu-ah *etc.*)

WAITING FOR THE ROBERT E LEE 1912
(L. Wolfe Gilbert & Lewis F. Muir)
American Ragtime Octette, Peter Bernard, Fanny Brice, Dolly Connolly, Al Jolson, The Two Bobs
From "The Honeymoon Express", Winter Garden, New York

Now for a song of the Deep South ... no, not Croydon (*or local*) ... but old Alabamy, where we find Mr N on the levee, waiting for a paddle-steamer named after that great soldier, General Robert E Lee. So let us wait no longer but extend a hearty British welcome to—Mr N! / Mr N with a popular American song. I think they're coming along quite well, don't you?

WAITING FOR THE TRAIN *See* CHARMING YOUNG LADY I MET IN THE TRAIN, THE

WAIT TILL THE CLOUDS ROLL BY 1881
(J. T. Wood: H. J. Fulmer)
Mohawk Minstrels, Will Oakland (Moore & Burgess Minstrels)

We continue with one of the most moving and affecting ballads in our musical heritage: Wait Till the Clouds Roll By. To do justice to this fine melody requires a very special artiste—one in a million. Unfortunately the artiste we've got was won in a raffle. So, direct from O'Grady's Kosher Curry House in the (*local*) Road, is Mr N. / Mr N with Wait Till the Clouds Roll By as you've never heard it before, and with any luck...

(*For other two-handers and/or possible concerted items see page 199*)

WAIT TILL THE SUN SHINES, NELLIE   1905
(Andrew B. Sterling: Harry Von Tilzer)
Winona Banks, Emma Carus, Byron G. Harlan, Harry Talley, Gladys Fisher

Probably the most successful and prolific song-writer of today is Mr Harry Von Tilzer, the man responsible for Down at the Old Bull and Bush, Give Me the Moonlight, A Bird in a Gilded Cage, and No X, Wait Till the Sun Shines, Nellie. I'm sure that Mr Von Tilzer himself would heartily approve of the zestful performance of Mr N. / Showing us his paces—excellent work from Mr N.

WAIT TILL THE WORK COMES ROUND   1906
(Gus Elen & C. Cornell & T. Leybourne)
Gus Elen

It is said that hard work never killed anyone. That may be so, but our Mr N doesn't intend to be the first, as we shall discover in No X, Wait Till the Work Comes Round. So in a portrayal of the labouring classes positively reeking of authenticity, is Mr N. / Mr N, proving that you can't beat the British working man.

WALKING HOME WITH ANGELINE   1902
(G. Totten Smith: John E. Roundbach)
Eily Helene, Stanley Kirkby
From "Kitty Grey", Apollo

A quiet item now, and nonetheless welcome, especially when delivered by Mr N, outlining the particulars of a romantic ramble in which he walked his light-of-love to her home. Her name is Angeline which explains the title of No X on your song-sheets, Walking Home With Angeline. Ladies and gentlemen, on the case is the dapper and debonair Mr N!

WALTZ ME AROUND AGAIN WILLIE   1906
(Will D. Cobb: R. E. N. Shields)
Margaret Cooper, Florrie Forde, George Grossmith jnr, Blanche Ring

Originally from the short-lived "His Honor The Mayor" (New York, New York) but the following year included in "Miss Dolly Dollars", 14th Street, New York. In London included in "The New Aladdin", Gaiety

Miss N dedicates her next song to any Willies who may be in the house—see No X, "Waltz Me Around Again Willie." So now, giving her all—or as much as propriety allows—oh, my fur and whiskers!—is that flirtatious firebrand Miss N. / Miss N, a lady of inexhaustible energies.

WALTZ SONG 1907
(Charles H. Taylor: Edward German)
Ruth Vincent
From "Tom Jones", Apollo

Mr Edward German has written many notable songs, and we hear now one of the highlights from his musical comedy Tom Jones, currently enjoying a most successful run at the Apollo Theatre in London's West End. This is the Waltz Song, also known as For Tonight. And singing it for us tonight is that sparkling soprano supreme, Miss N!

WATCHING THE TRAINS COME IN 1916
(Frank Leo)
Jack Pleasants

We take you now to (*local*) station, Platform 2, where we find our Mr N utterly in thrall to the romantic appeal of the railways, though there is perhaps an ulterior motive behind his passion for train-spotting. As we shall now discover from that somewhat seedy songster, Mr N. / Mr N watching the trains come in and certainly making his points...

(*See also* Casey Jones *etc.*)

WATCHMAN! WHAT OF THE NIGHT? 1905
(anon.: James B. Sarjeant)
Ivor Foster & Hubert Cave

A grand dramatic treat for us all now, a duet from two artistes—as opposed to a duet from three artistes—entitled "Watchman! What of the Night?". Now to be musically enacted by two gentlemen singing in full evening dress and indeterminate pitch: Messrs M & N. / Mr M & Mr N. I think we'd better put that behind us, don't you...?

(*For other two-handers and/or possible concerted items see page 199*)

Song Introductions

WE ALL CAME IN THE WORLD WITH NOTHING 1907
(Charles Collins & W. H. Wallis)
Tennyson & Wallis, Billy Williams

Our next artiste might be described as a *reductio ad absurdum* of the Music Hall arts as he stands poised in the wings about to embark upon what he fondly imagines will be a whole new career. With No X, We All Came in the World With Nothing, and appearing by kind permission of the Official Receiver, is Mr N. / Mr N, assuring us that you can't take it with you. If I can't take my train set, I'm not going.

WE ALL WENT UP UP UP THE MOUNTAIN 1933
(Elton Box & Desmond Cox & Ralph Butler)
George Jackley, The Midnight Minstrels

Mr N continues with what is described as a novelty song, the novelty being that he sings it not for pleasure but for spite. Yes, here and now, making a determined assault upon the north face of No X, We all went Up the Mountain, is the man with a crimp in his crampon: Mr N. / Mr N, up the mountain and up the pole.

WEDDING MARCH, THE 1902
(J. P. Harrington: George Le Brunn)
Marie Lloyd

I would imagine that for many of us the most memorable day of our lives was our wedding day—I'll never forget mine and God knows I've tried. But as we shall now hear one lady who underwent the liveliest of nuptials was the Belle of Bethnal Green herself, Miss N. / Miss N with memories of her wedding day in song—going from bed to verse, as it were.

(*See page 201 for further songs of London*)

WE DON'T WANT TO FIGHT (BUT BY JINGO! IF WE DO) *See* MACDERMOTT'S WAR SONG

WEE DEOCH-AN-DORIS, A 1910
(Whit Cunliffe & Gerald Grafton & Harry Lauder)
Harry Lauder

Though Music Hall started in London the movement spread rapidly, each part of the country developing its own distinctive style. Scotland has given us many fine artistes, and we're delighted now to welcome a comedian all the way from Glasgow, from Pollokshields. So giving us a load of Pollokshields Patter, Mr N! / A wee deoch-an-doris, aye ... actually, I'm Scotch myself ... not so much by birth as by absorption.

(*See also* Annie Laurie *etc.*)

WEEPIN' WILLER, THE   1865
(Harry Clifton)
Harry Clifton

We all know what a fine singing voice Mr N possesses, in fact I understand his neighbours regularly break his windows in order to hear him better. He now gives us a song from the earliest days of the Halls, and all the more welcome for that, an elegiac aria entitled The Weepin' Willer. So the best of order if you please for that Professor of Pleasure: Mr N. / A ripely Dickensian performance there from Mr N.

WE PARTED ON THE SHORE   1906
(Harry Lauder)
Harry Lauder

Now to North Britain—Scotland—and the glad return of Miss N with the tale of a love-lorn Scots lassie We Parted On The Shore. A lilting if lugubrious lay from the pen of Mr Harry Lauder himself, and presented by—(*If girl*)—the Flora Macdonald of Finsbury Park (*or local*) Miss N. (*If boy*)—the Rob Roy of Ravenscourt Park (*or local*) Mr N. / (*In heavy phoney Scots accent*) Mr N, dreeing his weird ... no, I don't know what it means either...

(*Note: Harry Lauder was knighted in 1919 so until then he was plain Mr. See* Annie Laurie *etc.*)

WE USED TO GATHER AT THE OLD DUN COW   1918
(T. W. Connor)
Ernie Mayne

The first time I saw the next act I have to say it gave me a nasty turn. But then the nasty turns of today are the stars of tomorrow, so let us give a hearty welcome to a man who at least has the courage of his many convictions: Mr N! / That was Mr N, making his last appearance with us...

(*See* 'Arf A Pint of Ale *etc.*)

WHAT A MOUTH!   1906
(R. P. Weston)
Harry Champion

Song Introductions

Mr N serenades us now with the tale of one Jimmy Binks who has a pronounced physiognomical peculiarity—an exceptionally large mouth, or norf and sarf as they say in the vehicular. Yes, it's that celebrated patter song What A Mouth!, and to sing it we have that immense favourite Mr N! / Mr N with a pithy little song, pithily sung, by a pithy artiste.

WHAT CHEER 'RIA   1885
(Bessie Bellwood: Will Herbert)
Bessie Bellwood, Nellie Farren

Miss N now assumes the roles of a greengroceress on the spree at a Music Hall where, she decides to eschew her usual bench in the gallery and to try instead a seat in the stalls, right by the Chairman. How this experiment turned out we shall now discover from the irrepressible, the irresistible, Miss N! / Thank you, Miss N. I'm sure everyone at Cheltenham Ladies' College must be very proud of you.

WHAT DID SHE KNOW ABOUT RAILWAYS?   1897
(C. G. Cotes: Bennett Scott)
Marie Lloyd
Note: "Railways" was Edwardian slang for women's red stockings, this being the point of the joke in the last line of the third verse.

Railway journeys can be fraught with difficulties even for the most experienced traveller. How much more daunting then for an innocent young country maiden, whose first trip on a train led her into—well, let's see exactly where it did lead her. Here she is, our very own Sweetheart of the Sidings: Miss N. / There's a girl worth taking a sleeper from Victoria to Clapham for (alter to suit).

(See also Casey Jones etc.)

WHAT D'YER THINK OF THAT? (MY OLD MAN'S A DUSTMAN)

(J. P. Long)   1922
Ernie Shand

Britain is said to be a class-obsessed society, with those from good homes and old-established families tending to look askance at those of inferior stock. I regret to say that our Mr N is quite insufferable in this regard, so tug your forelocks, please, for that thoroughgoing thoroughbred: Mr N. / Thank you Mr N, bachelor of this parish—stud fee half a guinea.

(See also Golden Dustman, The)

WHAT IS THE USE OF LOVING A GIRL IF THE GIRL DON'T LOVE YOU? 1902
(Frank Leo)
Sable Fern

Mr N now addresses that fascinating conundrum What Is the Use of Loving a Girl if the Girl Don't Love You?, a dilemma which has exercised the greatest intellects throughout the ages and will now be dissected by the skittish and suggestible: Mr N! / An energetically elegiac performance from Mr N.

WHAT I WANT IS A PROPER CUP OF COFFEE 1926
(R. P. Weston & Bert Lee)
Ernie Mayne

I am advised that during his performance of No X, What I Want is a Proper Cup of Coffee, Mr N will not only sing but may also dance! ... in which case there will be a special collection. So tripping the light sarcastic is that proper perisher Mr N! / Mr N, with a Proper Cup of Coffee—a really stirring song.

(*See* 'Arf A Pint of Ale *etc.*)

WHAT'S THAT FOR, EH? 1892
(J. P. Harrington: George Le Brunn)
Marie Lloyd

All parents know of the difficulties—nay, the embarrassments—of informing their children of the facts of life. One little girl said to her mother, "Mummy, how do Buffaloes make love?" Her mother said, "I don't know—your father's a Mason." Education then, is the topic to be pursued now by Little Dolly Nightmare herself, Miss N. / Thank you, Miss N. A fine little artiste and such a nice girl. She's very good to her mother ... never goes home.

(*See also* Boers Have Got My Daddy, The *etc.*)

WHEN A FELLOW IS TWENTY-ONE 1904
(A. J. Mills & Bennett Scott)
Hetty King

From the remarkable song-writing team of Mills and Scott who gave us When I Take my Morning Promenade, All the Nice Girls Love A Sailor, Fall in and Follow Me, and so many others we now present No X on your songsheets: When a Fellow is Twenty-One. A less well-known song and all the more agreeable therefore, especially when performed with the utmost polish and sly charm by Mr N! / I remember when I was twenty-one—the girls flocked round me like moths round a flame. Even Miss Florence Nightingale carried a torch for me...

(*See also* I'm Twenty-one Today)

WHEN ARE YOU GOING TO LEAD ME TO THE ALTAR, WALTER?
(Walter Dore: Billy Desmond)   1933
Randolph Sutton

The burden of Miss N's next aria is the pathological inability of one Walter to lead her to the altar. If he doesn't pop the question soon she may well turn her attentions elsewhere—and who shall blame her, the saucy jade? Here she is, the Jezebel of (*local*), Miss N! / Walter must need his head examining to let such a prize slip, I'm sure we'd all agree.

WHEN FATHER PAPERED THE PARLOUR
(R. P. Weston & Fred J. Barnes)   1909
Billy Williams

Our next artiste needs no introduction—he just needs an act. The best he can do is a descriptive song with which he assures me he has had a runaway success. If only he would... But now we hear of the time Mr N's Father Papered the Parlour, a saga offering us a glimpse into the life of the lower orders, as represented by Mr N! / Mr N. It won't happen again.

WHEN I DISCOVERED YOU
(Irving Berlin & E. Ray Goetz)   1914
Irene & Vernon Castle
From "Watch Your Step", New Amsterdam, New York. London: Empire, 1915

I imagine we are all aware that the United States is a country of immigrants. One young man of a Russian family is rapidly making his mark in the field of popular song. Born Israel Baline he now calls himself Irving Berlin, and Miss N now demonstrates one of his latest successes, When You Discovered Me. With this witty song let us now discover the sultry and the sparky Miss N.

WHEN I LEAVE THE WORLD BEHIND
(Irving Berlin)   1915
Gertie Gitana, Al Jolson, Fritzi Scheff

Time for us all to sing once again, and I know you will need no second asking as we are in for a double treat—first of all the song, which is that haunting melody No X, When I Leave the World Behind, and secondly the singer, for it is none other than Miss N. / Does your heart good, doesn't it?, to hear that again, especially so beautifully sung.

WHEN IRISH EYES ARE SMILING 1912
(George Graff & Chauncey Olcott: Ernest R. Ball)
Ernest R. Ball, Nora Delaney, John McCormack, Chauncey Olcott, Gerald Orme
From "The Isle o' Dreams", Grand Opera House, New York

A song with the happiest of sentiments and a most wonderful lilt is No X, When Irish Eyes are Smiling. And I know our eyes will be smiling too for a fine forthright performance of this most popular of ballads by Mr N. / A vintage performance indeed from Mr N.

(See also Band Played On, The *etc.; for further "eye" songs see* Algy *etc.)*

WHEN I TAKE MY MORNING PROMENADE 1910
(A. J. Mills: Bennett Scott)
Marie Lloyd

Now to a lady with whom I've had the pleasure of performing on numerous occasions ... no, please. I mean she's a marvellous turn ... show some respect. Telling us of her pre-prandial perambulatory peregrinations on the promenade is that acknowledged arbitress of fashion: Miss N. / Miss Flirty Boots herself ... makes me go weak at the knees...

WHEN OTHER LIPS *See* THEN YOU'LL REMEMBER ME

WHEN SHE WALKS 1906
(Harry Boden: W. Skerry & Harry Ford)
Harry Ford

So many Music Hall songs propagate a rather negative attitude to romance and the tender affections that it's nice to hear Mr N enthusiastically extolling the sterling attributes of the fortunate young woman to have won his heart, as we shall learn from the dignified and decidedly decorous Mr N.

WHEN THERE ISN'T A GIRL ABOUT 1906
(Harry Castling & Charles Collins)
Arthur Reece, Billy Williams

Next on the agenda is a gentlemen of good address, as they say.

Song Introductions   187

From No X When There Isn't A Girl About we may infer that he is a man besotted with the opposite (*whisper*) gender ... and indeed the ladies seem just as taken with the fastidious, fashionable and eminently fanciable Mr N. / Isn't he a caution?

WHEN THE SUMMER COMES AGAIN   1895
(Harry Bedford)
Kate Carney, Fred Mason

We take you back to the spring (*alter to suit*) when our Mr N, in the guise of an itinerant flower-seller, was looking forward to summertime in order to "roam around the country, with a girl who's ever willing. He can buy, she can cry "Three pots a shilling"". I'm sure you recognise that quotation from No X, When The Summer Comes Again, brought to us now by Mr N. (*For two hander:* in company with his light of love Miss M)! / A cockney romance.

(*For other two-handers and/or possible concerted items see page 199*)

WHEN YOU AND I WERE YOUNG, MAGGIE   1866
(George W. Johnson: J. A. Butterfield)
Harry MacDonough, Will Oakland, Jan Peerce

(*Comedy duet version*) A touching old ballad now: When You and I Were Young, Maggie to be sung by two well-known local artistes, Miss M and Mr N. There has, I must confess, been a little difficulty with this item—Miss M has been on the day-shift and Mr N on the night-shift so tonight is in fact the first time they've done it together. And so, remembering love's young dream for us now are Miss M and Mr N. / When You and I Were Young, Maggie, memorably rended-rendered by the constricted tenor Mr N, and the messy-soprano was Miss M.

(*For other two-handers and/or possible concerted items see page 199*)

WHEN YOU LIVE OPPOSITE TO ME   1911
(C. W. Murphy & Dan Lipton)
Daisy Dormer

The great house curtains will rise to reveal a tastefully arranged empty space ... into which come cavorting no fewer than two artistes, soulmates each ... aaah... With an oblique look at the age-old mystery of human infatuation are the redoubtable Mr N and the achingly attractive Miss M! / An exemplary performance by Miss M and her partner Mr N, the lucky dog.

(*For other two-handers and/or possible concerted items see page 199*)

WHEN YOU WERE SWEET SIXTEEN 1898
(James Thornton)
Hamilton Hill, Bonnie Thornton, Julius P. Witmark

We continue in romantic vein with the commendable Mr N, who gives us a taste of his quality with No X, When You Were Sweet Sixteen. Taxing our memories to the utmost now then is our very own troubadour of song, Mr N.

WHERE ARE THE LADS OF THE VILLAGE TONIGHT? 1914
(R. P. Weston: Herman Darewski)
Harry Cove, George Lashwood

It was Dr Johnson who remarked that "every man thinks meanly of himself for not having been a soldier, or not having been at sea." In time of strife our young men are not found wanting; off they go, leaving towns and communities bereft. Even the West End of London, known to habitués as "the village", is strangely quiet. No X—"Where are the Lads of the Village Tonight?" And the answer will be supplied by Mr N.

(*See also* Army of Today's All Right, The *etc. and page 201 for further songs of London*)

WHERE DID YOU GET THAT HAT? 1888
(James Rolmaz or Joseph J. Sullivan)
J. C. Heffron, Millie Hylton, Joseph J. Sullivan

We're scraping the top of the barrel now as Mr N lurches into view. Recently his old grandad dropped off the twig leaving him some property, money and a hat. But what a very important hat it is we shall now discover from that chirpy cockney cocksparrow, all the way from his yacht on the Hackney Marshes (*or local*): Mr! / That was Mr N, proving the old saying: "If you want to get ahead, get a hat".

(*See also* Any Old Iron? *etc.*)

WHERE'S THE GOOD? 1911
(Harry Boden: Bert Brantford)
Harry Ford

There have been great changes in thought during this 19th century, new attitudes towards man's place in the cosmos led by great British intellects such as Darwin, Huxley, N... N? Yes, our Mr N now offers some fresh insights into the human condition, and so it is my honour to introduce the Sage of Streatham Hill (*or local*), Mr N. / There are several more stanzas to that song but Mr N thought What's the Good?

Song Introductions

WHICH SWITCH IS THE SWITCH MISS FOR IPSWICH?   1915
(Worton David & J. Barnett & Herman Darewski)
Murray Johnson, Jack Norworth
From "Rosy Rapture", Duke of York's

The subject of our next item is that most useful modern device the telephone. But the problem with this means of communication is having to obtain your number through the operator. Which is where the troubles start as we shall now discover from that silver-tongued charmer Mr N! / *(To person in front row)* Are you sitting in front of somebody with a lisp? They should have given you oilskins and a sou'wester.

(*See also* Hello! Ma Baby etc.)

WHILE STROLLING THRU THE PARK   1880
(Robert Keiser: E. D. Haley)
Du Rell Twin Brothers, Tom Howard & Patsy Barrett

Now we proudly present two artistes, each of either gender—ingenuity can surely go no further—two artistes who in No X re-enact the immortal and eternal theme of boy meets girl. So here Strolling Through the Park and into view are Miss M and Mr N. / Takes you back, doesn't it?

(*For other two-handers and/or possible concerted items see page 199*)

WHITE DOVE, THE   1912
(F. Clifford Grey: Franz Lehar)
Robert Michaelis, Lawrence Tibbett
From "Zigeunerliebe", Carltheater, Vienna 1910, London: Daly's

We always like to include a ballad in our programme, and so we continue with a number from Herr Franz Lehar's latest success Zigeunerliebe, known to us as Gypsy Love, from which Mr N has selected that sumptuous melody, The White Dove. Let us now relax to the silvery lyric tones of Mr N! / A delightful song, delightfully sung.

WHITE WINGS   1870
(Banks Winter)
Peter Dawson, Mohawk Minstrels, J. P. O'Keefe, Will Oakland, Manuel Romain, Thatcher Primrose & West Minstrels, Banks Winter

Certain songs sear themselves into our hearts and minds, and I'm sure you would agree that one which falls firmly into that category is White Wings. And here now to execute this wonderful ballad—and I choose my words carefully—are the gentlemen of the company (*alter to suit*). / White Wings, given the full treatment there—though I doubt if it'll ever recover—by (*give names*).

(*See also* And the Great Big Saw Came Nearer and Nearer *etc.*)

WHO'LL CARE FOR THE CHILDREN? 1899
(Charles Osborne)
Arthur Reece

Never far from our minds nowadays is the nagging awareness that in South Africa they're revolting. But our brave young men flock to the colours knowing that should they fall in battle their wives and in particular their children will be cared for. So it is my honour now to introduce a charitably-minded member of the leisured classes: Lady Virginia Water. / Makes you proud to be British, doesn't she?

(*See also* Army of Today's All Right, The *etc.*)

WHO PUT THE BRICKS IN BRIXTON? 1920
(Herbert Rule)
Syd Walker

We all like riddles and conundrums don't we? Which is why in his next turn Mr N will be posing some deuced puzzling brain-teasers. Thinking caps on then for the man who'll be tickling our curiosity and anything else within reach, Professor N. / God knows what that was all about...

(*See page 201 for further songs of London*)

WHO'S COMING UP IN THE GALLERY? 1894
(Bennett Scott)
Katie Lawrence

In No X Miss N reminds us of the popular melodramas to be seen nowadays in the penny gaffs and blood tubs of London and indeed any major British city. As Shakespeare himself said, "Rough winds do shake the darling buds of May," but here is a little darling welcome at any time of year Miss N. (*Encourage audience responses*) / Thank you, Miss N. A respite now from the exalted heights of the drama as we continue with...

WHO WERE YOU WITH LAST NIGHT? 1912
(Fred Godfrey & Mark Sheridan)
Mark Sheridan

Song Introductions 191

Mr N now moves the show along with No X, Who Were You With Last Night?, I suppose really that should be With Whom Were You Last Night?... This song was written and first sung by Mr Mark Sheridan, a major star of the Halls who alas in a fit of depression and feeling—wrongly—that he had lost his public, shot himself in Kelvingrove Park in Glasgow. (*Abruptly change from sombre mood to smiling brightness*) So let's see how Mr N gets on with it, shall we...? A frisky little number given a frisky little performance by a frisky little artiste: Mr N. / And who were you with last night, sir? I must say the one you've brought in this evening's much prettier...

WHY AM I ALWAYS THE BRIDESMAID? 1917
(Charles Collins & Fred W. Leigh)
Lily Morris

Consider the lot of Miss N, a lady who might be described as an involuntary spinster. Is Miss N forever doomed to that solitary cup of bedtime cocoa? Is her nightie forever fated to remain around her ankles? Here then hot-foot from a low church high altar is Miss N! / Any offers? Please yourselves... (*OR for a positive response*) Ah! One brave and charitable man amongst you. Well done, sir—not a missionary, are you? (*If she has played to a man in the audience*) Looks like you're on a promise!

(*See also* Joshu-ah *etc.*)

WHY DID I LEAVE MY LITTLE BACK ROOM IN BLOOMSBURY?
(Frank W. Carter & A. J. Mills)
Alf Chester   1898

Mr N now emerges from his dressing-room to ask us in No X why he left his Little Back Room in Bloomsbury. Perhaps it was simply to come and sing for us here tonight. Whatever the reason, it is always a pleasure to appreciate the quiet charm and the consummate artistry of Mr N.

(*See page 201 for further songs of London*)

WHY DID YOU MAKE ME CARE? 1912
(Sylvester Maguire: Alfred Solman)
Manuel Romain

No X, Why Did You Make Me Care?, a song which Miss N invests with that intensity of feeling which make her appearances before us so very special. Thrill now to that wonderfully vibrant and authentic voice of the Halls: Miss N. / A mighty talent—and a great heart...

WHY DO THEY ALWAYS PICK ON ME? *See* THEY ALWAYS PICK ON ME

WILD WILD WOMEN, THE 1917
(Al Wilson & Al Piantadosi)
The Versatile Three
From "Doing Our Bit", Winter Garden, New York

Ever since Eve failed to turn over a new leaf we wretched males have been helplessly in thrall to the charms of the fair sex. To be surrounded by Wild, Wild Women may sound ever man's idea of Nirvana but I fancy the reality would be somewhat—debilitating. Our next artiste relishes the prospect, however, so let us now relish the manly talents and charms of Mr N. / Mr N, who must be stronger than he looks.

WILL YOU LOVE ME IN DECEMBER AS YOU DO IN MAY? 1905
(James J. Walker: Ernest R. Ball)
Janet Allen, American Quartet, Ernest R. Ball, Norman Blair, Haydn Quartet, Spook Minstrels

The lyrics of our next song were written by a future Mayor of New York, Mr James J Walker. But the message remains universal—that tremulous plea from one lover to another, No X, Will You Love Me In December As You Do In May? Naturally the answer must be a resounding "yes", most especially when the question is posed by most earnest of enquirers, Mr/Miss N.

WITH MY LITTLE WIGGER WAGGER IN MY HAND 1909
(Fred Earle & Frank W. Carter & Gilbert Wells)
Fred Earle

The modish thoroughbred Mr N now gives a masterly demonstration of a certain auxiliary item of fashion essential for any gentleman wishing to cut a dash. Here he is, that perfect paragon of poise and panache, the Beau Brummell of the Halls, Mr N. / A dandy performance there from Mr N.

WITH THIS HAT ON 1911
(Fred J. Barnes: R. P. Weston)
Tom Woottwell

Mr N puts his cheery face round the proscenium arch with song new to me concerning the changes that the acquisition of a hat, tile, lid or tarpot can make to a man's fortunes. So now straining his talents to breaking point is Mr N. / He spent so much money on the hat there was nothing left over for the costume.

W.O.M.A.N. 1902
(Fred W. Leigh)
George Lashwood

Mr N reckons that he knows all there is to know about women, except the origin of the word Woman. Delving now then into the derivation of this interesting term in what might be called an etymological aria is the footloose and fancy-free Mr N.

WON'T YOU BUY MY PRETTY FLOWERS? 1876
(Arthur W. French: G. W. Persley)
George Clare (Mohawk Minstrels)

Despite Britain's greatness as a nation, her power and affluence, there are many in our society engaged in a constant wearisome battle against hunger, poverty and despair. In No X we meet one of these unfortunates, an innocent and vulnerable young flower-girl. Won't You Buy My Pretty Flowers? cries Miss N. / A most expressive portrayal by Miss N.

WON'T YOU PLAY A SIMPLE MELODY? See PLAY A SIMPLE MELODY

WORK, BOYS, WORK 1867
(Harry Clifton & J. Williams)
Harry Clifton, Fred French
Note: air, Tramp Tramp Tramp the Boys are Marching (GF Root's American Civil War song)

What can I saw about Mr N that hasn't so often been censored? The salt of the earth is our N. An honest man, a sincere man, a moral man— yes, he's a real brick... So here now with No X, an improving aria entitled Work Boys Work and Be Contented. And certainly contentment is our lot for the next few minutes as we meet and greet the late and great Mr N! / Mr N will be appearing again later on, but I'll give you due warning, never fear.

WOT CHER! 1891
(Albert Chevalier: Charles Ingle)
Albert Chevalier

And what's next...? Ah, yes ... a representative of shall we say?, the lower stratum of society (*if in London: coming as he does from sarf of the river ... shall we all try that?* sarf *of the river...*) but full of *joie de vivre* nonetheless, due to an unexpected legacy. Bursting to tell us all about this stroke of good fortune is the effervescent and the ebullient Mr N! / Mr N, a classic song and a classic rendition.

(*See also* Any Old Iron? *etc. for legacy songs and page 201 for further songs of London*)

WOTCHER, 'RIA *See* WHAT CHEER 'RIA

YARN OF THE NANCY BELL, THE 1869
(W. S. Gilbert)

Mr WS Gilbert, apart from his legendary collaboration with Sir Arthur Sullivan, has written any number of plays and comic poems. Mr N now regales us with one of the latter, those I'm bound to say I find it not so much comic as gruesome, especially when one realises that it is based on actual events. "The Yarn of the Nancy Bell" will now be given a suitably lip-smacking performance by Mr N. / Well done, sir. Well done, indeed. I think I'll cancel that summer cruise...

(*See also* Billy's Rose *etc.*)

YES, WE HAVE NO BANANAS 1923
(Frank Silver: Irving Cohn)
Eddie Cantor, Florrie Forde
Interpolated into "Make It Snappy", Winter Garden, New York

Question: what popular chorus melody starts with the Hallelujah Chorus, continues with I Dreamt That I Dwelt in Marble Halls and finishes up with four bars of My Bonnie Lies Over the Ocean? Give up? Well, it's No X, the fruiterer's theme song Yes, We Have No Bananas, as dished up by the man who has been described as the Banana of the Halls—he's thick-skinned and yellow—Mr N! / The gluttonous and glutinous Mr N.

(*See also* Boiled Beef and Carrots *etc. also* Girl that I M.A.R.R.Y, The*)*

YES YOU ARE 1891
(Arthur West)
Jenny Valmore

Miss N returns with a number which draws up the lines of battle between us chaps and the fair sex. *Vive la différence*, as the French say, so let us gird our loins—I love saying that—so let us gird our loins for the Grande Dame of the Halls: Miss N! (*Encourage audience to* respond "No, we're not!") / (Looking after her) No, we're not! A challenging performance there from Miss N.

YIP-I-ADDY-I-AY 1908
(Will D. Cobb: John H. Flynn)
George Grossmith jnr, Blanche Ring
From "The Merry Widow And The Devil", a burlesque version of "The Merry Widow", Weber & Fields' Music Hall, New York. In London interpolated into "Our Miss Gibbs", (Gaiety, 1909) and sung by George Grossmith jnr who also largely rewrote the lyrics.

It is said of our Mr N that he has an infinite capacity for taking praise, not surprising in one so talented and attractive and with so much charm and... (peering at notes) ... his writing's terrible. But here he comes, with the quaint story of Herr Bellow who played the cello, Mr Personality himself, N! / What about those lyrics in the last verse?! "Such excitement he was in, he bought some more rosin..." They don't write 'em like that any more... thank God.

(For performance in German costume and accent) And so to a gentlemen from the continong, a foreign personage from a little Austrian village called Klaxen-Geshtumfen-Poofen, who will be appearing in traditional costume—showing his bare knees! Is (local) ready for this? A touch of the Tyrol now from Herr (cod-German version of singer's name)! / Well done, sir—excellent—I have to say that or he becomes a very sour kraut indeed.

YOU AIN'T ASHAMED OF ME, ARE YOU, BILL? 1895
(J. P. Harrington: George Le Brunn)
Alec Hurley, Rosie Lloyd

The young wife, nervous and perhaps lacking in self-confidence, must find dealings with her new husband's friends and family such a dreadful ordeal. A pitiful concern for her man's approval is the subject of No X, a song with that most heart-breaking of titles You Ain't Ashamed of Me, Are You, Bill? (If a male) So let's find out for here is Bill, in the person of our very own Mr N. (If female) So let's do what we can to encourage and to reassure Miss N. / I don't think N has anything to worry about, do you?

YOU CAN DO A LOT OF THINGS AT THE SEASIDE THAT YOU CAN'T DO IN TOWN 1911
(Charles Ridgewell & George A. Stevens)
Mark Sheridan

According to No X You Can Do A Lot of Things by the Seaside that You Can't Do In Town. A list of these activities, or at least those that won't lose us our licence, will now be adumbrated by the big Heavy Swell of the Sea himself: Mr N! / We'd like to congratulate Mr N on his engagement next summer entertaining on the Goodwin Sands… (*or local danger spot*)… Has pom-poms, can swim…

(*See also* All the Girls are Lovely by the Seaside *etc.*)

YOU CAN'T DO THAT THERE 'ERE 1935
(Raymond Wallace: Jack Rolls)
Mrs Jack Hylton, Jack Payne & his Band

Onwards and upwards with a gentleman who now warbles his way through a song called You Can't Do That There 'Ere. Ignoring this injunction and doing it both here and now is the rollicking and rip-roaring Mr N. / That's put us all in a good mood, I'm sure.

YOU CAN'T DO WITHOUT A BIT OF LOVE 1916
(Andrew Allen & Bert Lee)
Kirkby & Hudson

Our next artiste is a lady who needs no encomium from me, so highly is she held in your regard, especially in the style of song she is about to favour us with now. No X, You Can't Do Without a Bit of Love, and who would wish for one moment to challenge that sumptuous stunner, Miss N. / Miss N, without the slightest suggestion of the suggestive.

YOU DO SOON CHANGE YOUR MIND 1903
(Harry Boden: Bert Brantford)
Harry Ford

Now to a lamentable lay from Mr N, who has been mucked about, ladies and gentlemen—mucked about something cruel. So let's give a positive welcome if you please to one who has been a veritable victim of vacillation, Mr N.

YOU'LL HAVE TO MARRY ME NOW 1895
(Charles Brighton)
Charles Brighton

You'll Have to Marry Me Now trills our Miss N. What has she been up to? The mind boggleth. A somewhat suggestive title it's true but I'm sure we need fear no embarrassment from that frankly forward female, Miss N. / (*If busty*) There's a lady who'll never be left on the shelf—she carries it round with her.

YOU MADE ME LOVE YOU 1913
(Joseph McCarthy: Jimmie V. Monaco)
Al Jolson, Grace La Rue, Ella Retford, Florence Smithson, Willie Solar, Beth Tate, Lee White
Included in "Keep Smiling", Alhambra

1. (*For male*) You Made Me Love You sighs Mr N, and I'm sure every lady in the audience sighs in sympathy. Here then, plunging us into the turgid waters of emotional torment, is the suavely susceptible Mr N. / (*To couple*) Did you enjoy that, madam? She's nicely warmed up for you now, sir. I should get her home quick if I were you. Don't both with the rest of the show...

2. (*For female*) You Made Me Love You sighs the next lady to grace our stage. Yes, plunging us into the turbulent waters of emotional torment is an artiste who never fails to delight, desport, nay disarm: Miss N. / I don't know who that song was directed to but he'll need to be fit. (*If she vamps the chairman put your fingers in your collar and say: "I wish it was the interval..."*)

YOUNG MAN WHO WORKED AT THE MILK SHOP 1901
(A. J. Mills & Frank W. Carter)
Marie Kendall

Miss N tells us of the romantic entanglement between one Florrie and the Young Man who worked at the Milk Shop. With this lacteous lay is the young lady whose dark-blonde beauty and steadfast virtue make my every waking moment a torment: Miss N. / Miss N, may her cream never curdle.

(*See also* Polly Perkins of Paddington Green)

YOUR BABY 'AS GORN DAHN THE PLUG'OLE 1944
(Jack Spade)
Elsa Lanchester
From "Ditties from the Ditty Box" by "Jack Spade", a composite name for Elton Box, Desmond Cox and Lewis Ilda, this last being a pseudonym of the original publisher, Irwin Dash. A version by Morey Amsterdam and Kay Patrick was published in the US in 1946 under the title Your Baby Has Gone Down the Drainpipe.

We pay tribute now to the finest, most selfless of womanly virtues: mother-love. To my surprise I've found this admirable quality exists not just in people like us—you know, our sort—but in the common people as well. And to prove it let us hear a quite remarkable story of maternal devotion from Miss N. / She's not really upset—only acting.

YOU'RE THE FLOWER OF MY HEART (SWEET ADELINE)   1903
(R. Husch Gerard: Harry Armstrong)
George Donaldson (Symphony Quartet), Haydn Quartet, Peerless Quartet, Quaker City Four

An American song written in 1896 caused no great stir under the title Down Home In Old New England, but when a Mr Richard Gerard re-wrote the lyrics it became a roaring success. We know it now as Sweet Adeline, and to sing it for us: Mr N. / Mr N with Sweet Adeline. Having mentioned the lyricist, Mr Richard H Gerard, it's only fair that I mention the composer, Mr Harry Armstrong, who also wrote another song beloved of barbershop quartets: Nellie Dean—but that's for another time, perhaps.

SONGS FOR TWO-HANDED OR CONCERTED PERFORMANCE

Across the Bridge
And the Great Big Saw Came Nearer and Nearer
Buttercup, The
By the Light of the Silvery Moon
Comrades
Dance of the Grizzly Bear, The
Excelsior
Folkestone for the Day
Four-'Oss Sharrybang, The
Green Eye of the Little Yellow God
Happy Eliza and Converted Jane
Hard Times Come Again No More
He's Going There Every Night
If You Were the Only Girl in the World
(In the) Dingle Dongle Dell
Keys of Heaven, The
Let's Wait and See the Pictures
Merry Widow Waltz, The
Moon Has Raised Her Lamp Above, The
Moonlight Bay
More Work for the Undertaker
Nonsense! Yes! by Jove!
Oh Flo! (Why Do You Go?)
Paradise for Two, A
Play a Simple Melody
Rum-tiddley-um-tum-tay
Tell Me Pretty Maiden
Tenor and Baritone
There's Danger on the Line
They Didn't Believe Me
Those Wedding Bells Shall Not Ring Out
Wait Till the Clouds Roll by

Watchman! What of the Night?
When the Summer Comes Again
When You and I Were Young, Maggie
When You Live Opposite to Me
While Strolling Thru the Park
White Wings

Many seaside songs are amenable to concerted treatment—See *All the Girls are Lovely by the Seaside* etc, as are railway songs—see *Casey Jones* etc.

SONGS OF LONDON

Across the Bridge
Algy, or the Piccadilly Johnny with the Little Glass Eye
Bond Street Tea-walk, The
Burlington Bertie from Bow
Can London Do Without Me?
Chalk Farm to Camberwell Green
Coffee Shop at Pimlico, The
Coster Girl in Paris, The
Coster's Serenade, The
Dancing on the Streets
Dear Old Shepherd's Bush
From Marble Arch to Leicester Square
Give My Regards to Leicester Square
Hampstead is the Place to Ruralize
If It Wasn't for the 'Ouses in Between
I Live in Trafalgar Square
I Think I'll Buy Piccadilly
Lambeth Walk, The
Let's All Go Down the Strand
Lord Mayor's Coachman, The
Mystery of a Hansom Cab, The
Patchwork Garden, The
Percy from Pimlico
Piccadilly
Polly Perkins of Paddington Green
Postman's Holiday, The
Ratcatcher's Daughter, The
She Told Me to Meet Her at the Gate
Since I Came to London Town
Take a Look at Me Now
Take Me in a Taxi, Joe
They Built Piccadilly for Me
Trixie of Upper Tooting

Wedding March, The
Where are the Lads of the Village Tonight?
Who Put the Bricks in Brixton?
Why Did I Leave My Little Back Room in Bloomsbury?
Wot Cher!

The Ballad of Sam Hall, Down at the Old Bull and Bush, Ev'rybody Knows Me in My Old Brown Hat, Fall in and Follow Me and *She Was Poor But She Was Honest* also mention London incidentally. Not included in the introductions but recommended is Harry Dacre's lovely quiet melody *While London's Fast Asleep* (first sung by Marie Tyler in 1896).

INDEX

1. Artistes

Adams, Annie, 70, 103, 176
Alabama Barnstormers, 43
Albert, Arthur, 47
Albert, Fred, 41
Allen, Janet, 31, 192
Allin, Norman, 56, 134
American Quartet, 55, 99, 192
American Ragtime Octette, 75, 100, 133, 178
Anderson, Harry, 67
'Ary, Armand, 158

Baker, Bobby, 129
Baker, Elsie, 142
Baldwin, Minnie, 72
Ball, Ernest R., 121, 186, 192
Banks, Winona, 179
Bard, Wilkie, 45, 79, 91, 101, 102, 153, 154
Barnes, Fred, 51, 58, 66, 136
Barr, Ida, 54, 133
Barrett, George, 130
Barrett, Patsy, 189
Barrie, Leonard, 171
Barry, H. C., 64
Barry, Leonard, 49
Barry, Lydia, 54
Bass, George, 37, 148
Bastow, George, 39, 62, 117, 155, 176
Bates, Thorpe, 26, 27, 57, 139
Bayes, Nora, 71, 93, 118, 148, 156
Beauchamp, George, 64, 155
Beaufoi, Percy, 143
Beck, Clara, 86
Bedford, Harry, 86, 111, 135
Belfry, Venie, 82
Bell, Frank, 42
Bell, May A., 31, 87
Bellwood, Bessie, 74, 183
Bennett, Billy, 70, 156

Bennett, T. C. Sterndale, 162
Bentley, Irene, 139
Bernard, Peter, 178
Bignell, Charles, 121
Billings, Bud & Joe, 88
Birch, Harry, 148
Blair, Norman, 163, 192
Blakemore, Nora, 101
Blanchard, Miss E., 164
Blaney, Norah, 133
Bliss, Louise, 24
Blyth, Vernon, 48, 185
Bordini, Irene, 51
Bori, Lucrezia, 112
Brett, Marie, 107
Brice, Elizabeth, 29
Brice, Fanny, 178
Brighton, Charles, 196
Brogden, Gwendoline, 86
Bronson, Percy, 72
Brothers, Hedges, 130
Brothers, Leighton, 61
Brough, Robert, 130
Brunne, Adrienne, 171
Burchell, Kathleen, 78
Burnand, Lily, 175
Burns, Joe, 46
Bury, Felix, 63
Butt, Clara, 106, 107, 113, 114, 123

Cabella, Mlle C., 47
Caine, Georgia, 77
Cameron, Violet, 68
Campanini, Italo, 58
Campbell, Herbert, 130
Campobello, Signor, 93
Cantor, Eddie, 194
Carlton, Harry, 19
Carney, Kate, 23, 48, 62, 84, 112, 137, 172, 187
Carrington, Nell, 160
Carus, Emma, 17, 28, 46, 71, 80, 179

Caruso, Enrico, 27, 36, 60, 68, 113, 117
Cash, Morny, 86
Castle, Irene & Vernon, 48, 185
Castleton, Kate, 163
Cave, Herbert, 76
Cave, Hubert, 119, 180
Cavendish, Harry, 1
Celli, Frank, 157
Chambers, Miss E., 109
Champion, Harry, 22, 33, 45, 54, 55, 65, 88, 90, 111, 146, 168, 182
Charles-Hirsch, Caroline, 109
Cheetham, Joseph, 44, 150
Chester, Alf, 191
Chester, Fred, 18
Chevalier, Albert, 45, 56, 62, 103, 125, 193
Christian, Albert, 161
Christy Minstrels, 27, 43, 65, 149, 157
Clare, George, 193
Clare, Jenny, 81
Clarke, Henri, 103, 154
Clarke, Lucy, 137
Clarke, Tom, 110
Cliff, Laddie, 110, 163
Clifton, Harry, 49, 53, 144, 146, 178, 182, 193
Cline, Maggie, 24
Coates, John, 44, 117, 163
Coborn, Charles, 116, 175
Coffin, Hayden, 119, 125, 161
Cohen, Meyer, 121
Collins, Arthur, 17, 100, 127, 148
Collins, José, 139
Collins, Lottie, 167
Colquhoun, Ian, 134
Connolly, Dolly, 120, 178
Conor, Harry, 33
Cooper, Margaret, 77, 92, 140, 179
Coote, Bert, 80
Cornille, Marguerite, 73
Costello, Tom, 25, 32, 44, 68, 125, 156
Cotton, Billy, 116
Courtney, Maud, 76
Cove, Harry, 160, 188
Cove, Kate, 68

Cowell, Sam, 130, 147, 177
Cowl, Jane, 160
Cox, Jimmie, 129
Coyne, Fred, 174
Coyne, Joe, 118
Crumit, Frank, 61
Cunliffe, Whit, 56, 93, 96, 110, 169
Curtis, Mae, 109
Cuthburt, Sisters, 71

Dacre, Harry, 131
Dagmar, Alexandra, 39
Damerell and Rutland, 159
Daniels, Fred T., 24
Danvers, Johnny, 9, 71, 99
Davenport, Harry, 114
Davies, Ben, 117
Dawn, Hazel, 123
Dawson, Peter, 31, 56, 57, 58, 76, 106, 136, 141, 150, 189
Day, Edith, 18
de Rance, Haidee, 171
de Savigny, Julie, 92
De Vere, Flo, 112
Dee, Kitty, 158
Delaney, Nora, 186
Dockstader, Lew, 118
Donaldson, George, 198
Doreen, Lilian, 45
D'Orme, Aileen, 176
Dormer, Daisy, 16, 81, 85, 102, 123, 144, 187
Douglas, Eileen, 150
Drever, Constance, 118, 124, 177
Dryden, Leo, 119
Du Four Boys, 36
Du Maurier, George, 36
Du Rell Twin Brothers, 189
Duggan, Maggie, 89, 116
Dunning, Alice, 176
Dunville, T. E., 89

Earle, Fred, 59, 81, 153, 192
Earle, Hamilton, 106
Edgar, Marriott, 151
Ediss, Connie, 34
Edwards, Gus, 171
Eisdell, Hubert, 56, 107, 139, 150
Elen, Gus, 23, 52, 53, 54, 67, 83, 96,

Index

122, 127, 128, 179
Elliott, G. H., vii, ix, 73, 100, 110
Ellis, Harry, 68
Elsie, Lily, 113, 118, 177
Emerald, Nora, 119
Emerson, Ida, 73
Emmett, J. K., 149
Essex, Clifford, 76
Essex, Violet, 74

Fair, W. B., 173
Farkoa, Maurice, 63, 140
Farren, Nellie, 183
Faulkner, Edith, 73
Fawn, James, 25
Federici, Frederick, 152
Fern, Sable, 184
Fields, Gracie, 29, 31
Fields, Happy Fanny, 37
Finette, Mlle, 38
Fink, Edith, 133, 145
Fisher, Gladys, 179
Fisher, Sallie, 142
Fletcher, Lizzie, 159
Florence, Evangeline, 112
Florence, Mrs W. J., 39
Flory, Regine, 144
Ford, Harry, 186, 188, 196
Forde, Florrie, 17, 31, 41, 47, 52, 58, 60, 62, 66, 68, 71, 72, 94, 97, 103, 116, 117, 133, 138, 145, 154, 155, 165, 171, 174, 179, 194
Formby, George, 94, 102, 105, 132, 142
Foster, Charles, 32, 155
Foster, Ivor, 106, 119, 180
Fox, Della, 87
Fox, Harry, 1
Foy, Ernest, ix
Fragson, Harry, 19, 73
Francis, James, 153
Freear, Louie, 117, 175
Freeman, Harry, 39, 64, 109
French, Fred, 103, 193
French, Percy, 141
Fyffe, Will, 78, 90

Galbraith, Beatrice, 109
Gallimore, Florrie, 98, 124

Geistinger, Marie, 47
Gigli, Beniamino, 117, 121, 169
Gilson, Lottie, 111, 118, 121, 157
Girardi, Alexander, 119
Gitana, Gertie, 51, 94, 127, 128, 185
Glaser, Lulu, 76
Gluck, Alma, 113
Glynne, Walter, 160
Godfrey, Charles, 16, 67, 126
Godwin, Will, 83
Gordon, Alf, 82, 148, 153
Gordon, Harry, 89
Grain, Corney, 61, 143
Graves, George, 50
Green, Evie, 176
Green, Gene, 133
Green, Mabel, 85
Grosse, Charles, 130
Grossmith jnr, George, 104, 122, 171, 174, 179, 195
Grover, Russell, 35
Guilbert, Yvette, 21, 57, 107, 111
Gunther, Mizzie, 118, 177

Hallam, Basil, 65
Harlan, Byron G., 17, 100, 127, 179
Harrison, Charles W., 121
Harrison, Denham, 66
Harrison, John, 56, 117
Harrison, William, 119, 169
Hart, Annie, 165
Hawthorne, Lil, 80, 86, 123, 165
Haydn Quartet, 192, 198
Haydon, Ethel, 108
Hayes, Catherine, 173
Hayes, Milton, 70
Heffron, J. C., 188
Held, Anna, 85
Helene, Eily, 179
Henson, Leslie, 70, 122
Hetherington, Dot, 33
Hicks, Seymour, 21
Hill, Hamilton, 32, 45, 68, 188
Hill, Jenny, 33
Hite, Mabel, 127
Holloway, Stanley, 34, 70, 151
Hooey, William, 116
Howard, Joe, 73
Howard, Tom, 189

Hudson, Harry, 161
Hudson, Olga & Elga & Eli, 163
Hudson, Thomas, 163
Hughes, Tom E., 38, 102
Hunter, G. W., 158
Hurley, Alec, 24, 78, 108, 195
Hylton, Jack, 135, 152
Hylton, Millie, 111, 188
Hylton, Mrs Jack, 196

Irwin, May, 87, 100

Jackley, George, 181
Jacks, Jacques, 77
Jacobson, 23, 130
James, Daisy, 100
Janis, Elsie, 66, 160
Jerome, Daisy, 22, 150
Johnson, Carroll, 29
Johnson, Murray, 100, 189
Jolson, Al, 17, 35, 37, 55, 60, 99, 160, 162, 163, 178, 185, 197
Jones, Ada, 29, 85, 144, 170
Jones, Alma, 117, 175
Judge, Jack, 97

Keen, Kit, 167
Kellogg, Shirley, 161
Kendall, Marie, 31, 50, 86, 106, 107, 126, 165, 175, 197
King, Charles, 29, 142
King, Hetty, viii, ix, 20, 87, 88, 141, 184
Kirby, Gerald, 72
Kirkby and Hudson, 161, 196
Kirkby, Stanley, 106, 161, 168, 179
Knowles, R. G., 34

La Rue, Grace, 197
Labette, Dora, 107, 169
Lanchester, Elsa, 197
Lane, Jack, 147
Lashwood, George, 16, 18, 94, 97, 134, 148, 188, 193
Latona, Jen, 100
Lauder, Harry, 87, 149, 151, 163, 181, 182
Laurier, Jay, 80, 165
Lawlor, Charles B., 157

Lawrence, Katie, 47, 52, 133, 190
Laye, Evelyn, 135
Leamar, Alice, 21, 167
Leamore, Tom, 140, 164
Legarde, Millie, 73, 77
Lena, Lily, 165
Lennard, Arthur, 110, 160
Leno, Dan, vii, 69, 122, 165
Lenton, Olive, 156
Leslie, William, 106
Lester, Alfred, 124, 138
Lester, Frank, 50
L'Estrange, Nellie, 134
Levey, Ethel, 17, 54, 118, 142
Lew Hearn and Bonita, 75
Leybourne, George, 9, 41, 49, 59, 103, 132, 154, 176
Leyton, George, 34
Lherie, Paul, 58
Libbey, J. Aldrich, 16
Lillie, Beatrice, 100, 169
Lindon, Millie, 60, 113, 159, 160
Liston, Harry, 103
Lloyd, Arthur, 46, 116, 145
Lloyd, Edward, 76, 169
Lloyd, Florence, 139
Lloyd, Marie, vii, x, 21, 22, 27, 33, 44, 51, 55, 59, 96, 99, 112, 122, 129, 131, 133, 147, 151, 152, 153, 170, 172, 173, 181, 183, 184, 186
Lloyd, Marie jnr, vii-viii
Lloyd, Rosie, 195
Lloyd, Sisters, 113
Lockett, Lou, 84
Loftus, Cissie, 111
Loftus, Marie, 74, 168
Lomax, Fawcett, 130
Loraine, Violet, 70, 84, 90, 110
Lorraine, Lillian, 37, 150
Lunn, Louise Kirkby, 113
Lupino, Stanley, 85

McCormack, John, 27, 31, 44, 103, 106, 115, 121, 149, 160, 163, 164, 186
McCullough, Carl, 161
Macdermott, G. H., 53, 114, 169
MacDonough, Harry, 68, 80, 187
McHugh, John, 49

Index

McIntyre, Leila, 139
Mackay, Julie, 73, 80, 93
Mackinder, Lionel, 174
Majilton, Madeline, 81
Marshall, Edward, 63
Marshall, Eric, 128
Mason, Fred, 187
Matthews, H. P., 113
May, Maggie, 176
Maybrick, Michael, 76
Mayne, Clarice, 17, 35, 44, 56, 63, 66, 82, 97, 98, 101, 103, 105, 131, 133, 147
Mayne, Ernie, 79, 126, 154, 182, 184
Mayo, Sam, 81, 104, 146, 153, 154
Melba, Nellie, 24
Merson, Billy, 128, 136, 162
Michaelis, Robert, 189
Midnight Minstrels, The, 181
Mill, Paul, 139
Millar, Gertie, 40, 120, 175
Miller, Max, 165
Minstrel Companies, All, 69
Mohawk Minstrels, 178, 189, 193
Monks, Victoria, 29, 38, 67, 84
Moore and Burgess Minstrels, 135, 178, 157
Moore-Duprez, May, 37, 166
Mora, Helene, 171
Morell, Frank, 19
Morgan, Lloyd, 28
Morley, Victor, 77
Morris, Lily, 51, 79, 136, 174, 191
Mortimer, Maude, 82, 97
Mudge, Eva, 29
Muir, Minnie, 97
Mullane, Frank, 100
Munroe, Walter, 95, 126, 165
Murray, Billy, 17, 29, 118, 133, 142
Murray, Elizabeth, 17, 87
Murray, Slade, 43

Neagle, Anna, 18
Nicholls, Harry, 130
Nichols, Emma J., 39
Nilsson, Christine, 173
Nolan, Michael, 111
Norman, Horace, 43
Norrice, James, 31

Norrie, James, 65
North, Bobby, 72
Norworth, Jack, 60, 69, 107, 156, 160, 189
Nugent, Maude, 165

Oakland, Will, 46, 93, 121, 135, 157, 164, 178, 187, 189
O'Keefe, J. P., 189
Olcott, Chauncey, 121, 186
O'Neil, Denis, 141
O'Neill, Dan, 107
Orme, Gerald, 186
O'Shea, Tessie, 129

Parsons, Phil, 127
Passmore, Walter, 139
Pastor, Tony, 132, 173
Patti, Adelina, 76, 173
Paul, Howard, 153
Payne, Edmund, 175
Payne, Herbert, 66, 82, 120, 130, 149
Payne, Jack & His Band, 196
Payne, Millie, 71
Pearce, Albert, 37
Pearce, Lizzie, 35
Peerce, Jan, 187
Peerless Quartet, 109, 198
Pelissier, H. G., 159
Petrova, Olga, 124
Phillips, Mrs F. R., 103
Piccolomini, Maria, 35
Pike, Ernest, 27, 56, 65, 82, 150, 168, 169
Pitt, Archie, 50
Pleasants, Jack, 43, 91, 97, 129, 173, 180
Pounds, Courtice, 167
Pounds, Louie, 33
Power, Nellie, 33, 176
Price, Denham, 27
Price, Georgie, 37
Primrose and Dockstader Minstrels, 68
Pryde, Peggy, 162
Purcell, Annie, 37
Pyne, Louisa, 81

Quaker City Four, 198

Radford, Robert, 56
Rafferty, Pat, 165
Rainforth, Elizabeth, 81
Ramsden, Cissy, 84
Randall, Harry, 64, 98, 102
Randall, W., 41
Ray, Phil, 83
Raymond, Ruby, 54
Read, John, 69
Reece, Arthur, 32, 162, 171, 186, 190
Reeve, Ada, 37, 88, 169, 174
Reeves, Sims, 44
Rene, Ida, 35
Retford, Ella, 19, 20, 37, 72, 73, 75, 85, 87, 100, 101, 119, 144, 145, 154, 161, 166, 171, 197
Rhodes, John, 1-2
Rhodes, William, 2
Richardson, Foster, 56
Rickaby, J. W., 95, 115, 140, 171
Rickards, Harry, 71, 75
Ridley, George, 46
Rigolboche, 38
Ring, Blanche, 93, 98, 130, 179, 195
Ritchard, Cyril, 70
Ritte, Philip, 150
Roberts, Arthur, 16, 47
Robey, George, vii, 22, 27, 84, 92, 95, 141
Robson, Frederick, 177
Romain, Manuel, 46, 189, 191
Romaine, Violet, 19
Rooney, Pat, 87
Rosewood, Lillian, 93
Ross, W. G., 26
Rowland, Adele, 138
Royle, Kate, 53
Rudd, Austin, 32
Rule, Herbert, 79
Rumford, Kennerley, 107
Russell, Bobbie, 100
Russell, Henry, 69, 163
Russell, Leonard, 27
Russell, Lillian, 26, 43

Sablon, Jean, 57
Samuels, Rae, 100
Sanders, Madge, 171
Sanderson, Julia, 171
Santley, Charles, 119
Sarony, Leslie, 21, 85
Sara, Mlle (Sarah Wright), 38
Scheff, Fritzi, 185
Scott, Maidie, 31, 57, 76, 83, 87, 89, 104
Seeley, Blossom, 160
Seeley, Frank, 20
Shand, Ernest, 25, 37
Shand, Ernie, 183
Sharman, Jack, 170
Shelley, Lilian, 144
Sheridan, Mark, 28, 37, 73, 74, 80, 170, 190, 195
Sherrington, Louie, 176
Shields, Ella, 36
Shine, J. L., 130
Sisters, Farber, 55
Smiles, Jack, 60, 91
Smithson, Florence, 142, 150, 197
Solar, Willie, 100, 197
Soldene, Emily, 157
Spencer, Elizabeth, 29
Spook Minstrels, 192
Spurr, Mel B., 172
Stanford, Molly Wood, 36
Steele, Albert, 70
Stella, Esta, 120
Sterling, Antoinette, 113, 114
Stewart and Gillen, 93
Stimson, Fred, 130
Stratton, Eugene, 110
Sullivan, Joseph J., 188
Sutton, Randolph, vii, viii, 66, 136, 185
Symphony Quartet, 198

Talley, Harry, 179
Tate, Beth, 30, 166, 197
Tate, Harry, 68
Taylor, Evelyn, 25
Taylor, Harry, 60, 131
Tempest, Marie, 20, 119
Temple, Madge, 30, 54, 90
Templeton, Fay, 115
Tennyson and Wallis, 181
Terriss, Ellaline, 17, 76, 98, 111, 112, 139, 158

Index

Terry, Will "Alf Gordon", 153
Tetrazzini, Luisa, 24
Teyte, Maggie, 27, 123
Thatcher Primrose & West Minstrels, 189
Thorne, Mabel, 165
Thornton, Bonnie, 118, 126, 188
Thornton, Edna, 49, 114, 123
Thorpe, Herbert, 56
Three Rascals, The, 72, 75, 100
Thurber, Leona, 93
Thursby, Emma, 173
Tibbett, Lawrence, 136, 189
Tich, Little, vii, x, 160
Tierney, Harry, 84
Tiffany, Maud, 17, 54
Tilley, Vesta, vii, 16, 18, 24, 59, 61, 105, 118, 120, 152, 164
Tomlin, Blanche, 142
Toole, J. L., 130, 177
Tree, Maria, 76
Treumann, Louis, 118
Trevelyan, Hilda, 117, 175
Troupe, Colonna, 38
Tucker, Sophie, 48, 69, 161
Twist, Quentin, 36
Two Bobs, The, 17, 40, 60, 138, 178
Two Rascals, The, 23
Tyler, Marie, 202

Valmore, Jenny, 194
Van Blunt, Walter, 29
Vance, Alfred, 41, 103, 130
Vance, Clarice, 80
Vance, Eunice, 21
Vane, Sybil, 106
Varney, A. Frank, 107
Vaughan, Kate, 134
Versatile Three, The, 192
Vestris, Lucy, 39
Victoria, Vesta, 47, 72, 95, 96, 101, 128, 131, 134, 137, 144, 166, 178
Vincent, Ruth, 180
Vokes, May, 87

Waldron, Jack, 84
Walker, Syd, 190
Wallace, Nellie, 176
Ward, Dorothy, 77, 99, 166

Ward, May, 31
Ware, Mrs G., 103
Wentworth, Fanny, 172
West, Arthur, 39
Wheatley, Horace, 175
Whelan, Albert, vii, viii, 40, 45, 141, 145
White, Lee, 56, 69, 161, 197
Whitney, Ann, 16
Whittle, Charles R., 30, 48, 56, 68, 71, 109, 119, 124, 146
Williams, Billy, 132, 181, 185, 186
Williams, Bransby, 70, 141, 157
Williams, Gus, 118
Williams, Norman, 61
Williams, W. H., 19
Williams, Walter, 107
Wilton, Robb, 26
Windom, Constance, 79
Windom, W. H., 171
Winter, Banks, 189
Winters, Mike & Bernie, viii
Witmark, Julius P., 188
Wood, Daisy, 68, 100
Wood, Sisters, 42
Woottwell, Tom, 192
Wyndham, S. W., 155
Wynn, Bessie, 19
Wynne, Wish, 137

Yohe, May, 111

Zigeuner Quartet, 82
Zimbalist, Efrem, 113
Zolari, C. A., 35

2. Lyricists and Composers

Abrahams, Maurice
   HE'D HAVE TO GET UNDER (GET OUT AND GET UNDER), 72
Abrahams, Maurice and Muir, Lewis F.
   HITCHY-KOO, 75
Adams, Harry
   GOLDEN WEDDING, THE, 67
Adams, Harry and Coyne, Fred
   TUNER'S OPPOR-TUNER-TY,

174
Adams, J.
  See Dance, George, 175
Adams, Stephen
  HOLY CITY, THE, 76
Ager, Milton and Meyer, George W.
  EVERYTHING IS PEACHES DOWN IN GEORGIA, 55
Aïdé, Hamilton
  CZARDAS, 47
  LAUGHING SONG, THE, 109
"AJC"
  MARRIED TO A MERMAID, 116
Albert, Arthur
  See Snape, P. H., 47
Allen, Andrew
  See Stanley, Wynn, 37
Allen, Andrew and Lee, Bert
  YOU CAN'T DO WITHOUT A BIT OF LOVE, 196
Amsterdam, Morey and Patrick, Kay
  YOUR BABY HAS GONE DOWN THE DRAINPIPE, 197
Andrews, C. Bond
  SIGNALMAN ON THE LINE, THE, 157
Anonymous
  BIRMINGHAM JAIL, 31
  FRANKIE AND JOHNNY, 61
  IN JERSEY CITY, 92
  KEYS OF HEAVEN, THE, 107
  PHILOSOPHY (A BEE ONCE LIGHTED ON A FLOWER), 140
  RATCATCHER'S DAUGHTER, THE, 147
  RIDING DOWN FROM BANGOR, 148
  SHE WAS POOR BUT SHE WAS HONEST, 156
  SPIDER AND THE FLY, THE, 163
  VILLIKINS AND HIS DINAH, 177
  WATCHMAN! WHAT OF THE NIGHT?, 180
Anstey, F.
  BURGLAR BILL, 35

Arden, Hope
  RIDING ON A LOAD OF HAY, 148
Armstrong, A. E.
  SAILOR'S FAREWELL, THE, 152
Armstrong, Harry
  NELLIE DEAN, 127
  YOU'RE THE FLOWER OF MY HEART (SWEET ADELINE), 198
Arthurs, George
  See David, Worton, 79, 91, 101
  See Lee, Bert, 105
  See Leigh, Fred W., 98, 112
  IT'S A DIFFERENT GIRL AGAIN!, 96
Arzonia, Joe
  PREACHER AND THE BEAR, THE, 145
Asaf, George
  PACK UP YOUR TROUBLES IN YOUR OLD KITBAG, 138
Asher, Angelo A.
  TA-RA-RA-BOOM-DE-AY, 167
Atteridge, Harold R.
  BY THE BEAUTIFUL SEA, 36
Austin, Fred
  I'M GOING BACK TO HIMAZAS, 89
Ayer, Nat D.
  See Brown, A. Seymour, 133
  DEAR OLD SHEPHERD'S BUSH, 50
  IF YOU WERE THE ONLY GIRL IN THE WORLD, 84
  IN OTHER WORDS, 92
  LET THE GREAT BIG WORLD KEEP TURNING, 110
  VICAR AND I WILL BE THERE, THE, 177
Ayer, Nat D. and Lee, Bert
  NOBODY NOTICED ME, 129

Balfe, Michael W.
  COME INTO THE GARDEN, MAUD, 44
  EXCELSIOR, 56
  I DREAMT THAT I DWELT IN MARBLE HALLS, 81

THEN YOU'LL REMEMBER ME, 169
Ball, Ernest R.
  WHEN IRISH EYES ARE SMILING, 186
  WILL YOU LOVE ME IN DECEMBER AS YOU DO IN MAY?, 192
Ball, Ernest R. and Olcott, Chauncey
  MOTHER MACHREE, 121
Barclay, Lawrence
  HE CALLS ME HIS OWN GRACE DARLING, 72
Barclay, Lawrence and Murray, Fred
  OUR LODGER'S SUCH A NICE YOUNG MAN, 137
Barnes, Fred J.
  See Weston, R. P., 93, 98, 132, 185
  WITH THIS HAT ON, 192
Barnes, Fred J. and Collins, Charles
  SWEET LITTLE ROSE OF PERSIA, 164
Barnes, Fred J. and Weston, R. P.
  KISS THE GIRL IF YOU'RE GOING TO, 107
Barnes, Paul
  GOOD-BYE, DOLLY GRAY, 68
Barnett, J.
  See David, Worton, 189
Barrett, Lester
  HELLO, SUSIE GREEN, 73
Barrett, Oscar
  NONSENSE! YES! BY JOVE!, 130
Barri, Odoardo
  OLD BRIGADE, THE, 134
Barry, H. C.
  GHOST OF SHERLOCK HOLMES, THE, 64
Bastow, George
  See Leigh, Fred W., 39, 155
  GALLOPING MAJOR, THE, 62
Bateman, Edgar
  See Murphy, C. W., 122
  FOLKESTONE FOR THE DAY, 59
  IF IT WASN'T FOR THE 'OUSES IN BETWEEN, 83
  IT'S A GREAT BIG SHAME, 96
  LIZA JOHNSON, 112
  MY OLD PAL JOE, 125
Bateman, Edgar and Baynes, Eustace
  NICE QUIET DAY, A, 128
Bateman, Edgar and Mill, Paul
  PATCHWORK GARDEN, THE, 139
Bay
  HOW CAN A LITTLE GIRL BE GOOD?, 76
Bayes, Nora and Norworth, Jack
  SHINE ON HARVEST MOON, 156
Bayly, Thomas Haynes
  CAPTAIN WITH HIS WHISKERS, THE, 39
Baynes, Eustace
  See Bateman, Edgar, 128
Bays, R. E.
  PLEASE WILL YOU HOLD THE BABY, SIR?, 143
Beaton, Bob
  See Lauder, Harry, 151
Beauchamp, George and Osborne, Charles
  GET YOUR HAIR CUT, 64
Bedford, Harry
  IF YOU CAN'T DO ANY GOOD DON'T DO ANY HARM, 84
  WHEN THE SUMMER COMES AGAIN, 187
Bedford, Harry and Sullivan, Terry
  IT'S A BIT OF A RUIN THAT CROMWELL KNOCKED ABOUT A BIT, 96
Bedford, Harry and Weston, R. P.
  I LIKE YOUR TOWN, 86
Bell, Frank
  COFFEE SHOP AT PIMLICO, THE, 42
Bellwood, Bessie
  WHAT CHEER 'RIA, 183
Benedict, Jules
  MOON HAS RAISED HER LAMP ABOVE, THE, 119
Berlin, Irving
  See Snyder, Ted, 127
  ALEXANDER'S RAGTIME

BAND, 17
DANCE OF THE GRIZZLY BEAR, THE, 48
EVERYBODY'S DOIN' IT NOW, 54
I WANT TO BE IN DIXIE (I WANT TO GO BACK TO DIXIE), 100
I WANT TO GO BACK TO MICHIGAN (DOWN ON THE FARM), 100
IF THE MANAGERS ONLY THOUGHT THE SAME AS MOTHER, 83
PLAY A SIMPLE MELODY, 142
WHEN I LEAVE THE WORLD BEHIND, 185
Berlin, Irving and Goetz, E. Ray
WHEN I DISCOVERED YOU, 185
Bicknell, G.
CRUEL MARY HOLDER, 46
Bingham, C. Clifton
LOVE'S OLD SWEET SONG, 114
Birch, Harry
RIDING ON A LOAD OF HAY, 148
Bishop, Henry R.
HOME! SWEET HOME!, 76
Bizet, Georges
FLOWER SONG, 58
Black, H. Broughton
TENOR AND BARITONE, 168
Blake, James W. and Lawlor, Charles B.
DANCING ON THE STREETS, 48
SIDEWALKS OF NEW YORK, THE, 157
Blamphin, Charles
JUST TOUCH THE HARP GENTLY, 106
Blanchard, E. L.
'NORRIBLE TALE, A, 130
Boden, Harry
WHEN SHE WALKS, 186
WHERE'S THE GOOD?, 188
YOU DO SOON CHANGE YOUR MIND, 196
Bowers, F. V.
LUCKY JIM (HOW I ENVY HIM), 114
Bowyer, Fred
ACROSS THE BRIDGE, 16
DOWN WENT THE CAPTAIN, 53
Bowyer, Fred and Powell, Orlando
AFTER THE BALL, 16
Box, Elton and Cox, Desmond and Butler, Ralph
WE ALL WENT UP UP UP THE MOUNTAIN, 181
Box, Elton and Cox, Desmond and Ilda, Lewis
See Spade, Jack, 197
Bradley, Rev. Edward
RATCATCHER'S DAUGHTER, THE, 147
Brahe, May H.
BLESS THIS HOUSE, 31
Brantford, Bert
WHERE'S THE GOOD?, 188
YOU DO SOON CHANGE YOUR MIND, 196
Brennan, Robert H.
RING DOWN THE CURTAIN, 149
Brighton, Charles
YOU'LL HAVE TO MARRY ME NOW, 196
Broadwood, Lucy
I'M A MAN THAT'S DONE WRONG TO MY PARENTS, 88
Brooks, Shelton
SOME OF THESE DAYS, 161
Brown, A. Seymour and Ayer, Nat D.
OH, YOU BEAUTIFUL DOLL, 133
Brown, Lew
GIVE ME THE MOONLIGHT, 66
Bunn, Alfred
I DREAMT THAT I DWELT IN MARBLE HALLS, 81
THEN YOU'LL REMEMBER ME, 169

Index

Burley, Joe
  GIRLS, STUDY YOUR COOKERY BOOK, 66
Burley, Joe and Johnson, Cecil
  AYESHA, MY SWEET EGYPTIAN, 25
Burnand, F. C.
  BUTTERCUP, THE, 36
Butler, Ralph
  See Box, Elton, 181
Butterfield, J. A.
  WHEN YOU AND I WERE YOUNG, MAGGIE, 187

Caesar, Irving
  SWANEE, 163
Callahan, J. Will
  SMILES, 160
Cannon, Hughie
  BILL BAILEY, WON'T YOU PLEASE COME HOME?, 29
Cape, Fred
  TIN GEE-GEE, THE, 172
Carroll, Harry
  BY THE BEAUTIFUL SEA, 36
Carroll, Peter
  MILLER'S DAUGHTER, THE, 119
Carter, Frank W.
  See Earle, Fred, 192
  See Mills, A. J., 191, 197
Carter, Frank W. and Kind, John A. Glover
  LET'S WAIT AND SEE THE PICTURES, 110
Carter, Frank W. and Mills, A. J.
  HAS ANYBODY SEEN MY TIDDLER?, 71
  WHY DID I LEAVE MY LITTLE BACK ROOM IN BLOOMSBURY?, 191
Carter, Frank W. and Weston, R. P.
  BOYS OF THE CHELSEA SCHOOL, 34
Caryll, Ivan
  MY BEAUTIFUL LADY, 123
Castling, Harry
  See Mills, A. J., 32, 98
  DID YOUR FIRST WIFE EVER DO THAT?, 50
  LET'S HAVE FREE TRADE AMONGST THE GIRLS, 110
  NO, 'ARRY, DON'T ASK ME TO MARRY, 129
  ONE OF THE SHABBY GENTEEL, 135
  OUR THREEPENNY HOP, 137
  THOUGH ALL YOUR FRIENDS MAY LEAVE YOU, 172
  UNDER THE BED, 176
Castling, Harry and Collins, Charles
  ARE WE TO PART LIKE THIS, BILL?, 23
  SHE TOLD ME TO MEET HER AT THE GATE, 155
  WHEN THERE ISN'T A GIRL ABOUT, 186
Castling, Harry and Mills, A. J.
  JUST LIKE THE IVY, 106
Castling, Harry and Murphy, C. W.
  LET'S ALL GO DOWN THE STRAND, 109
Castling, Harry and Rule, Herbert
  TURNED UP, 174
Castling, Harry and Walsh, James
  DON'T HAVE ANY MORE, MRS MOORE, 51
Champion, Harry
  See Leigh, Fred W., 146
  THAT GORGONZOLA CHEESE, 168
Cherry, Andrew
  DEAR LITTLE SHAMROCK, THE, 49
Chester, Fred
  ALGY'S ABSOLUTELY FULL OF TACT, 18
Chevalier, Albert
  COSTER'S SERENADE, THE, 45
  FALLEN STAR, A, 56
  FUTURE MRS 'AWKINS, THE, 62
  MY OLD DUTCH, 125
  WOT CHER!, 193
Clarke, Billy
  NELLIE DEAN, 127
Clarke, Cuthbert
  GREEN EYE OF THE LITTLE

YELLOW GOD, THE, 70
SHOOTING OF DAN McGREW,
  THE, 157
Clarke, Grant
  EVERYTHING IS PEACHES
  DOWN IN GEORGIA, 55
Clarke, Grant and Leslie, Edgar
  HE'D HAVE TO GET UNDER
  (GET OUT AND GET UNDER),
  72
Cliffe, Fred
  EVERY LITTLE MOVEMENT
  HAS A MEANING OF ITS
  OWN, 55
Clifford, Nat
  MY WIFE'S FIRST HUSBAND,
  126
  OH! JACK, YOU ARE A HANDY
  MAN, 133
Clifton, Harry
  DARK GIRL DRESS'D IN BLUE,
  THE, 49
  DUTCHMAN'S COURTSHIP,
  THE, 53
  POLLY PERKINS OF PADDING-
  TON GREEN, 144
  PULLING HARD AGAINST
  THE STREAM, 146
  WAIT FOR THE TURN OF THE
  TIDE, 178
  WEEPIN' WILLER, THE, 182
Clifton, Harry and Williams, J.
  WORK, BOYS, WORK, 193
Cobb, George L.
  ALABAMA JUBILEE, 17
  ARE YOU FROM DIXIE?, 23
Cobb, Will D.
  COULD YOU BE TRUE TO EYES
  OF BLUE?, 45
  GOOD-BYE, DOLLY GRAY, 68
  I CAN'T TELL WHY I LOVE
  YOU BUT I DO, 80
  WALTZ ME AROUND AGAIN
  WILLIE, 179
  YIP-I-ADDY-I-AY, 195
Cobb, Will D. and Smith, Harry B.
  I JUST CAN'T MAKE MY EYES
  BEHAVE, 85
Coborn, Charles
  TWO LOVELY BLACK EYES,
  175
Cohn, Irving
  YES, WE HAVE NO BANANAS,
  194
Collins, Charles
  See Barnes, Fred J., 164
  See Castling, Harry, 23, 155, 186
  FATHER'S GOT THE SACK
  FROM THE WATERWORKS, 57
  SWEET LITTLE ROSE OF
  PERSIA, 164
Collins, Charles and Godfrey, Fred
  NOW I HAVE TO CALL HIM
  FATHER, 131
Collins, Charles and Leigh, Fred W.
  DON'T DILLY DALLY, 51
  EV'RYBODY KNOWS ME IN
  MY OLD BROWN HAT, 55
  NOW YOU'VE GOT YER
  KHAKI ON, 131
  WHY AM I ALWAYS THE
  BRIDESMAID?, 191
Collins, Charles and Mellor, Tom
  I WOULDN'T LEAVE MY
  LITTLE WOODEN HUT FOR
  YOU, 102
Collins, Charles and Murray, Fred
  BOILED BEEF AND CARROTS,
  33
Collins, Charles and Sheppard, E. A.
  ANY OLD IRON?, 22
  COVER IT OVER QUICK
  JEMIMA, 45
Collins, Charles and Wallis, W. H.
  WE ALL CAME IN THE
  WORLD WITH NOTHING, 181
Connor, Tommie and Haines, Will
E. and Harper, Jimm
  BIGGEST ASPIDISTRA IN THE
  WORLD, THE, 29
Connor, T. W.
  LITTLE BIT OF CUCUMBER, A,
  111
  OLD DICKY BIRD, 134
  SHE WAS ONE OF THE EARLY
  BIRDS, 155
  WE USED TO GATHER AT THE
  OLD DUN COW, 182

Conroy, Peter
  HIS LORDSHIP WINKED AT THE COUNSEL, 75
Cooke, Leonard
  SUNSHINE OF YOUR SMILE, 163
Cooper, George
  SWEET GENEVIEVE, 164
Coote, Charles
  WAIT FOR THE TURN OF THE TIDE, 178
Cornell, C.
  See Elen, Gus, 179
Costa, P. Mario
  SINCE I CAME TO LONDON TOWN, 158
Cotes, C. G.
  See Scott, Bennett, 89
  COME DOWN AND OPEN THE DOOR, 42
  OH, HOW RUDE!, 132
  PIANO TUNER, THE, 141
  WHAT DID SHE KNOW ABOUT RAILWAYS?, 183
Cove, W. H.
  CHARMING YOUNG WIDOW I MET IN THE TRAIN, THE, 41
Coverdale, Charlie
  BACK ANSWERS, 26
Cox, Desmond
  See Box, Elton, 181
Cox, Jimmie
  NOBODY KNOWS YOU WHEN YOU'RE DOWN AND OUT, 129
Coyne, Fred
  See Adams, Harry, 174
  TUNER'S OPPOR-TUNER-TY, 174
Crispen, Minnie G.
  TALE OF ACKMED KURD, THE, 167
Crook, John
  COSTER'S SERENADE, THE, 45
  JERUSALEM'S DEAD, THE, 103
Cunliffe, Whit and Grafton, Gerald and Lauder, Harry
  WEE DEOCH-AN-DORIS, A, 181

Dacre, Harry
  DAISY BELL, 47
  GHOST OF BENJAMIN BINNS, THE, 64
  I'LL BE YOUR SWEETHEART, 86
  OH, FLO! (WHY DO YOU GO?), 131
  WHILE LONDON'S FAST ASLEEP, 202
Daly, Brian
  JERUSALEM'S DEAD, THE, 103
  SIGNALMAN ON THE LINE, THE, 157
Damerell, Stanley J. and Hargreaves, Robert
  RILEY'S COWSHED, 148
Damerell, Stanley J. and Rutland, John
  SING! SING! SING!, 159
Dance, George
  HIS LORDSHIP WINKED AT THE COUNSEL, 75
  MARTHA SPANKS THE GRAND PIANNA, 117
Dance, George and Adams, J.
  TWIDDLEY BITS, 175
Danks, H. P.
  SILVER THREADS AMONG THE GOLD, 157
Darewski, Herman
  See David, Worton, 189
  See Weston, R. P., 90
  HELLO, SUSIE GREEN, 73
  IN THE TWI-TWI-TWILIGHT, 94
  SISTER SUSIE'S SEWING SHIRTS FOR SOLDIERS, 160
  WHERE ARE THE LADS OF THE VILLAGE TONIGHT?, 188
Darnley, Herbert
  SWIMMING MASTER, THE, 165
Davenport, Arthur
  SINCE I WALKED OUT WITH A SOLDIER, 159
David, Worton
  See Ellerton, Alf, 127
  See Murphy, C. W., 75, 81, 94, 103

See Weston, R. P., 54
BOBBING UP AND DOWN LIKE THIS, 32
FOUR-AND-NINE, 60
David, Worton and Arthurs, George
I CAN SAY "TRULY RURAL", 79
I CAN'T REACH THAT TOP NOTE (AH! AH! AH!), 79
I WANT TO SING IN OPERA, 101
I'M WAITING HERE FOR KATE, 91
David, Worton and Barnett, J. and Darewski, Herman
WHICH SWITCH IS THE SWITCH MISS FOR IPSWICH?, 189
David, Worton and Lee, Bert
ALGERNON, GO H'ON!, 17
ALL THE GIRLS ARE LOVELY BY THE SEASIDE, 19
AT THE VICAR'S FANCY BALL, 25
HELLO! HELLO! WHO'S YOUR LADY FRIEND?, 73
I DO LIKE A S'NICE S'MINCE S'PIE, 80
NURSIE-NURSIE, 131
David, Worton and Long, J. P.
REST OF THE DAY'S YOUR OWN, THE, 147
David, Worton and Murphy, C. W.
I PARTED MY HAIR IN THE MIDDLE, 94
THEY'RE ALL SINGLE BY THE SEASIDE, 171
David, Worton and Powell, Orlando
AND THE PARROT SAID, 22
Day, David G.
LORD MAYOR'S COACHMAN, THE, 113
Dempsey, J. E.
IF I COULD ONLY MAKE YOU CARE, 82
Dent, Harry and Goldburn, Tom
NEVER MIND, 128
Desmond, Billy
WHEN ARE YOU GOING TO LEAD ME TO THE ALTAR, WALTER?, 185
D'Hardelot, Guy
BECAUSE, 27
CHALK FARM TO CAMBERWELL GREEN, 40
Dillon, Will
I WANT A GIRL JUST LIKE THE GIRL WHO MARRIED DEAR OLD DAD, 99
Dix, J. Arlie
PATCHWORK GARDEN, THE, 139
Dixon, Mason
DO IT AGAIN, 51
Dodson, Gerald
FISHERMEN OF ENGLAND, THE, 57
Donaldson, Walter
HOW 'YA GONNA KEEP 'EM DOWN ON THE FARM?, 77
Dore, Walter
WHEN ARE YOU GOING TO LEAD ME TO THE ALTAR, WALTER?, 185
Douglas Scott, Lady John
ANNIE LAURIE, 22
Douglas, William
ANNIE LAURIE, 22
Dryden, Leo and Godwin, Will J.
MINER'S DREAM OF HOME, 119
Duffy, H. A. and Harrison, J. M.
SIMPLE LITTLE MAID IN THE CORNER, THE, 158
Durandeau, A. E.
ASK A P'LICEMAN, 25
MYSTERY OF A HANSOM CAB, THE, 126
NEVER INTRODUCE YER DONAH TO A PAL, 127
Durandeau, A. E. and Ellis, Albert E.
NEVER INTRODUCE YER DONAH TO A PAL, 127

Earle, Fred
SEAWEED, 153
Earle, Fred and Carter, Frank W.

Index

andWells, Gilbert
  WITH MY LITTLE WIGGER WAGGER IN MY HAND, 192
Edgar, Marriott
  RUNCORN FERRY, THE, 151
Edwards, Gus
  BY THE LIGHT OF THE SILVERY MOON, 37
  COULD YOU BE TRUE TO EYES OF BLUE?, 45
  I CAN'T TELL WHY I LOVE YOU BUT I DO, 80
  I JUST CAN'T MAKE MY EYES BEHAVE, 85
Elen, Gus
  DOWN THE DIALS, 52
Elen, Gus and Cornell, C. and Leybourne, T.
  WAIT TILL THE WORK COMES ROUND, 179
Ellerton, Alf
  BELGIUM PUT THE "KIBOSH" ON THE KAISER, 28
  NATURE'S MADE A BIG MISTAKE, 127
  SHE PUSHED ME INTO THE PARLOUR, 154
Ellerton, Alf and David, Worton
  NATURE'S MADE A BIG MISTAKE, 127
Elliott, Zo
  See King, Stoddard, 169
Ellis, Albert E.
  See Durandeau, A. E., 127
Elton, Richard
  See Harrison, E. Denham, 66
Emerson, Ida
  HELLO! MA BABY, 73
Emmell, David
  PHILOSOPHY (A BEE ONCE LIGHTED ON A FLOWER), 140
Eplett, Fred
  'E DUNNO WHERE 'E ARE, 54
  GET YOUR HAIR CUT, 64
  OLD DICKY BIRD, 134
Evans, George "Honeyboy"
  IN THE GOOD OLD SUMMER-TIME, 93
Everard, George
  IS YOUR MOTHER IN MOLLY MALONE?, 95
  OLD MAN'S DARLING, AN, 134
Everard, George and Murray, Fred
  IT'S ALL RIGHT IN THE SUMMER TIME, 96
  NEXT HORSE I RIDE ON, THE, 128

Farnie, H. B.
  GENDARMES' DUET, 63
Ferguson, Sir Samuel
  LARK IN THE CLEAR AIR, THE, 108
Field, L.
  HAPPY ELIZA AND CONVERTED JANE, 71
Finck, Herman
  GILBERT, THE FILBERT, 65
  I'LL MAKE A MAN OF YOU, 86
Fink, Harry
  CURSE OF AN ACHING HEART, THE, 46
Fitz, Albert H. and Penn, William H.
  HONEYSUCKLE AND THE BEE, THE, 76
Flynn, John H.
  YIP-I-ADDY-I-AY, 195
Folloy, Frank
  See Lauder, Harry, 163
Forbes, Cedric
  TALE OF ACKMED KURD, THE, 167
Ford, Harry
  See Skerry, W., 186
Ford, Lena Guilbert
  KEEP THE HOME FIRES BURNING, 106
Forman, Edmund
  COME DOWN AND OPEN THE DOOR, LOVE, 43
  I'VE GOT THE OOPERZOOTIC, 99
  MY NELLIE'S BLUE EYES, 175
Formby, George
  I WAS STANDING AT THE CORNER OF THE STREET, 102
  JOHN WILLIE, COME ON, 105

Formby, George and Hunt, J.
   I WAS STANDING AT THE
   CORNER OF THE STREET, 102
Formby, George and Kendal, Alec
   PLAYING THE GAME IN THE
   WEST, 142
Foster, Stephen
   BEAUTIFUL DREAMER, 27
   HARD TIMES COME AGAIN
   NO MORE, 71
   JEANIE WITH THE LIGHT
   BROWN HAIR, 103
Fragson, Harry
   ALL THE GIRLS ARE LOVELY
   BY THE SEASIDE, 19
   HELLO! HELLO! WHO'S YOUR
   LADY FRIEND?, 73
French, Arthur W.
   WON'T YOU BUY MY PRETTY
   FLOWERS?, 193
French, Percy
   PHIL THE FLUTER'S BALL, 141
Friedman, Leo
   LET ME CALL YOU SWEET-
   HEART, 109
Fulmer, H. J.
   WAIT TILL THE CLOUDS ROLL
   BY, 178
Fyffe, Will
   I BELONG TO GLASGOW, 78
   I'M 94 THIS MORNIN', 90
Fyleman, Rose
   THERE ARE FAIRIES AT THE
   BOTTOM OF OUR GARDEN,
   169

Gaunt, Percy
   BOWERY, THE, 33
Gay, Noel
   ONLY A GLASS OF CHAM-
   PAGNE, 135
Gerard, R. Husch
   YOU'RE THE FLOWER OF MY
   HEART (SWEET ADELINE), 198
German, Edward
   WALTZ SONG, 180
Gershwin, George
   SWANEE, 163
Gheel, Henry E.
   FOR YOU ALONE, 60
Gibson, Fred
   HE LED ME UP THE GARDEN,
   73
Gifford, Harry
   See Lawrance, Alf J., 123
   See Mellor, Alf J., 85
   See Mellor, Tom, 100
   IS ANYBODY LOOKING FOR A
   WIDOW?, 95
   SHE SELLS SEA-SHELLS, 154
Gifford, Harry and Lawrance, Alf J.
   and Mellor, Tom
   KITTY, THE TELEPHONE GIRL,
   107
Gilbert, Fred
   AT TRINITY CHURCH I MET
   MY DOOM, 25
   BRIGHTON, 34
   DOWN THE ROAD, 53
   MAN THAT BROKE THE BANK
   AT MONTE CARLO, THE, 116
Gilbert, L. Wolfe
   HITCHY-KOO, 75
Gilbert, L. Wolfe and Muir, Lewis F.
   WAITING FOR THE ROBERT E
   LEE, 178
Gilbert, W. S.
   YARN OF THE NANCY BELL,
   THE, 194
Glover, Alfred
   ARCHIBALD, CERTAINLY
   NOT!, 22
Glover, Charles W.
   ROSE OF TRALEE, 149
Goard, Henry A.
   GIPSY'S WARNING, THE, 65
Goddard, J.
   SAILOR'S FAREWELL, THE,
   152
Godfrey, Charles
   GOLDEN WEDDING, THE, 67
Godfrey, Fred
   See Collins, Charles, 131
   See Mills, A. J., 166
Godfrey, Fred and Letters, Will
   MOLLY O'MORGAN, 119
Godfrey, Fred and Sheridan, Mark
   WHO WERE YOU WITH LAST

Index

NIGHT?, 190
Godwin, Will J.
  See Dryden, Leo, 119
  See Ridgewell, Charles, 83
  GLORIOUS BEER, 67
  I WANT TO PLAY WITH LITTLE DICK, 101
Goetz, E. Ray
  See Berlin, Irving, 185
Goldburn, Tom
  See Dent, Harry, 128
Golden, John L.
  POOR BUTTERFLY, 144
Goodwin, Joe
  BILLY (FOR WHEN I WALK), 30
Graff, George and Olcott, Chauncey
  WHEN IRISH EYES ARE SMILING, 186
Grafton, Gerald
  See Cunliffe, Whit, 181
  See Lauder, Harry, 87
Graham, Charles
  TWO LITTLE GIRLS IN BLUE, 175
Grain, Corney
  FOUR-'OSS SHARRYBANG, THE, 61
  POLKA AND THE CHOIRBOY, THE, 143
Gray, Barry
  FIACRE, LE, 57
Green, Eddie
  GOOD MAN IS HARD TO FIND, A, 69
Green, F. W.
  CLICQUOT!, 41
Greenbank, Harry H.
  AMOROUS GOLDFISH, THE, 20
  GAY BOHEMIA, 63
  IF I ONLY KNEW THE WAY, 82
Greenbank, Percy
  MY OWN LITTLE GIRL, 125
Grey, F. Clifford
  DEAR OLD SHEPHERD'S BUSH, 50
  IF YOU WERE THE ONLY GIRL IN THE WORLD, 84
  IN OTHER WORDS, 92
  LET THE GREAT BIG WORLD KEEP TURNING, 110
  VICAR AND I WILL BE THERE, THE, 177
  WHITE DOVE, THE, 189
Grock, A. and Silberman, L. and Thurban, T. W.
  DO IT AGAIN, 51
Grossmith jnr, George
  JOHNNY AT THE GAIETY, 104

Haines, Will E.
  See Connor, Tommie, 29
Haley, E. D.
  WHILE STROLLING THRU THE PARK, 189
Hansell, I.
  ALL ROUND MY HAT, 19
Hargreaves, James and Mayo, Sam
  SHE COST ME SEVEN AND SIXPENCE, 153
Hargreaves, Robert
  See Damerell, Stanley J., 148
Hargreaves, Robert and Hargreaves, William
  I PUT ON MY COAT AND WENT HOME, 94
Hargreaves, William
  See Hargreaves, Robert, 94
  BURLINGTON BERTIE FROM BOW, 36
  CAN LONDON DO WITHOUT ME?, 38
  GIVE MY REGARDS TO LEICESTER SQUARE, 67
  IF YOU WANT TO HAVE A ROW WAIT TILL THE SUN SHINES, 84
  LITTLE YELLOW-BIRD, 112
  NIGHT I APPEARED AS MACBETH, THE, 128
  OH, I MUST GO HOME TONIGHT, 132
  P.C. 49, 140
  THEY BUILT PICCADILLY FOR ME, 171
Hargreaves, William and Lipton, Dan
  DANCE WITH YOUR UNCLE

JOSEPH, 48
Harper, Jimmy
   See Connor, Tommie, 29
Harrington, J. P.
   AND THE LEAVES BEGAN TO FALL, 21
   BATHING, 27
   BELLA WAS A BARMAID, 28
   BOND STREET TEA-WALK, THE, 33
   EVERYTHING IN THE GARDEN'S LOVELY, 55
   GIDDY LITTLE GIRL SAID "NO!", THE, 64
   GOLDEN DUSTMAN, THE, 67
   I LIKE YOUR APRON AND YOUR BONNET, 85
   IT'S A PITY TO WASTE THE CAKE, 97
   LEAVE A LITTLE BIT FOR YOUR TUTOR, 109
   PUT ON YOUR SLIPPERS, 147
   SALUTE MY BICYCLE, 152
   TRICKY LITTLE TRILBY, 173
   WEDDING MARCH, THE, 181
   WHAT'S THAT FOR, EH?, 184
   YOU AIN'T ASHAMED OF ME, ARE YOU, BILL?, 195
Harris, Charles K.
   AFTER THE BALL, 16
   DON'T GIVE ME DIAMONDS, ALL I WANT IS YOU, 51
Harris, F. Clifford
   BROKEN DOLL, A, 35
   EV'RY LITTLE WHILE, 56
   GIVE ME A LITTLE COSY CORNER, 66
   I WAS A GOOD LITTLE GIRL TILL I MET YOU, 101
   IT'S LOVELY TO BE IN LOVE, 97
   MY ACTOR MAN, 122
Harris, F. Clifford and Valentine
   BACHELOR GAY, A, 26
   PARADISE FOR TWO, A, 139
Harrison, E. Denham and Elton, Richard
   GIVE ME A TICKET TO HEAVEN, 66

Harrison, J. M.
   See Duffy, H. A., 158
Hasting, Walter
   SONG OF THE THRUSH, THE, 162
Hayes, Billie
   I AIN'T 'ARF A LUCKY KID, 78
Hayes, Charles
   I AIN'T 'ARF A LUCKY KID, 78
Hayes, J. Milton
   GREEN EYE OF THE LITTLE YELLOW GOD, THE, 70
Henty, Dick and Rihill, Louis
   MURDERS, 122
Herbert, Victor
   ART IS CALLING FOR ME, 24
Herbert, Will
   WHAT CHEER 'RIA, 183
Hersee, Henry
   FLOWER SONG, 58
Hill, Lady Arthur
   IN THE GLOAMIN', 93
Hobson, M.
   'NORRIBLE TALE, A, 130
Holmans, G.
   HAMPSTEAD IS THE PLACE TO RURALIZE, 70
Holt, Fred
   See Rule, Herbert, 136
   OURS IS A NICE 'OUSE OURS IS, 138
Hood, Basil
   MERRY WIDOW WALTZ, 118
Hood, Thomas
   OUR HANDS HAVE MET BUT NOT OUR HEARTS (THE FALSE FRIEND), 137
Hope, Lawrence
   KASHMIRI SONG (PALE HANDS I LOVED), 106
Horwitz, Charles
   LUCKY JIM (HOW I ENVY HIM), 114
Howard, Frank
   ONLY A PANSY BLOSSOM, 135
Howard, Joseph E.
   HELLO! MA BABY, 73
Hoyt, Charles
   BOWERY, THE, 33

Index

Hubbell, Raymond
  POOR BUTTERFLY, 144
Hudson, Thomas
  SPIDER AND THE FLY, THE, 163
Hunt, G. W.
  MACDERMOTT'S WAR SONG, 114
  SHE DOES THE FANDANGO ALL OVER THE PLACE, 154
  UP IN A BALLOON, 176
Hunt, J.
  See Formby, George, 102
Hunter, Harry
  I'VE GOT THE OOPERZOOTIC, 99
  LORD MAYOR'S COACHMAN, THE, 113
Hunting, Russell
  See Krone, Percy, 52
Hyde, Will
  JOHNNY MORGAN'S SISTER, 104

Ingle, Charles
  MY OLD DUTCH, 125
  WOT CHER!, 193
Ingraham, Herbert
  ALL THAT I ASK OF YOU IS LOVE, 19
Ison, George
  DOWN WENT THE CAPTAIN, 53

Jackson, William
  DEAR LITTLE SHAMROCK, THE, 49
Jerome, William
  BEDELIA, 28
  ROW, ROW, ROW, 150
John J. Stamford
  McNAMARA'S BAND, 115
Johnson, Cecil
  See Burley, Joe, 25
Johnson, George W.
  WHEN YOU AND I WERE YOUNG, MAGGIE, 187
Jones, E. Boyd and Rubens, Paul
  TELL ME, PRETTY MAIDEN, 167
Jones, Sidney
  AMOROUS GOLDFISH, THE, 20
  GAY BOHEMIA, 63
  LINGER LONGER LOO, 111
Jonghman, Edward
  THOSE WEDDING BELLS SHALL NOT RING OUT, 171
Judge, Jack and Williams, Harry J.
  IT'S A LONG, LONG WAY TO TIPPERARY, 97

Kalmar, Bert
  IF YOU CAN'T GET A GIRL IN THE SUMMERTIME, 84
Keen, Walter P.
  SINCE I BECAME A MARRIED MAN, 158
Keiser, Robert
  WHILE STROLLING THRU THE PARK, 189
Kelly, J. T.
  SHE'S ONLY A WORKING GIRL, 155
Kelly, W. B. and Woodhouse, J. H.
  SING US ONE OF THE OLD SONGS, 159
Kendal, Alec
  See Formby, George, 142
  COME IN AND CUT YOURSELF A PIECE OF CAKE, 43
  I'M TWENTY-ONE TODAY, 91
  TO CHEER HIM UP AND SEND HIM ON HIS WAY, 173
Kendis, James and Paley, Herman
  BILLY (FOR WHEN I WALK), 30
Kern, Jerome
  HOW'D'YA LIKE TO SPOON WITH ME?, 77
  THEY DIDN'T BELIEVE ME, 171
Kind, John A. Glover
  See Carter, Frank W., 110
  BY THE SEA (BY THE BEAUTIFUL SILVERY SEA), 37
  I DO LIKE TO BE BESIDE THE SEASIDE, 80
  LET'S HAVE FREE TRADE

AMONGST THE GIRLS, 110
King, Harry
　MUFFIN MAN, THE, 122
King, Stoddard and Elliott, Zo
　THERE'S A LONG LONG TRAIL A-WINDING, 169
Kipling, Rudyard
　ON THE ROAD TO MANDALAY, 136
Knight, Charles
　FROM MARBLE ARCH TO LEICESTER SQUARE, 61
Knight, Charles and Lyle, Kenneth
　HERE WE ARE! HERE WE ARE!! HERE WE ARE AGAIN!!!, 74
Krone, Percy and Hunting, Russell and Sterling, Andrew B.
　DOWN AT THE OLD BULL AND BUSH, 52
Kummer, Clare
　IN THE DINGLE DONGLE DELL, 92

Lalo, Clarence
　IN OLDEN SPAIN, 92
Lalo, Edward
　IN OLDEN SPAIN, 92
Lamb, Arthur
　BIRD IN A GILDED CAGE, A, 31
　MANSION OF ACHING HEARTS, THE, 116
Lamb, Arthur and Solman, Alfred
　BIRD ON NELLIE'S HAT, THE, 31
Langley, Percival
　I'M GLAD I TOOK MY MOTHER'S ADVICE, 89
Laska, Edward
　HOW'D'YA LIKE TO SPOON WITH ME?, 77
Lauder, Harry
　See Cunliffe, Whit, 181
　I LOVE A LASSIE, 87
　ROAMIN' IN THE GLOAMIN', 149
　SAFTEST O' THE FAMILY, THE, 151
　STOP YER TICKLIN', JOCK, 163

WE PARTED ON THE SHORE, 182
Lauder, Harry and Beaton, Bob
　SAFTEST O' THE FAMILY, THE, 151
Lauder, Harry and Folloy, Frank
　STOP YER TICKLIN', JOCK, 163
Lauder, Harry and Grafton, Gerald
　I LOVE A LASSIE, 87
Lawlor, Charles B.
　See Blake, James W., 48, 157
Lawrance, Alf J.
　See Mellor, Tom, 100
　I LIKE YOUR APRON AND YOUR BONNET, 85
Lawrance, Alf J. and Gifford, Harry
　MY CASTLE IN SPAIN, 123
Le Brunn, George
　'ARRY 'ARRY 'ARRY, 24
　ACROSS THE BRIDGE, 16
　AND THE LEAVES BEGAN TO FALL, 21
　BATHING, 27
　BELLA WAS A BARMAID, 28
　BOND STREET TEA-WALK, THE, 33
　EVERYTHING IN THE GARDEN'S LOVELY, 55
　FOLKESTONE FOR THE DAY, 59
　GOLDEN DUSTMAN, THE, 67
　HE'S GOING THERE EVERY NIGHT, 74
　IF IT WASN'T FOR THE 'OUSES IN BETWEEN, 83
　IT'S A GREAT BIG SHAME, 96
　I'VE NEVER LOST MY LAST TRAIN YET, 99
　LEAVE A LITTLE BIT FOR YOUR TUTOR, 109
　LIZA JOHNSON, 112
　MY SON (MY SON, MY ONLY SON), 126
　NO, 'ARRY, DON'T ASK ME TO MARRY, 129
　OH! MR PORTER, 133
　SALUTE MY BICYCLE, 152
　SONG OF THE THRUSH, THE, 162

Index

THERE THEY ARE—THE TWO OF THEM ON THEIR OWN, 170
TRICKY LITTLE TRILBY, 173
WEDDING MARCH, THE, 181
WHAT'S THAT FOR, EH?, 184
YOU AIN'T ASHAMED OF ME, ARE YOU, BILL?, 195

Le Brunn, Thomas
  OH! MR PORTER, 133

Le Clerq, Arthur
  NOBODY LOVES A FAIRY WHEN SHE'S FORTY, 129

Leamore, Tom
  PERCY FROM PIMLICO, 140

Lee, Alfred
  CHAMPAGNE CHARLIE, 41
  FLYING TRAPEZE, THE (THE DARING YOUNG MAN ON), 59

Lee, Bert
  See Allen, Andrew, 196
  See Ayer, Nat D., 129
  See David, Worton, 17, 19, 25, 73, 80, 131
  See Smith, Clay, 161
  See Weston, R. P., 16, 21, 34, 68, 70, 90, 97, 135, 138, 161, 165, 184
  SOPHY, 162

Lee, Bert and Arthurs, George
  JOSHU-AH, 105

Lee, Bert and Two Bobs, The
  FOUR-AND-NINE, 60

Leggett, Steve
  GLORIOUS BEER, 67

Lehar, Franz
  LOVE, GOODBYE, 113
  MERRY WIDOW WALTZ, 118
  VILIA, 177
  WHITE DOVE, THE, 189

Lehmann, Liza
  THERE ARE FAIRIES AT THE BOTTOM OF OUR GARDEN, 169

Leigh, Fred W.
  See Collins, Charles, 51, 55, 131, 191
  See Murray, Fred, 41, 74, 78, 111, 170
  AMATEUR WHITEWASHER, THE, 20
  ARMY OF TODAY'S ALL RIGHT, THE, 24
  COSTER GIRL IN PARIS, THE, 44
  GALLOPING MAJOR, THE, 62
  I AIN'T NOBODY IN PERTICULAR, 78
  JOLLY GOOD LUCK TO THE GIRL WHO LOVES A SOLDIER, 105
  MARY ANN SHE'S AFTER ME, 117
  MORE WORK FOR THE UNDERTAKER, 121
  POOR JOHN, 144
  PUT ON YOUR TAT-TA, LITTLE GIRLIE, 147
  RIDING ON TOP OF THE CAR, 148
  RUM-TIDDLEY-UM-TUM-TAY, 151
  THAT GORGONZOLA CHEESE, 168
  TIDDLY-OM-POM, 172
  W.O.M.A.N., 193
  WAITING AT THE CHURCH, 178

Leigh, Fred W. and Arthurs, George
  I'VE GOT MY EYE ON YOU, 98
  LITTLE OF WHAT YOU FANCY DOES YOU GOOD, A, 112

Leigh, Fred W. and Bastow, George
  CAPTAIN GINJAH, O.T., 39
  SHE'S PROUD AND SHE'S BEAUTIFUL, 155

Leigh, Fred W. and Champion, Harry
  PUT A BIT OF TREACLE ON MY PUDDEN, MARY ANN, 146

Leigh, Fred W. and Murray, Fred
  'ARRY 'ARRY 'ARRY, 24

Leigh, Fred W. and Pether, Henry E.
  ROSIE'S YOUNG MAN, 150

Lemon, Laura G.
  MY AIN FOLK, 123

Lennard, Arthur
  See Mills, A. J., 159

Leo, Frank
  COWSLIP AND THE COW, THE, 45
  I DO LIKE AN EGG FOR MY TEA, 80
  I WISH I'D BOUGHT DUCKS, 102
  WATCHING THE TRAINS COME IN, 180
  WHAT IS THE USE OF LOVING A GIRL IF THE GIRL DON'T LOVE YOU?, 184

Leoncavallo, Ruggiero
  MATTINATA, 117

Leslie, Edgar
  See Clarke, Grant, 72

Letters, Will
  See Godfrey, Fred, 119
  See Murphy, C. W., 58, 71

Lewis, Sam M. and Young, Joe
  HOW'YA GONNA KEEP 'EM DOWN ON THE FARM?, 77

Leybourne, George
  CHAMPAGNE CHARLIE, 41
  FLYING TRAPEZE, THE (THE DARING YOUNG MAN ON), 59

Leybourne, T.
  See Elen, Gus, 179

Lipton, Dan
  See Hargreaves, William, 48
  See Murphy, C. W., 18, 54, 82, 102, 133, 146, 187

Lipton, Dan and Murphy, C. W. and Neat, John
  SHE'S A LASSIE FROM LANCASHIRE, 154

Lipton, Dan and Murray, Fred
  MY GIRL'S A YORKSHIRE GIRL, 124

Lloyd, Arthur
  CRUEL MARY HOLDER, 46
  PRETTY LIPS, 145

Long, J. P.
  See David, Worton, 147
  I CAN'T DO MY BALLY BOTTOM BUTTON UP, 79
  MARY'S TICKET, 117
  THEY ALL WALK THE WIBBLY WOBBLY WALK, 170
  WHAT D'YER THINK OF THAT? (MY OLD MAN'S A DUSTMAN), 183

Long, J. P. and Mayne, Ernie
  BACK AT THE FARM, 100

Longfellow, Henry W.
  EXCELSIOR, 56

Lonsdale, T. S.
  TOMMY MAKE ROOM FOR YOUR UNCLE, 173

Lyle, Kenneth
  See Knight, Charles, 74
  ARMY OF TODAY'S ALL RIGHT, THE, 24
  FROM MARBLE ARCH TO LEICESTER SQUARE, 61
  JOLLY GOOD LUCK TO THE GIRL WHO LOVES A SOLDIER, 105

McCarthy, Joseph
  ALICE BLUE GOWN, 18
  YOU MADE ME LOVE YOU, 197

McCree, Junie
  NORA MALONE (CALL ME BY PHONE), 130

MacDonald, Ballard
  COME OVER THE GARDEN WALL, 44
  GEORGIE TOOK ME WALKING IN THE PARK, 63
  I LOVE TO GO SWIMMIN' WITH WIMMIN, 87
  IF I SHOULD PLANT A TINY SEED OF LOVE, 82

McGlennon, Felix
  AND HER GOLDEN HAIR WAS HANGING DOWN HER BACK, 21
  COMRADES, 44
  DOWN AT THE FARM-YARD GATE, 52
  SHIP I LOVE, THE, 156
  SMILES, 160
  SONS OF THE SEA, 162
  THAT IS LOVE!, 168

McHugh, Jimmy and Gilbert, J. E.

Index

and Conley, Steve
  SARAH (SITTING IN THE SHOE SHINE SHOP), 152
MacKenzie, Scott
  I AIN'T NOBODY IN PERTICULAR, 78
MacMurrough, Dermott
  MACUSHLA, 115
Madden, Edward
  BY THE LIGHT OF THE SILVERY MOON, 37
  MOONLIGHT BAY (ON), 120
Madden, Edward and Morse, Dolly
  BLUE BELL, 32
Magini
  See Murphy, C. W., 102
Maguire, Sylvester
  WHY DID YOU MAKE ME CARE?, 191
Malone, Edgar
  I WANT TO BE A PRIMA DONNA, 24
Marks, Edward B.
  MOTHER WAS A LADY (IF JACK WERE ONLY HERE), 121
Marshall, Henry I.
  BE MY LITTLE BABY BUMBLE BEE, 29
Maurice, George
  LINGER LONGER LOO, 111
Mayne, Ernie
  See Long, J. P., 100
Mayne, Will
  SHE PUSHED ME INTO THE PARLOUR, 154
Mayo, Sam
  See Hargreaves, James, 153
  JOHNNIE, 104
  PUSHING YOUNG MAN, THE, 146
Meen, George
  OH, FRED! TELL THEM TO STOP, 132
Meher, Donovan and Tate, James W.
  GEORGIE TOOK ME WALKING IN THE PARK, 63
Mellor, Tom
  See Collins, Charles, 102
  MY CASTLE IN SPAIN, 123

Mellor, Tom and Lawrance, Alf J. and Gifford, Harry
  I LIKE YOUR OLD FRENCH BONNET, 85
  I WANT TO GO TO IDAHO, 100
Merson, Billy
  ON THE GOOD SHIP "YACKI HICKI DOO LA", 136
  SPANIARD THAT BLIGHTED MY LIFE, THE, 162
Meyer, George W.
  See Ager, Milton, 55
Mill, Paul
  See Bateman, Edgar, 139
Milliken, Richard A.
  'TIS THE LAST ROSE OF SUMMER, 173
Mills, A. J.
  See Carter, Frank W., 71
  See Castling, Harry, 106
  ALL THE NICE GIRLS LOVE A SAILOR (SHIP AHOY!), 20
  BY THE SIDE OF THE ZUYDER ZEE, 37
  COME AND PUT YOUR ARMS AROUND ME, GEORGIE DO, 42
  DARLING MABEL, 49
  FALL IN AND FOLLOW ME, 56
  HAS ANYBODY SEEN A GERMAN BAND?, 72
  I DON'T CARE WHAT BECOMES OF ME, 81
  IS YOUR MOTHER IN MOLLY MALONE?, 95
  LOST, STOLEN OR STRAYED, 113
  POPSY WOPSY, 144
  TAKE ME IN A TAXI, JOE, 166
  WHEN I TAKE MY MORNING PROMENADE, 186
Mills, A. J. and Carter, Frank W.
  YOUNG MAN WHO WORKED AT THE MILK SHOP, 197
Mills, A. J. and Castling, Harry
  BOERS HAVE GOT MY DADDY, THE, 32
  IT'S THE POOR THAT HELP THE POOR, 98

Mills, A. J. and Godfrey, Fred and Scott, Bennett
  TAKE ME BACK TO DEAR OLD BLIGHTY, 166
Mills, A. J. and Lennard, Arthur
  SISTER 'RIA, 159
Mills, A. J. and Scott, Bennett
  KNOCK THE TWO ROOMS INTO ONE, 108
  MY BOY'S A SAILOR MAN, 123
  WHEN A FELLOW IS TWENTY-ONE, 184
Mills, Kerry
  MEET ME IN ST LOUIS, LOUIS, 118
Mills, Wilfrid
  MY AIN FOLK, 123
Mitchell, Samuel N.
  JUST TOUCH THE HARP GENTLY, 106
Molloy, J. L.
  LOVE'S OLD SWEET SONG, 114
Monaco, Jimmie V.
  ROW, ROW, ROW, 150
  YOU MADE ME LOVE YOU, 197
Monckton, Lionel
  CHALK FARM TO CAMBERWELL GREEN, 40
  MOONSTRUCK, 120
  MY MOTTER, 124
  MY OWN LITTLE GIRL, 125
  PIPES OF PAN, THE, 142
  SIMPLE LITTLE STRING, A, 158
  TWO LITTLE SAUSAGES, 175
  UNDER THE DEODAR, 176
Moor-King, Alfred
  TA-RA-RA-BOOM-DE-AY, 167
Moore, J. Charles
  CALL ROUND ANY OLD TIME, 38
  DON'T STOP MY 'ARF A PINT O' BEER, 52
  EVERY LITTLE MOVEMENT HAS A MEANING OF ITS OWN, 55
Moore, Thomas
  'TIS THE LAST ROSE OF SUMMER, 173
Morande, Paul
  PICCADILLY, 141
Morse, Dolly
  See Madden, Edward, 32
Morse, Theodore
  BLUE BELL, 32
Morton, Hugh
  MY BEAUTIFUL LADY, 123
Morton, Richard
  BRIGHTON, 34
  GHOST OF SHERLOCK HOLMES, THE, 64
  SINCE I CAME TO LONDON TOWN, 158
  TA-RA-RA-BOOM-DE-AY, 167
Moss, Katie
  FLORAL DANCE, THE, 58
Muir, Lewis F.
  See Abrahams, Maurice, 75
  See Gilbert, L. Wolfe, 178
Mulchinock, William P.
  ROSE OF TRALEE, 149
Mullen, Alfred and Nelson, Sidney
  CAPTAIN WITH HIS WHISKERS, THE, 39
Murphy, C. W.
  See Castling, Harry, 109
  See David, Worton, 94, 171
  See Lipton, Dan, 154
  See Weston, R. P., 90
  I LIVE IN TRAFALGAR SQUARE, 86
  LITTLE YELLOW-BIRD, 112
  MRS CARTER, 122
  THEY ALWAYS PICK ON ME, 170
Murphy, C. W. and Bateman, Edgar
  MRS CARTER, 122
Murphy, C. W. and David, Worton
  HOLD YOUR HAND OUT, NAUGHTY BOY, 75
  I DO LIKE YOU SUSIE IN YOUR PRETTY LITTLE SUNDAY CLOTHES, 81
  IN THE VALLEY OF GOLDEN DREAMS, 94
  JERE-JEREMIAH, 103
Murphy, C. W. and Letters, Will

Index

FLANAGAN, 58
  HAS ANYBODY HERE SEEN KELLY?, 71
Murphy, C. W. and Lipton, Dan
  ALL HANDS ON DECK, 18
  ESAU TAKE ME ON THE SEESAW, 54
  IF I HAD A GIRL AS NICE AS YOU, 82
  OH! OH! ANTONIO, 133
  PUT ME AMONGST THE GIRLS, 146
  WHEN YOU LIVE OPPOSITE TO ME, 187
Murphy, C. W. and Lipton, Dan and Magini
  I WONDER WHAT IT FEELS LIKE TO BE POOR?, 102
Murphy, Stanley
  BE MY LITTLE BABY BUMBLE BEE, 29
Murray, Fred
  See Barclay, Lawrence, 137
  See Collins, Charles, 33
  See Everard, George, 96, 128
  See Leigh, Fred W., 24
  See Lipton, Dan, 124
  AMATEUR WHITEWASHER, THE, 20
  GINGER, YOU'RE BALMY, 65
  OLD MAN'S DARLING, AN, 134
  SHE'D NEVER HAD A LESSON IN HER LIFE, 153
Murray, Fred and Leigh, Fred W.
  CHARLIE ON THE MASH, 41
  HE'S GOING THERE EVERY NIGHT, 74
  I 'AVEN'T TOLD HIM NOT UP TO NOW, 78
  LITTLE BIT OFF THE TOP, A, 111
  THERE THEY ARE—THE TWO OF THEM ON THEIR OWN, 170
Murray, Fred and Weston, R. P.
  I'M HENRY THE EIGHTH I AM, 90
Murray, Slade
  See Sutherd, A., 43

Neat, John
  See Lipton, Dan, 154
  PRETTY LITTLE GIRL FROM NOWHERE, THE, 145
Nelson, Sidney
  See Mullen, Alfred, 39
Nevin, Ethelbert
  NARCISSUS, 170
Newton, Eddie
  CASEY JONES, 40
Nicholls, Harry
  NONSENSE! YES! BY JOVE!, 130
Nolan, Michael
  LITTLE ANNIE ROONEY, 111
Norman, George P.
  THERE'S DANGER ON THE LINE, 169
Norris, Harry B.
  ALGY, or THE PICCADILLY JOHNNY WITH THE LITTLE GLASS EYE, 18
  SEASIDE GIRLS, THE, 152
Norworth, Jack
  See Bayes, Nora, 156
  SHINE ON HARVEST MOON, 156
Novello, Ivor
  KEEP THE HOME FIRES BURNING, 106
  LITTLE DAMOZEL, THE, 112
Nugent, Maude
  SWEET ROSIE O'GRADY, 165

O'Connor, Shamus
  McNAMARA'S BAND, 115
Offenbach, Jacques
  GENDARMES' DUET, 63
O'Hara, Geoffrey
  K-K-K-KATY, 107
Olcott, Chauncey
  See Ball, Ernest R., 121
  See Graff, George, 186
Oliver, Will
  HAPPY ELIZA AND CONVERTED JANE, 71
O'Reilly, P. J.

FOR YOU ALONE, 60
Orred, Meta
   IN THE GLOAMIN', 93
Osborne, Charles
   See Beauchamp, George, 64
   FOR OLD TIMES' SAKE, 60
   I'M GLAD I TOOK MY MOTHER'S ADVICE, 89
   WHO'LL CARE FOR THE CHILDREN?, 190
O'Shaughnessy, Terrence
   McNAMARA'S BAND, 115
Oxenford, John
   MOON HAS RAISED HER LAMP ABOVE, THE, 119

Paley, Herman
   See Kendis, James, 30
Palmer, J. F.
   BAND PLAYED ON, THE, 26
Patrick, Kay
   See Amsterdam, Morey, 197
Payne, John Howard
   HOME! SWEET HOME!, 76
Pelham, Paul
   THEY ALL WALK THE WIBBLY WOBBLY WALK, 170
Pelham, Paul and Rule, Herbert
   FROM POVERTY STREET TO GOLDEN SQUARE, 62
   GOOD MORNING, MR POSTMAN, 69
Pelissier, H. G.
   SINCE I WALKED OUT WITH A SOLDIER, 159
Penn, Arthur A.
   SMILIN' THRU, 160
Penn, William H.
   See Fitz, Albert H., 76
   PANSY FACES, 139
Persley, G. W.
   WON'T YOU BUY MY PRETTY FLOWERS?, 193
Pether, Henry E.
   See Leigh, Fred W., 150
   POOR JOHN, 144
   WAITING AT THE CHURCH, 178
Petrie, H. W.

   I DON'T WANT TO PLAY IN YOUR YARD, 81
Philips, Montague F.
   FISHERMEN OF ENGLAND, THE, 57
Piantadosi, Al
   See Wilson, Al, 192
   CURSE OF AN ACHING HEART, THE, 46
Piave, F. Mario
   BRINDISI, 35
Pink, Wal and Randall, Harry
   IT'S ONLY A FALSE ALARM (GREAT EXPECTATIONS), 98
Pinna, Herbert De
   DOES THIS SHOP STOCK SHOT SOCKS?, 50
Potter, Sam
   DADDY'S ON THE ENGINE, 47
Powell, Felix
   PACK UP YOUR TROUBLES IN YOUR OLD KITBAG, 138
Powell, George
   See Asaf, George, 138
Powell, Orlando
   See Bowyer, Fred, 16
   See David, Worton, 22
   COSTER GIRL IN PARIS, THE, 44
   GIDDY LITTLE GIRL SAID "NO!", THE, 64
   IT'S A PITY TO WASTE THE CAKE, 97
   PUT ON YOUR SLIPPERS, 147
   RUM-TIDDLEY-UM-TUM-TAY, 151
   SHE'D NEVER HAD A LESSON IN HER LIFE, 153
   TIDDLY-OM-POM, 172
Pratt, Cornelius
   DON'T STOP MY 'ARF A PINT O' BEER, 52
Pratt, Mrs F. B.
   PLEASE SELL NO MORE DRINK TO MY FATHER, 143
Procter, Adelaide A.
   LOST CHORD, THE, 113

Randall, Harry

Index

See Pink, Wal, 98
Ray, Lilian
  SUNSHINE OF YOUR SMILE, 163
Ray, Phil
  IF THE MISSUS WANTS TO GO LET HER DROWN, 83
Reave, Norman
  BOBBING UP AND DOWN LIKE THIS, 32
Redmond, Walter
  SHE'D A BROTHER IN THE NAVY, 153
Reeve, Ada
  TRIXIE OF UPPER TOOTING, 174
Reeves, Charles
  I'M A LITTLE TOO YOUNG TO KNOW, 88
Rexford, Eben E.
  ONLY A PANSY BLOSSOM, 135
  SILVER THREADS AMONG THE GOLD, 157
Rick, Alfred E.
  SWING ME HIGHER, OBADIAH, 165
Ridg(e)well, Charles
  BILLY MUGGINS, 30
Ridgewell, Charles and Godwin, Will J.
  IF THOSE LIPS COULD ONLY SPEAK, 83
Ridgewell, Charles and Stevens, George A.
  I'M SHY, MARY ELLEN, I'M SHY, 91
  YOU CAN DO A LOT OF THINGS AT THE SEASIDE THAT YOU, 195
Ridley, George
  CUSHIE BUTTERFIELD, 46
Rihill, Louis
  See Henty, Dick, 122
Riviére, J.
  CLICQUOT!, 41
Roberts, Lees
  SMILES, 160
Robey, George
  See St John, John L., 22

Robey, George and Rohmer, Sax
  BANG WENT THE CHANCE OF A LIFETIME, 27
Robson, T. F. and Wells, Gilbert
  VARMER GILES, 176
Rogers, E. W.
  ASK A P'LICEMAN, 25
  CALL ROUND ANY OLD TIME, 38
  FOLLOWING IN FATHER'S FOOTSTEPS, 59
  LAMBETH WALK, THE, 108
  MIDNIGHT SON, THE, 118
  MOONLIGHT BLOSSOMS, 120
  MY SON (MY SON, MY ONLY SON), 126
  MYSTERY OF A HANSOM CAB, THE, 126
  PRETTY LITTLE GIRL FROM NOWHERE, THE, 145
  SKYLARK!, 160
  SWEETHEARTS STILL, 164
Rohmer, Sax
  See Robey, George, 27
  PIGTAIL OF LI FANG FU, THE, 141
Rollit, George
  I'VE NEVER LOST MY LAST TRAIN YET, 99
Rolls, Jack
  YOU CAN'T DO THAT THERE 'ERE, 196
Rolmaz, James
  WHERE DID YOU GET THAT HAT?, 188
Romberg, Sigmund
  I LOVE TO GO SWIMMIN' WITH WIMMIN, 87
Root, G. F.
  RING THE BELL, WATCHMAN, 149
  TRAMP TRAMP TRAMP THE BOYS ARE MARCHING, 193
Rosenfeld, Monroe H.
  AND HER GOLDEN HAIR WAS HANGING DOWN HER BACK, 21
  THOSE WEDDING BELLS SHALL NOT RING OUT, 171

Ross, Adrian
  LOVE, GOODBYE, 113
  MILLER'S DAUGHTER, THE, 119
  TELL ME, DEAR FLOWER, 167
  TWO LITTLE SAUSAGES, 175
  UNDER THE DEODAR, 176
  VILIA, 177
Roundbach, John E.
  WALKING HOME WITH ANGELINE, 179
Rourke, M. E.
  THEY DIDN'T BELIEVE ME, 171
Rowe, Josephine V.
  MACUSHLA, 115
Royle, Kate
  DOWN WENT THE CAPTAIN, 53
Rubens, Paul
  See Jones, E. Boyd, 167
  BRIGHTON, 34
  HERE'S TO LOVE AND LAUGHTER, 74
  I CAN'T TAKE MY EYES OFF YOU, 79
  TRIXIE OF UPPER TOOTING, 174
Rubens, Paul and Wimperis, Arthur
  BRIGHTON, 34
Rule, Herbert
  See Castling, Harry, 174
  See Pelham, Paul, 62, 69
  FROM POVERTY STREET TO GOLDEN SQUARE, 62
  OURS IS A NICE 'OUSE OURS IS, 138
  WHO PUT THE BRICKS IN BRIXTON?, 190
Rule, Herbert and Holt, Fred
  ONLY A WORKING MAN, 136
Russell, Henry
  COME HOME, FATHER, 43
Rutland, John
  See Damerell, Stanley J., 159

St John, John L. and Robey, George
  ARCHIBALD, CERTAINLY NOT!, 22

Sanderson, Wilfrid
  FRIEND O' MINE, 61
Sarjeant, James B.
  WATCHMAN! WHAT OF THE NIGHT?, 180
Sarony, Leslie
  I LIFT UP MY FINGER AND I SAY "TWEET TWEET", 85
Sayers, Henry J.
  TA-RA-RA BOOM-DER-E, 167
Schmid, Johann C.
  IF I COULD ONLY MAKE YOU CARE, 82
Schubert, Franz
  TELL ME, DEAR FLOWER, 167
Schwartz, Jean
  BEDELIA, 28
Scott, Bennett
  See Mills, A. J., 108, 123, 166, 184
  ALL THE NICE GIRLS LOVE A SAILOR (SHIP AHOY!), 20
  BY THE SIDE OF THE ZUYDER ZEE, 37
  COME AND PUT YOUR ARMS AROUND ME, GEORGIE DO, 42
  COME DOWN AND OPEN THE DOOR, 42
  DARLING MABEL, 49
  FALL IN AND FOLLOW ME, 56
  HAS ANYBODY SEEN A GERMAN BAND?, 72
  I DON'T CARE WHAT BECOMES OF ME, 81
  IT'S A DIFFERENT GIRL AGAIN!, 96
  LOST, STOLEN OR STRAYED, 113
  OH, HOW RUDE!, 132
  POPSY WOPSY, 144
  TAKE ME IN A TAXI, JOE, 166
  WHAT DID SHE KNOW ABOUT RAILWAYS?, 183
  WHEN I TAKE MY MORNING PROMENADE, 186
  WHO'S COMING UP IN THE GALLERY?, 190
Scott, Bennett and Cotes, C. G.
  I'M GOING TO GET MARRIED

Index

TODAY—HOORAY!, 89
Scott, Maurice
  AYESHA, MY SWEET EGYPTIAN, 25
  GIRLS, STUDY YOUR COOKERY BOOK, 66
  I'VE GOT RINGS ON MY FINGERS, 98
  MY OLD PAL JOE, 125
  NICE QUIET DAY, A, 128
  OH, I'M ONE OF THE BOYS, 132
  SWING ME HIGHER, OBADIAH, 165
Scott-Gatty, Charles
  HULLO! TU-TU, 77
Scott-Gatty, Muriel
  HULLO! TU-TU, 77
Searson, E. A.
  HE LED ME UP THE GARDEN, 73
Seibert, T. Lawrence
  CASEY JONES, 40
Sellen, Edgar
  ALL THAT I ASK OF YOU IS LOVE, 19
Service, Robert
  SHOOTING OF DAN McGREW, THE, 157
Sheppard, E. A.
  See Collins, Charles, 22, 45
Sheridan, Mark
  See Godfrey, Fred, 190
Sherman, Tom
  I WANT TO BE A PRIMA DONNA, 24
Shields, R. E. N.
  IN THE GOOD OLD SUMMERTIME, 93
  WALTZ ME AROUND AGAIN WILLIE, 179
Siebert, Edrich
  MARROW SONG, THE, 116
Sievier, Bruce
  See Williams, Walter, 141
Silberman, L.
  See Grock, A., 51
Silver, Frank
  YES, WE HAVE NO BANANAS, 194
Sims, George R.
  BILLY'S ROSE, 30
Skerry, W. and Ford, Harry
  WHEN SHE WALKS, 186
Smith, Clay and Weston, R. P. and Lee, Bert
  SOMEBODY'S COMING TO TEA, 161
Smith, Edgar
  MA BLUSHIN' ROSIE, 115
Smith, G. Totten
  WALKING HOME WITH ANGELINE, 179
Smith, Harry B.
  See Cobb, Will D., 85
  ART IS CALLING FOR ME, 24
  PANSY FACES, 139
Smith, Robert H.
  COME DOWN, MA EVENING STAR, 43
Snape, P. H. and Albert, Arthur
  DADDY'S ON THE ENGINE, 47
Snyder, Ted
  I WANT TO BE IN DIXIE (I WANT TO GO BACK TO DIXIE), 100
  IF THE MANAGERS ONLY THOUGHT THE SAME AS MOTHER, 83
Snyder, Ted and Berlin, Irving
  MY WIFE'S GONE TO THE COUNTRY, 127
Solman, Alfred
  See Lamb, Arthur, 31
  WHY DID YOU MAKE ME CARE?, 191
Spade, Jack
  YOUR BABY 'AS GORN DAHN THE PLUG-'OLE, 197
Speaks, Oley
  ON THE ROAD TO MANDALAY, 136
Spencer, E. Mordaunt
  ROSE OF TRALEE, 149
Stange, Stanislaus
  MY HERO, 124
Stanley, Wynn and Allen, Andrew
  CA-BAGES, CA-BEANS AND

CAR-ROTS, 37
Sterling, Andrew B.
  See Krone, Percy, 52
  MEET ME IN ST LOUIS, LOUIS, 118
  TAKE A LOOK AT ME NOW, 166
  UNDER THE ANHEUSER BUSH, 52
  WAIT TILL THE SUN SHINES, NELLIE, 179
Stern, Joe
  MOTHER WAS A LADY (IF JACK WERE ONLY HERE), 121
Sterndale Bennett, T. C.
  SOPHY, 162
Stevens, George A.
  See Ridgewell, Charles, 91, 195
  ON MOTHER KELLY'S DOOR-STEP, 136
Story, Pauline B.
  RING DOWN THE CURTAIN, 149
Straus, Oscar
  MY HERO, 124
Strauss II, Johann
  CZARDAS, 47
  LAUGHING SONG, THE, 109
Stromberg, John
  COME DOWN, MA EVENING STAR, 43
  MA BLUSHIN' ROSIE, 115
Stuart, Leslie
  LILY OF LAGUNA, THE, 110
  SOLDIERS OF THE QUEEN, 161
  SWEETHEART MAY, 164
  TELL ME, PRETTY MAIDEN, 167
Sullivan, Arthur
  BUTTERCUP, THE, 36
  LOST CHORD, THE, 113
Sullivan, Joseph J.
  WHERE DID YOU GET THAT HAT?, 188
Sullivan, Terry
  (FLOATING WITH) MY BOATING GIRL, 58
  See Bedford, Harry, 96
  FATHER'S GOT THE SACK

FROM THE WATERWORKS, 57
SHE SELLS SEA-SHELLS, 154
Sutherd, A. and Murray, Slade
  COME DOWN AND OPEN THE DOOR, LOVE, 43

Tabbush, Reginald
  HOW CAN A LITTLE GIRL BE GOOD?, 76
Tabrar, Joseph
  DADDY WOULDN'T BUY ME A BOW WOW, 47
  FOR MONTHS AND MONTHS AND MONTHS, 60
  HARD TIMES COME AGAIN NO MORE, 71
  HE'S GOING TO MARRY MARY ANN, 74
  I STOPPED I LOOKED AND I LISTENED, 95
  OH! YOU LITTLE DARLING, 134
Talbot, Howard
  IF I ONLY KNEW THE WAY, 82
  MARTHA SPANKS THE GRAND PIANNA, 117
Tate, James W.
  See Meher, Donovan, 63
  BACHELOR GAY, A, 26
  BROKEN DOLL, A, 35
  COME OVER THE GARDEN WALL, 44
  EV'RY LITTLE WHILE, 56
  GIVE ME A LITTLE COSY CORNER, 66
  I WAS A GOOD LITTLE GIRL TILL I MET YOU, 101
  IF I SHOULD PLANT A TINY SEED OF LOVE, 82
  IT'S LOVELY TO BE IN LOVE, 97
  MY ACTOR MAN, 122
  PARADISE FOR TWO, A, 139
Taylor, Charles H.
  WALTZ SONG, 180
Taylor, Helen
  BLESS THIS HOUSE, 31
Tempest, Charles
  'ARF A PINT OF ALE, 23

Index

Tennyson, Alfred
  COME INTO THE GARDEN, MAUD, 44
Terry, Fred
  ANY OLD IRON?, 22
Teschemacher, Edward
  BECAUSE, 27
  MATTINATA, 117
Thackeray, William M.
  See AJC
Thorn, Geoffrey
  SHE'D A BROTHER IN THE NAVY, 153
Thornton, James
  MY SWEETHEART'S THE MAN IN THE MOON, 126
  WHEN YOU WERE SWEET SIXTEEN, 188
Thurban, T. W.
  See Grock, A., 51
  PIGTAIL OF LI FANG FU, THE, 141
Tierney, Harry
  ALICE BLUE GOWN, 18
  IF YOU CAN'T GET A GIRL IN THE SUMMERTIME, 84
Tosti, F. Paolo
  GOOD-BYE!, 68
  PARTED, 139
Traditional
  BALLAD OF SAM HALL, THE, 26
  DANNY BOY, 49
  FLORAL DANCE, THE, 58
  I'M A MAN THAT'S DONE WRONG TO MY PARENTS, 88
Trevelyan, Arthur
  GIRL THAT I M.A.R.R.Y..., THE, 65
Tucker, Henry
  SWEET GENEVIEVE, 164
Two Bobs, The
  See Lee, Bert, 60
  See Weston, R. P., 138

Valentine
  See Harris, F. Clifford, 26, 139
Valentine, John
  ALL ROUND MY HAT, 19
Van Alystyne, Egbert
  I'M AFRAID TO COME HOME IN THE DARK, 87
  IN THE SHADE OF THE OLD APPLE TREE, 93
Venton, F. W.
  I'M A LITTLE TOO YOUNG TO KNOW, 88
Verdi, Guiseppe
  BRINDISI, 35
Von Tilzer, Albert
  GIVE ME THE MOONLIGHT, 66
  NORA MALONE (CALL ME BY PHONE), 130
Von Tilzer, Harry
  BIRD IN A GILDED CAGE, A, 31
  DOWN AT THE OLD BULL AND BUSH, 52
  I WANT A GIRL JUST LIKE THE GIRL WHO MARRIED DEAR OLD DAD, 99
  MANSION OF ACHING HEARTS, THE, 116
  RIDING ON TOP OF THE CAR, 148
  TAKE A LOOK AT ME NOW, 166
  THEY ALWAYS PICK ON ME, 170
  UNDER THE ANHEUSER BUSH, 52
  WAIT TILL THE SUN SHINES, NELLIE, 179

Waite, Ted
  I THINK I'LL BUY PICCADILLY, 95
  MAJOR-GENERAL WORTHINGTON, 115
Walker, James J.
  WILL YOU LOVE ME IN DECEMBER AS YOU DO IN MAY?, 192
Wallace, Raymond
  YOU CAN'T DO THAT THERE 'ERE, 196
Wallace, W. Vincent

OUR HANDS HAVE MET BUT
NOT OUR HEARTS (THE FALSE
FRIEND), 137
Wallis, W. H.
　See Collins, Charles, 181
Walsh, James
　See Castling, Harry, 51
Ware, George
　BOY IN THE GALLERY, THE,
　33
　JESSIE THE BELLE AT THE
　(RAILWAY) BAR, 103
Watson, M.
　MARRIED TO A MERMAID,
　116
Weatherly, F. E.
　DANNY BOY, 49
　FRIEND O' MINE, 61
　HOLY CITY, THE, 76
　LITTLE DAMOZEL, THE, 112
　OLD BRIGADE, THE, 134
　PARTED, 139
　ROSES OF PICARDY, 150
Wells, Gilbert
　See Earle, Fred, 192
　See Robson, T. F., 176
　MARY'S TICKET, 117
Wenrich, Percy
　MOONLIGHT BAY (ON), 120
West, Alfred H.
　FALLEN STAR, A, 56
West, Arthur
　CAPTAIN CALLED THE MATE,
　THE, 39
　YES YOU ARE, 194
Weston, R. Harris
　AIN' IT NICE?, 16
　AND THE GREAT BIG SAW
　CAME NEARER AND NEARER,
　21
　BRAHN BOOTS, 34
　OLGA PULLOFFSKI THE
　BEAUTIFUL SPY, 135
Weston, R. P.
　See Barnes, Fred J., 107
　See Bedford, Harry, 86
　See Carter, Frank W., 34
　See Murray, Fred, 90
　See Smith, Clay, 161

SISTER SUSIE'S SEWING
SHIRTS FOR SOLDIERS, 160
THERE ARE NICE GIRLS
EVERYWHERE, 169
WHAT A MOUTH!, 182
WHERE ARE THE LADS OF
THE VILLAGE TONIGHT?, 188
WITH THIS HAT ON, 192
Weston, R. P. and Barnes, Fred J.
　IN THESE HARD TIMES, 93
　I'VE GOT RINGS ON MY
　FINGERS, 98
　OH, I'M ONE OF THE BOYS,
　132
　WHEN FATHER PAPERED THE
　PARLOUR, 185
Weston, R. P. and David, Worton
　END OF MY OLD CIGAR, THE,
　54
Weston, R. P. and Lee, Bert
　AIN' IT NICE?, 16
　AND THE GREAT BIG SAW
　CAME NEARER AND NEARER,
　21
　BRAHN BOOTS, 34
　GOOD-BYE-EE, 68
　GYPSY WARNED ME, THE, 70
　I MIGHT LEARN TO LOVE HIM
　LATER ON, 90
　IT'S MY BATH NIGHT TO-
　NIGHT, 97
　OLGA PULLOFFSKI THE
　BEAUTIFUL SPY, 135
　SHE WAS POOR BUT SHE WAS
　HONEST, 156
　SOMEBODY WOULD SHOUT
　OUT "SHOP"!, 161
　SWIM! SAM! SWIM!, 165
　WHAT I WANT IS A PROPER
　CUP OF COFFEE, 184
Weston, R. P. and Lee, Bert and Two
　Bobs, The
　PADDY McGINTY'S GOAT, 138
Weston, R. P. and Murphy, C. W.
　and Darewski, Herman
　I'M LOOKING FOR MR
　WRIGHT, 90
White, C. A.
　PLEASE SELL NO MORE

Song Introductions

DRINK TO MY FATHER, 143
Whiting, George
  MY WIFE'S GONE TO THE COUNTRY, 127
Whitson, Beth Slater
  LET ME CALL YOU SWEETHEART, 109
Whyte-Melville, G. J.
  GOOD-BYE!, 68
Wilcock, Frank
  I WANT TO TAKE A YOUNG MAN IN (AND DO FOR HIM), 101
Williams, Harry H.
  I'M AFRAID TO COME HOME IN THE DARK, 87
  IN THE SHADE OF THE OLD APPLE TREE, 93
Williams, Harry J.
  See Judge, Jack, 97
Williams, J.
  See Clifton, Harry, 193
Williams, Walter and Sievier, Bruce
  PICCADILLY, 141
Williams, Watkyn
  HAMPSTEAD IS THE PLACE TO RURALIZE, 70
Wilmot, Charles
  IN THE TWI-TWI-TWILIGHT, 94
Wilson, Al and Piantadosi, Al
  WILD WILD WOMEN, THE, 192
Wilson, H. Lane
  TENOR AND BARITONE, 16
Wimperis, Arthur
  See Rubens, Paul, 34
  GILBERT, THE FILBERT, 65
  HERE'S TO LOVE AND LAUGHTER, 74
  I'LL MAKE A MAN OF YOU, 86
  MY MOTTER, 124
  ONLY A GLASS OF CHAMPAGNE, 135
  PIPES OF PAN, THE, 142
Wincott, Harry
  CAN'T STOP! CAN'T STOP!! CAN'T STOP!!!, 39
  DOWN THE DIALS, 52
  FOR ME! FOR ME!, 59
  I'M GETTING READY FOR MY MOTHER-IN-LAW, 88
Wingate, Philip
  I DON'T WANT TO PLAY IN YOUR YARD, 81
Winter, Banks
  WHITE WINGS, 189
Wood, Haydn
  ROSES OF PICARDY, 150
Wood, J. T.
  WAIT TILL THE CLOUDS ROLL BY, 178
Woodforde-Finden, Amy
  KASHMIRI SONG (PALE HANDS I LOVED), 106
Woodhouse, J. H.
  See Kelly, W. B., 159
  GRASS WIDOWER, THE, 69
Woodville, Ernie
  TWIDDLEY BITS, THE, 175
Work, Henry Clay
  COME HOME, FATHER, 43
  GRANDFATHER'S CLOCK, 69
Wright, Harry
  'E DUNNO WHERE 'E ARE, 54
Wynne, Wish
  OOH! 'ER! (THE SLAVEY), 137

Xanrof, L.
  FIACRE, LE, 57

Yellen, Jack
  ALABAMA JUBILEE, 17
  ARE YOU FROM DIXIE?, 23
Yorkston, James
  COCKLES AND MUSSELS, 42
Young, Joe
  See Lewis, Sam M., 77
  I'M ALONE BECAUSE I LOVE YOU, 88
Young, Rida J.
  I CAN'T TAKE MY EYES OFF YOU, 79
  MOTHER MACHREE, 121
Young, Willie
  LINGER LONGER LOO, 111

Zeller, Carl
MILLER'S DAUGHTER, THE,
119

www.ingramcontent.com/pod-product-compliance
Ingram Content Group UK Ltd.
Pitfield, Milton Keynes, MK11 3LW, UK
UKHW021842210426
5322IPUK00022B/427